T0245974

A Century of Labour

To Anna

A CENTURY OF LABOUR

Jon Cruddas

polity

Copyright © Jon Cruddas 2024

The right of Jon Cruddas to be identified as Author of this Work has been asserted in accordance with the UK Copyright, Designs and Patents Act 1988.

First published in 2024 by Polity Press

Polity Press
65 Bridge Street
Cambridge CB2 1UR, UK

Polity Press
111 River Street
Hoboken, NJ 07030, USA

All rights reserved. Except for the quotation of short passages for the purpose of criticism and review, no part of this publication may be reproduced, stored in a retrieval system or transmitted, in any form or by any means, electronic, mechanical, photocopying, recording or otherwise, without the prior permission of the publisher.

ISBN-13: 978-1-5095-5834-6

A catalogue record for this book is available from the British Library.

Library of Congress Control Number: 2023938517

Typeset in 11.5 on 14pt Adobe Garamond
by Fakenham Prepress Solutions, Fakenham, Norfolk NR21 8NL
Printed and bound in Great Britain by CPI Group (UK) Ltd, Croydon CR0 4YY

The publisher has used its best endeavours to ensure that the URLs for external websites referred to in this book are correct and active at the time of going to press. However, the publisher has no responsibility for the websites and can make no guarantee that a site will remain live or that the content is or will remain appropriate.

Every effort has been made to trace all copyright holders, but if any have been overlooked the publisher will be pleased to include any necessary credits in any subsequent reprint or edition.

For further information on Polity, visit our website:
politybooks.com

'The Cause of Labour is the Hope of the World'
W. Crane, The Workers Maypole, *Justice: The Organ of Social Democracy*, Social Democratic Federation, 1894.

Contents

Acknowledgements

Many people have helped with this book. In particular I would like to thank Adrian Pabst and Patrick Diamond for supplying detailed comments on sections of the draft. I must also acknowledge a debt of appreciation to the two anonymous readers of the draft for their detailed criticism and very helpful guidance. I wish to also thank Peter Nolan and Michael Sandel for conversations ranging over several years on key economic and philosophical themes covered in the book, and to Kenneth O. Morgan and John Shepherd for their guidance in relation to labour history as well as Eric Shaw and Emmanuelle Avril. I am also indebted to Francesca Klug for educating me on the history of human rights.

I also wish to thank Anne-Marie Green for her advice on under-standing decades of Labour's equalities legislation, as well as to David Evans, Matthew Jackson, Angela Cartwright, Helen Pearce and Fraser Welsh from Labour's Head Office for their help over membership data. Throughout the project, Sarah Hadden has been a brilliant help in working through the empirical data.

At Polity I would like to thank Louise Knight for initially suggesting the project and her continued support alongside Inès Boxman.

I wish to thank my staff and local party for their patience while I worked on this project – and the extraordinary support they have shown me since I was first selected as a candidate some 25 years ago. I have been active in the trade union and labour movement for 44 years and have worked for and represented the Labour Party for 35 years. During that time, I have been privileged to work alongside many thousands of members, activists, staff and Labour representatives. This book is my attempt to honour their commitment to the cause of Labour. I still believe it to be the hope of the world.

Finally, as my time as MP for Dagenham and Rainham comes to an end, I owe a tremendous debt of gratitude to my constituents across Dagenham and Rainham for allowing me to be their political representative.

Preface

'Lenin Dead (official). Ramsay MacDonald Premier'[1]

Following an inconclusive December election and six weeks of confusion, speculation and negotiation, Britain's first Labour government took office a century ago, on 22 January 1924. Yet there have only been six Labour Prime Ministers: Ramsay MacDonald, Clement Attlee, Harold Wilson, Jim Callaghan, Tony Blair and Gordon Brown. Only three, Attlee, Wilson and Blair, won a majority at a general election. Despite many extraordinary achievements, including the introduction of a welfare state and the National Health Service (NHS), Labour has only held power for a total of 33 years. Why has Labour underperformed in British politics? Why has the party often struggled to win elections and then hold on to power? The centenary of the first Labour government provides an opportunity to try to answer these questions, reassess the party's performance over the last 100 years and inspect the character and purpose of the modern party.

The first Labour government was led by Ramsay MacDonald, having been elected leader from the left of the party two years earlier. MacDonald was a magnetic force, arguably the most significant political figure of the 1920s. In the 15 years from 1914 to the election of the second Labour government in 1929, the party had successfully replaced the Liberals as the main opposition to the Conservatives. Few would have anticipated such events; there was no inevitability this would occur despite social and economic changes that undoubtedly helped a party of labour. That history unfolded in this way was in no small part due to the organizational skills and strategic genius, the agitation and struggle of a generation of Labour leaders, chief among them MacDonald. Yet in Labour mythology, MacDonald remains a traitor to the cause. For many of the party faithful so too does Blair, electorally Labour's most successful leader. Labour history is complicated; a deeply contested terrain.

It is unknown what the current Labour leader Keir Starmer will say or do to celebrate the centenary of the first Labour government. It was a short, arguably unremarkable government, although there haven't been that many to celebrate since then. How a leader addresses their party's history helps to reveal their own political character. This will be especially true for Starmer.

Even after four years in post, Keir Starmer remains an elusive leader, difficult to find. He is clearly an honest, decent man engaged in politics for principled reasons. Yet there are few contributions to help reveal an essential political identity and little in the way of an intellectual paper trail. He travels light compared to ideologues such as MacDonald. Apart from Brexit, there have been few interventions in the key internal party debates of the last 30 years. Notwithstanding vague associations with the 'soft left' of the party, he appears detached from the deeper intellectual traditions that have shaped the history of Labour. This book focuses on three of these traditions: the first, the ethical socialist tradition, seeks to nurture human virtue; the second attempts to expand human welfare; the third aims to promote liberty and human rights. Yet apart from his actual name, little ties Starmer to the ethical and spiritual concerns of Labour's early founders, figures such as Keir Hardie and George Lansbury. His approach to economics does not appear to be grounded in any specific theoretical understanding of inequality, material justice and welfare distribution. Despite a successful career as a human rights lawyer, as Labour leader Starmer appears disinterested in questions of liberty and freedom.

Starmer often seems detached from his own party and uncomfortable in communion with fellow MPs. In his immediate circle he appears to value the familiar and unchallenging. It is difficult to identify the purpose of a future Starmer government – what he seeks to accomplish beyond achieving office. Labour appears content for the coming election to amount to a referendum on the performance of the governing Conservatives, rather than a choice between competing visions of politics and justice. This book seeks to reassess Labour's history and the present condition of the party by returning to questions of justice. We explore competing visions of how society should be organized and how this has helped define a century of Labour. The argument of the book is that Labour's successes and failures can be understood in terms of its ability to unite and cohere three competing approaches to justice within an overall political organization and agenda for government.

The book is published a few months before, hopefully, a new period of Labour in power. Keir Starmer will have a troubled inheritance. Labour's history is a resource to be excavated to help inform the present. In one sense it is surprising that Labour might once more be on the verge of holding office given the industrial and demographic changes of the past century. Over the years we have regularly been told that the party's over, that Labour will never again hold power as it lies on the wrong side of history. Labour's very existence and current popularity might well reflect an enduring demand for the type of political change that the party represents and its ability to evolve with the times informed by a restless desire to serve. This book revisits Labour's history to aid the future of the party. Labour has a proud record and has altered the life opportunities of many millions of British people, and hopefully will do so again over the coming months.

History

The Labour Party grew out of the late nineteenth-century trade union movement and the expansion of the franchise. It was initially formed in 1900 as the Labour Representation Committee (LRC) with the cooperation of unions and three key organizations: the Independent Labour Party (ILP), the Social Democratic Federation (SDF) and the Fabian Society. In February 1906, having secured 29 MPs at that month's election, it reformed as the Labour Party. By the late 1920s it had successfully replaced the Liberal Party as the main opposition to the Conservatives.

Following two brief periods of minority government, in 1924 and between 1929 and 1931, the party split. Although imperilled, it survived. In 1940 Labour emerged as a junior partner in the wartime coalition and helped resist calls advocating a negotiated settlement with the Nazis. After a landslide victory in 1945, the Attlee government established the welfare state, created the NHS and, informed by Clause IV of the 1918 party constitution, nationalized a fifth of the economy.[1] It also embarked on a programme of decolonization and nuclear armament and helped to establish NATO.

Defeat in 1951 was followed by 'thirteen wasted years' in opposition and significant internal factional tension. In 1964 a programme of economic modernization was offered by the newly elected government of Harold Wilson. At a snap election 17 months later, Wilson's narrow majority turned into another landslide victory. Despite liberalizing social reforms and significant policy achievements, the parliament was overshadowed by a humiliating 1967 devaluation, ongoing economic difficulties and tensions over industrial relations reform. Yet defeat in 1970 and a Tory majority of 31[2] was considered by many commentators a surprise result. The oil price shocks of 1973, the three-day week and escalating industrial strife led to a minority Labour administration following the February 1974 election. A second October election saw

Wilson again returned, this time with a four-seat majority. It was to be Labour's last election victory until 1997.

Wilson resigned in March 1976, replaced by James Callaghan. A financial crisis and IMF-imposed austerity had, by late 1978, been transformed into economic growth and falling inflation. However, a failure to go to the country, the effect of a so-called 'Winter of Discontent', the return of inflationary pressures and the loss of a no-confidence vote produced a Conservative majority of 44 in 1979. Tensions over internal party democracy and wider policy disputes, including over Europe and economic strategy, resulted in a breakaway party – the Social Democratic Party (SDP) – and another 18 years in opposition, often referred to as 'the wilderness years'.

Tony Blair and New Labour provided the party with its longest sustained period in office. It returned a 178-seat majority at the 1997 election, reduced to 166 in 2001, then to 65 in 2005, and brought forward a substantial package of economic, social and constitutional reforms. Yet the government was undermined by the Iraq War and the failure to find weapons of mass destruction and by its approach to economic regulation, which culminated in recession and austerity. Under Gordon Brown, Labour was defeated in 2010 following the effects of the global economic crisis and forced into opposition against a Conservative/ Liberal Democratic coalition, after Labour's own negotiations with Nick Clegg's party stalled. Despite the effects of austerity, a collapse in support for the Lib Dems and the rise of UKIP, Labour suffered a further loss in 2015. Ed Miliband quickly resigned as leader and was replaced by Jeremy Corbyn with the party now facing a majority Conservative government. The Prime Minister David Cameron subsequently resigned following the 2016 vote to leave the European Union. In 2017 the Conservatives led by Theresa May lost their majority but remained in power, despite significant gains made by a radical Labour leadership. The 2019 election would be Labour's fourth defeat in less than a decade and produce an 81-strong majority for Boris Johnson, triggering an end to Corbyn and the ascent of Keir Starmer. Labour has now been in opposition for 14 years.

A basic history can be told through assembling and chronologically ordering the facts. But to explain how and why they occurred requires scrutiny of the people involved, their thinking, relationships and actions.

It needs to investigate the context and motivations behind decisions. History needs to study the personal battles, ideological differences, the successes and failures, the tragedies and triumphs that shape the dramatic arc of Labour's story. There is no single way to draw out this drama; we must choose a method to navigate Labour history.

One is through biography.[3] We could study the six Labour Prime Ministers or the biographies of every party leader from Keir Hardie to Keir Starmer, 23 if we include acting leaders, or other key figures. The danger with such a biographical lens is a focus on individual agency and personality at the expense of ideology or the structural difficulties leaders face in managing the party and in government decision making. Alternatively we might detail and evaluate Labour's achievements over the last century given the constraints of office.[4] Or rather than search for an overall party history, we might instead favour a more detailed study of specific Labour administrations or periods out of office, or significant years that stand out within this history, such as 1900, 1924, 1945 or 1997.[5] Another way might be to pinpoint key events and assess how the party dealt with them, for instance significant economic shocks. Or we could instead dissect key election victories and losses or route Labour's history through a prism of party factionalism.

Another variation could be to inspect how a specific constitutional feature of the party has helped shape its history. An obvious example is the trade union link, or battles over Clause IV of the original party constitution. Or we could instead scrutinize how war and conflict have shaped Labour's history, from the Boer War and 1900 'Khaki' election, through two world wars and the recent Iraq conflict. Alternatively, we could investigate the history of political thought within Labour and the changing ideological character of the party or through its shifting policy priorities. Or we might even rethink Labour's story through a counter-factual method; providing alternatives that are counter to the facts to explore events from a variety of angles. For instance, what if Keir Hardie had failed to be elected the first chairman of the Parliamentary Labour Party (PLP) in February 1906, in effect party leader, as Hardie won by only one vote over David Shackleton after several ballots? Or if Attlee had failed to survive any of the three times he was carried off First World War battlefields? What might have happened if both Hugh Gaitskell and John Smith had not died prematurely but instead faced the country as

Labour leaders in 1964 and 1997? Or Callaghan and Brown had decided in favour of early elections in 1978 and 2008 rather than suffer what came later? What if Blair had decided not to actively support George W. Bush over Iraq or David Miliband had been the victor over his brother Ed in September 2010?

There are numerous ways to navigate Labour history. Yet whatever the method, a number of themes continue to reappear. I will focus on just three and label them the *origin question*, the *death question* and the *purpose question*.

Origin, Death, Purpose

Whatever route is chosen through Labour history, three questions frequently recur.[6] The first we have already touched on: was the rise of a party of labour inevitable given the evolving nature of industrial capitalism? Or to rephrase this, given the social and economic changes brought about by the speed and timing of British industrialization, was a party of the organized working class always going to rise and crowd out the Liberal Party in the first quarter of the last century? Labour's rise to power was remarkably swift for a new political party. Whether it was inevitable that Labour would replace the Liberals is the source of much debate within labour history.[7] This is *the origin question*. The second question, *the death question*, complements the first by inverting it for a different era. Given the effects of deindustrialization and recent technological revolutions, is the party just painting over the cracks and managing its own decline? Is the party on the wrong side of history? Is the party over? Has the forward march of Labour halted?[8]

These two questions bookend party history and between them capture significant intellectual influences on the party. In the formative period these include Darwinian and secular Enlightenment influences, utopianism, various religious strands, especially dissenting traditions, and orthodox Marxism. All share some sense that Labour's political history can be understood because of evolving economic and social forces; they retain an essential determinism in assessing the way history unfolds and progresses. The obvious challenge is to suggest that history might not be that straightforward, and instead stress complexity and contingency. This is a familiar tension at the heart of much of the social sciences. In Labour's origins story, it was often assumed that political change approximated that of the natural sciences. Such thinking has remained influential throughout party history, for instance, through eugenics or post-war attempts to harness the expansion of sociology toward a science of social progress in aid of the party. It represents an ongoing belief in social and scientific progress, in human evolution and maturity, one consistently attached to the role of the party, its intellectual reasoning and policy formation.[9]

This optimistic vision surrounding Labour inverted into a fatalism following the defeat of the Attlee government, again driven by a certain class essentialism and view of economic and technological change which implied the potential eclipse of the party.[10] Such an approach informed the electoral pessimism of 1950s revisionism given widespread assumptions of the inevitable decline of Labour as a representative party of an organized working class. From a different perspective it also influenced the famous contribution of Eric Hobsbawm questioning the forward march of Labour, and debates surrounding the 'New Times' the party must adapt to. Such thinking also underpinned the arguments of 'modernizers' in the 1980s, as well as the diagnosis supplied later by New Labour. Such thinking has regularly inspired proposals to change the party name or constitution or policy priorities, or all three at once. Such intellectual and political concerns do not belong to one party faction. For instance, such an approach recently reappeared within the Corbyn project with the contributions of what is sometimes labelled the 'post-work' left in their understanding of automation and prophecy of a world without work or workers and advocation of a Universal Basic Income.

Questions of inevitability and contingency recur throughout the book. They reveal tensions at the heart of Labour history, first really exposed on coming to power between the wars. Two brief periods of minority Labour government were defined by the contingencies of conflict and economic crisis, bringing with them epic dilemmas for a party motivated by a spiritual sense of purpose. Throughout its early years Labour remained highly conflicted; consumed by the responsibilities of office and national duty, yet psychologically shaped by a crusading belief in inevitable socialist transformation. The drama is revealed in the lives of the key personalities and within the factions and traditions they helped create. Their political biographies vividly expose these tensions, often concluding in personal tragedy and defeat despite having helped sculpt Labour's remarkable early history. We draw out these tensions with a focus on the characters of Hardie, Ramsay MacDonald and George Lansbury, and demonstrate how they inform the Labour drama throughout the last century and still do today.

The book begins with the first two brief Labour governments. Unremarkable in terms of their achievements, constrained electorally by both a global pandemic and austerity, by the so-called 'Geddes Axe' and later the proposals of the May committee, contingencies which by the early 1930s threatened the very existence of the party. In 1931 MacDonald privately remarked his government was 'too much of the onlooker oppressed by circumstances'.

In 2024, after 14 years of opposition, and waves of pandemic, recession and austerity, this historic tension shadows Labour's contemporary existence. Structural hostility confronts the party, especially acute amongst the media. Such a climate engineers a psychology of appeasement to navigate any viable routes to office, but in turn dilutes any mandate for change and room to manoeuvre once in power. Offering efficient management and reassurance suggest the prospect of renewed austerity and will be unlikely to satisfy the demand for change amongst the membership and in the country. The politics of austerity has bedevilled Labour throughout its entire history.

Both the origin and death stories are driven by the composition of British class politics, long-term changes in the demand and supply of labour and Labour's understanding of capitalism. These concerns are shared by present-day historians and commentators preoccupied by who represents and what exists of the working class, especially given the modern political binaries of age, education, geography, of Brexit, and the collapse of the Red Wall. Yet the danger with both questions is an over-reliance on assumptions of inevitability regarding destiny and decline. They also foreshadow an additional problem, a certainty about the role of the party; a political essentialism. This leads to the third question, the *purpose question*.

R.H. Tawney's 1934 essay *The Choice before the Labour Party* is a famous expression of the purpose question, highly relevant in any analysis of the position facing Labour today.[11] It was written in response to Labour's first real crisis as a party. Ramsay Macdonald, the first secretary of the ILP and Labour's first Prime Minister, the man whose contribution stands second only to Hardie in the party's formation, led a National Government from 1931. Tawney highlights the dilemma at the heart of the party; its tense relationship between orthodoxy and radicalism. He identifies the problem as being driven by a lack of creed. As the hopes attached to that government died, he describes how the government 'did not fall with a crash, in a tornado from the blue. But crawled slowly to its doom.'

Despite the sense of destiny infecting much of the party's origins story, throughout history Labour's difficulties have often been blamed on external events, generally economic ones. But Tawney argues this is to deny socialist agency and responsibility. His words and diagnosis of Labour's inability to shape events echo down through the decades. 'The gravest weakness of British Labour is ... its lack of creed. The Labour Party is hesitant in action, because divided in mind. It does not achieve what it could, because it does not know what it wants.' He doesn't pull his punches. There is, he says, a 'void in the mind of the Labour Party' which leads us into 'intellectual timidity, conservatism, conventionality, which keeps policy trailing tardily in the rear of realities'.

Tawney implies the existence of a definitive party creed to shape socialist agency and inoculate against the dilemmas of office. Is he right to do so? Again, questions of certainty and essentialism reappear. Yet from the very beginning there was little certainty regarding the purpose of Labour. An early distinction was clear between those who saw its role as representing certain interests in distributional contests over resources, and others who considered it a vehicle to achieve a different type of society. Another question quickly followed: whether Labour was primarily a parliamentary party or anchored within wider movements. Questions of purpose have always remained unresolved because of Labour's hybrid quality. From its creation, the LRC was a coalition of different organizations and philosophies regarding questions of purpose. Labour has remained a brittle coalition of sectional interests, societies and, after 1918, members. These have aligned as factions, drawing from assorted political traditions in forming alternative programmes. Labour has always contained various liberal, Marxist, socialist, religious, national, regional and assorted municipal elements.[12] It has offered a home to thinkers and theories, those more concerned with factional battles and position, others with cold electoral calculation. Each has retained their own sense of political purpose in a party without a formal ideology or identity.

Lacking any overarching official ideology can bring strengths and weakness. It offers political agility and creativity in adapting to changing environments. Yet, as Sidney Webb suggested in 1894, without an essential purpose the movement might head in 'spurious' directions in search of instant solutions.[13] The elusive question of purpose creates clear dangers when interpreting history through factional alignment, however. It can lead to combatants erecting and inserting a formal ideological architecture and coherence back into a fluid party history filled with wide-ranging influences. Such tendencies are what psychologists might call 'the presenting problem', one we must move beyond to achieve historical understanding.

This becomes clear as we rehearse some of the historically specific philosophical influences on Labour. To name a few: Edwardian idealism, 1930s positivism, eugenics, the technological determinism of the Second International, later New Left reformulations, later still postmodernism, the concerns of the 'Third Way' and today's hyperindividualized identity politics. Labour's ever-changing ideological currents make it a difficult terrain to navigate. Suggesting a definitive purpose, or creed, might be the *wrong path* through such a history.

One obvious example of the dangers in such an approach to the purpose question is the regular attempt to encase an 'authentic' radical Labour tradition within a certain timeframe; specifically, in the years between 1918, with the adoption of Clause IV of the party constitution and publication of *Labour and the New Social Order*, and Labour's first majority in 1945 and the manifesto *Let Us Face the Future*. This approach suggests between 1918 and 1945 we can identify Labour's 'authentic' purpose defined by public ownership.[14] In these terms attempts to revise Clause IV – by Gaitskell in 1960 or Blair in 1995 – are swiftly considered heretical; at odds with an essential purpose. As are those interpretations of the 1945 victory and the achievements of the Attlee government which reject such a reading of Labour's purpose.

In 2024 there is an ever-present danger with such essentialism where the ideology and institutions of 70 years ago become the horizon of ambition, played out in a defensive backward-looking culture when confronted by, for instance, a revolution in liberal market economics. It might embed a language of institutional conservatism spoken by those who self-identify as egalitarians and reformers.

History is important to the labour movement. We take pride in it.[15] A sense of history – that history is on the side of the party – has helped hold Labour together at moments of crisis. Yet it also constrains Labour through sentimental attachment and an idealized sense of its past, one that is prone to misrepresentation and historical myth making and that promotes widely held false beliefs about the purpose of the party. This has regularly fostered disunity, for instance with myths of a leadership betrayal of an essential Labour purpose such as over the events of 1931, or *In Place of Strife* in 1969 or the actions of the New Labour government after 1997.

In contrast, we might investigate ideas less in terms of an essential socialist purpose than as contributions within a broad range of Labour thought, and create a method to appreciate and interpret these interventions. Rather than gauge the work of party intellectuals such as Sidney Webb or Tawney, G.D.H. Cole or Harold Laski, Tony Crosland or Tony Giddens, relative to an essential purpose, we might instead ask how they have helped shape a crossbred Labour history and inspect how they themselves are anchored within deeper traditions of thought that compete for power and influence. In such an approach, political ideas remain part of the ongoing war of position. In this sense Tawney's *The Choice* is seen as one contribution in the post 1931 battle to retrieve and reset the party, rather than seen as a definitive intervention regarding Labour's purpose, or creed. In a similar way E.P. Thompson's epic history of the English working class and biography of William Morris were both intimately connected to internal battles for supremacy within the Communist Party and remain significant interventions that helped shape post-war Labour politics. No one writing about Labour history does so from a position of absolute neutrality or objectivity. Crosland's *The Future of Socialism* was not an isolated academic contribution in search of an essential truth but powered by an internal contest for 1950s factional supremacy. Today, from a similar perspective, Patrick Diamond is assembling an impressive body of work on Labour history to aid the latest generation of revisionist actors. In contrast, the classic text on Labour's political thought provided by Geoffrey Foote comes from a more radical

Bennite perspective.[16] All these contributions help shape party history; they don't simply reflect and delineate some true purpose.[17] The question this book seeks to contribute towards is: How do we apply an intellectual coherence to Labour given its shape-shifting quality?

Justice

Addressing Labour's fluid quality, over 30 years ago David Marquand diagnosed *The Progressive Dilemma*, an alternative entry point into our three questions of origin, death and purpose.[18] Historically, how could progressive intellectuals secure durable economic, democratic and social change? When and where and through which political party could radicals help deliver enduring transformation given the forces of reaction and our democratic architecture – and at what collateral cost? For example, in the early part of the last century, what were the costs and benefits of supporting Labour – given its class composition and conservative 'labourist' traditions – at the expense of retaining support for liberalism? Alternatively, should the intellectual remain above the party-political fray, retaining independence and campaigning agility? This formed the basis of the *Progressive Dilemma* and the template for Marquand's study of British political history. Amongst the many consequences of failing to successfully traverse this dilemma was the high probability that you might lock in Conservative rule. It allowed for the contingencies of alliance and the heterogeneity of political parties; their shifting structure and purpose. For example, it helps account for how different groups of actors within Labour history – politicians, union leaders and academics or intellectuals – have combined and the way political leadership has had to negotiate with significant institutional power brokers whilst also looking to intellectuals for ideas and inspiration.

The *Progressive Dilemma* provides a method to inspect both our origin and death questions. It offers a different route to study the emergence of the party and the decline of the Liberals early in the century and how, across the UK as a whole,[19] there has only been one electorally successful centre-left political leader in the last 35 years. Tony Blair appeared to have subtly navigated the terrain of the Progressive Dilemma. His coalition held resilient and secured three major, unprecedented majorities. Today the dilemma remains intense given that Labour's traditional class constituencies are in long-term decline and the influence of a variety of nationalist forces. Meanwhile across the south of England advances by the Liberals and Greens remain distinct possibilities.

Rather than treat labour history as the search for an essential creed or purpose, Marquand's approach allows us to inspect the fluid nature of political formation. In this book we hope to achieve the same, but in a different way to Marquand. We suggest the inability to resolve the purpose question lies in the way that competing *conceptions of justice* have shaped the history of the party. We detail how three alternative visions of how society should be organized have shaped this past century of Labour, each grounded within different traditions of thought. These traditions operate behind the backs of the personalities, factions and movements within the political drama and offer an alternative understanding of Labour over the last century.

The pages that follow navigate Labour history through theories of justice. This is not to say the participants endlessly study Bentham, Locke or Aristotle, but that the traditions, factions and ideas these political actors espouse or reject do not simply fall out of the sky. Often unbeknown to the political combatants, they are carriers of thought and remain embedded within traditions of justice. The practical application of these assorted theories – the *praxis* of politics – plays out in the way various political and economic interest groups, factions and personalities fight for power and influence within the party or wider movement. As will become apparent, different individuals and political movements can be influenced by more than one tradition at the same time. We suggest that such a framework helps account for Labour's underperformance in British politics. Labour succeeds when it draws inspiration from all three competing traditions. Yet for this to occur requires extraordinary acts of leadership and a commitment to political pluralism and reconciliation within the party. These are elusive qualities. Hopefully the following discussion might contribute to developing a holistic Labour history. But it also requires some admissions on my part.

Admissions

I am not a trained historian. I have worked for or represented the Labour Party for 35 years. What follows is a contribution from within a political tradition. Although far from uncritical, it reflects my own background and political views. To give an example, I am writing this in my study in Ireland overlooked by various photographs and statues that reflect my outlook. On the wall in front of me is a *Vanity Fair* drawing of 'Queer Hardie', Labour's first leader. Hanging close by is a wirephoto of Clement Attlee on the campaign trail in conversation across a garden gate. Behind me is a 1934 *Daily Herald* photo of George Lansbury unveiling the headstone of James Hammett, the Tolpuddle Martyr. All mementoes from events celebrating these great figures. The only other bits of political memorabilia on display are a copy of an oil painting of Mayo native Michael Davitt by William Orpen, a small marble statue of John Fitzgerald Kennedy, as well as his funeral mass card, and a photo of dockers' leader Vic Turner being carried out of Pentonville Prison on the shoulders of my friend Brian Holmes. Apart from assorted books that's it. These belongings reveal personal preferences and prejudices. Lloyd George once said of a politician, 'he has sat on the fence so long that iron has entered his soul'. I admit I am not on the fence when it comes to the history of Labour.

What follows is an argument about party history. It is neither a neutral walk-through of dates, people and events, nor used to advance an essential political creed. I suggest that the history of the party is best understood by exploring how competing theories of justice have influenced Labour's traditions and personalities and informed the drama of Labour politics over the last century. Labour history can be reassessed through the interplay between three competing theories of justice which seek to maximize *human welfare, human freedom* or *human virtue*.

I freely admit I identify with the latter tradition and in the pages that follow I seek to locate figures such as Hardie, Lansbury and Attlee firmly within this approach. It is often associated with ethical socialist elements and, especially from 1893, with the early pioneers of the ILP, although I will attempt to pinpoint its significance in more recent Labour politics, for example in leaders such as John Smith and Tony Blair. So, I begin by admitting this preference over certain party traditions, memories and allegiances because drafting such historical narratives involves judgement in the present when interpreting the past. Labour Party history drips with mythology and political distortion. We need to tread carefully as the past is often used in selective, subjective and deeply contestable ways.

History is regularly deployed as political currency in ongoing internal contests, ones which increasingly involve a performative element aided by social media. But history is not memory, or parable or myth or spin; although Labour's history is filled with numerous vivid characters and includes all these. Chesterton once famously said history and tradition remain 'the democracy of the dead' but, in the case of Labour's history and tradition, these democratic stories are deeply contested.[20]

2

Justice

The centenary of Britain's first Labour government offers a moment to rethink the history of the party. Labour history is, however, deeply contested. Over the past century the party has regularly appeared trapped, caught between a doctrinaire left who claim ownership of an essential socialist creed and liberal perspectives for whom Labour's historical class associations restrict the progressive cause. Today party ideology has truncated. State socialism is widely considered a historic failure, while social democracy appears a pale, hollow, technocratic project, offering limited resistance to the global rise of authoritarian populism, and when in power ill-equipped to achieve enduring change. Labour lacks definition and appears hollow.

Yet since first gaining power Labour has achieved many extraordinary successes in pursuit of material change, social reform and equality, in challenging patriarchy, racism and the legacy of imperialism, promoting human rights and delivering significant democratic and constitutional renewal. In comparison with other progressive movements, Labour has successfully forged a path shaped by unique national conditions given our early industrialization.[1] Yet any honest assessment cannot fail to acknowledge a political century littered with failures and missed opportunities. Today we inhabit a country disfigured by escalating inequality, populist upheaval and democratic discontent. Navigating such a history is a challenge. How can we account for the achievements as well as the missed opportunities?

Assessing the record of the party is especially difficult given the changing nature of capitalism and British society over the last century. A fixed political ideology and policy prospectus would be ill-equipped for the complexities of such a journey. What was appropriate and necessary for a minor party emerging in the Edwardian era is not what was demanded in war time or when propelled into the minority governments of the 1920s. A very different party would re-emerge in the inter-war period. One that withstood both left- and right-wing authoritarian forces after Labour's near fatal collapse following the Wall Street Crash; one which successfully transitioned into a wartime coalition in 1940. Post-war reconstruction bent into factional tension as the party sought to navigate the demands of a new social and economic order. Later still, the effect of oil shocks and heightened class struggle throughout the 1970s were difficult for the Labour Party as were the extra-parliamentary demands of radical liberation movements. Thatcherism, deindustrialization, and the collapse of the corporatist state further upended a party historically rooted within male trade unionism and manufacturing. How this culminated in the creation of New Labour remains unfinished business in the ongoing assessment of Labour's purpose, its strengths and weaknesses; whether it has pushed the boundaries beyond anything recognizably part of the Labour tradition or travelled full circle and retrieved its historical purpose in reuniting with early liberal concerns. This shifting terrain has demanded organizational, political and ideological dexterity in maintaining electoral coalitions to gain and retain power whilst brokering factional tensions against a regular drumbeat asserting 'betrayal'.

It is a highwire act for any party leader, especially such an unknown one as Keir Starmer. His elusiveness might prove to have been necessary to obtain the leader's crown in 2019 and traverse from brutal defeat to victory barely five years later. We shall see. Even so, to gain and retain power and navigate the complexities of government, having ditched the commitments upon which he was first elected leader, guarantees a complicated future relationship with his party.

The journey would not be so difficult if not for the limited electoral successes of the party since first gaining power a century ago. Labour formed two brief minority administrations in 1924 and 1929. Its first overall majority wasn't until 1945 following the unique demands of wartime planning and after having entered coalition. Even then, despite some extraordinary achievements, by 1951 it had been thrown from office and would remain in opposition for another 13 years. From then until 1997 there was only one significant Labour majority, in 1966. Despite appearing to buck the trend with landslides and significant majorities in 1997, 2001 and 2005, these wins were followed by major defeats in 2010 and 2015 and from which, despite a brief 2017 uplift, the party's position deteriorated further in the winter of 2019.

Such an uncomfortable relationship with the electorate has produced tension between ideas and the sources of ideological innovation and renewal, and the practical policy concerns and the demands of leadership. The study of ideas and of the intellectual resources available to the party over the past century is limited. There is an extraordinarily rich and growing tradition of labour history to draw on yet little real evaluation of the political and social thought that has shaped a century of Labour. In its place is a growing scholarship surrounding Labour leaders. These excellent materials tend to focus on the dilemmas of power and personality, struggles within real and shadow cabinets, of factional tension and organization, revealed through diaries and testimonies to portray the characters at the heart of Labour. More elusive is a method of understanding the changing ideological influences at work behind this drama.

Justice and the Left

In their interpretations of Labour politics, historians often rely on a left/right factional fault line to assess the actions of individuals, their achievements and failures, and the movements that battle for internal supremacy. This is an important route through the Labour story, but is it sufficient? The book will offer a different perspective because, despite appearances, different factions regularly share certain political characteristics as they emerge from similar traditions of thought. Instead, we introduce a three-part justice schema to reassess Labour history.

The basic argument is that political debate is grounded within alternative philosophical approaches to questions of justice; competing conceptions of how society should be organized. In general, these are concerned with maximizing *human welfare, human freedom* or *human virtue*.[2] The first tends to consider the material wellbeing of the people as the measure of justice. The second is concerned with a respect for, and the extension of, personal rights and freedoms. The third is the promotion of human virtue. This schema helps establish an alternative historical framework to rethink the often-impenetrable divisions and factions on the left and how competing visions of socialism have shaped the Labour Party over the last 100 years. Such a lens helps us account for both the successes and failures of Labour over the last century.

Three Visions of Justice

Welfare

The first approach shaping Labour history seeks to maximize questions of human welfare. The political philosophy of utilitarianism, the series of theories that argue an intervention should be assessed by its ability to promote the greatest happiness for the greatest number of people, can be traced back to the work of Jeremy Bentham and philosophers such as John Stuart Mill and Henry Sidgwick.[3] Bentham was heavily influenced by David Hume and other thinkers of the Enlightenment, with deep roots in Scottish Calvinist traditions, which endeavoured, especially between the 1740s and 1790s, to establish a framework to consider historical progress.[4] Unlike its French counterpart, it lacked any fundamental attack on established systems of political and economic order.

Utilitarianism focuses on questions of aggregative happiness and the application of philosophy to make people better off. Jeremy Bentham sought pleasure in the absence of pain and proposed you could calculate this and in so doing establish a science of society, whereby ethics would become a branch of the natural sciences. Actions would be judged in terms of rational outcomes; the amount of utility derived from any action to promote happiness.

Several philosophical concerns emerge from this, most notably what constitutes pleasure and is it a measurable good? For instance, G.E. Moore's famous attack on utilitarianism argued that it could not cater for questions of friendship and beauty in accounting for our happiness. John Stuart Mill consequently rejected the pure quantitative calculation of utility, and instead distinguished between higher and lower pleasures in human development. Other questions remain, however, regarding human motivations and intentions, such as do we have a desire to be kind for reasons other than self-interest?

Less abstract concerns relating to the practical application of the philosophy regularly appear, such as how our desire to maximize the good might collide with how it is distributed. This might lead us to question the morality, in rational terms, of doing the most good in terms of aggregate pleasure. Subsequent variations on classical utilitarianism introduced criteria for deciding the quality of the outcome, including questions of distributive justice. However, the question of motivation persists. For instance, are there duties and responsibilities to our immediate family or community which challenge the idea of the aggregate maximization of outcomes? Does such a science withdraw from other specific duties and obligations that define our humanity and how we live and what we cherish? Moreover, strictly speaking, acts of stealing, or killing of the innocent could be justified in terms of aggregate utility, so too other inequalities which might under certain conditions boost overall happiness. Such ethical approaches can endanger life.

Utilitarian thinking has retained an extraordinarily powerful influence, arguably the dominant influence, on political philosophy and public policy, especially in welfare economics and politics. Its attractiveness for politicians and policy makers lies in its focus on the rules required to organize society to maximize the welfare of others.[5] Questions of utility dominate politics.

The appeal of this philosophy for Labour is obvious for a party concerned with the allocation of resources and questions of material inequality. Welfare models of justice tend to rely on utilitarian philosophical assumptions to craft interventions which seek to maximize the happiness of the maximum number of people. This is generally translated to mean their material wellbeing, their welfare, and tends to be primarily interested in the allocation of economic resources. Within the UK left, this approach has historically been associated with the work and policies of the Fabian Society and a generation of economists and planners that took hold of the top strata of the Labour Party throughout the 1930s under the sponsorship of the great economist, politician and eventual Chancellor Hugh Dalton. It is often described as 'labourist', a term associated with modest economic reform and redistribution executed by a central government aided by strong institutional union support.

In the pages that follow we identify three basic inter-related utilitarian approaches that have influenced Labour history. First, the idea of *labourism* that relates to Labour's relationship to its affiliated unions. Although this relationship tends to be defined by rules and customs rather than through ideology, it rests on the enhancement of material living standards through political action. Its political concerns are primarily distributional and material. In 1900 the LRC was founded both 'to promote legislation in the direct interests of labour' through higher wages, reduced hours and improved working conditions and to defend these material working-class interests. The second utilitarian tradition we identify within Labour history we describe as *welfarism*. This seeks to maximize the economic wellbeing of the people through the distribution of economic resources. The third tradition we describe as *statism* has been linked primarily to debates around nationalization. This approach promotes the view that the state has a major, necessary and legitimate role in directing critical aspects of the economy to enhance the overall wellbeing of the people, either directly through state ownership and state planning or indirectly through economic interventions and macroeconomic regulation.

Questions of power and democracy tend to be downplayed within this tradition – consequently it can be labelled 'economistic' or economically 'deterministic'. This approach tends to envision the task of left politics as one of state capture to redistribute and maximize the welfare of the people. As such, it attracts criticism for technocratic forms of administration and a centralizing, bureaucratic statecraft. Crucially it is not the preserve of any one faction on the left as it remains the hallmark of *both* the traditional Labour 'right' and 'left'. A 'left/right' framework to interpret party history obscures this reality.

This economistic or distributional tradition continues to dominate contemporary left thinking. For instance, under New Labour, the welfarism favoured by Gordon Brown was of remedial money transfers – tax credits – to buttress the disposable incomes of workers as wages flatlined due to global competitive pressures; an approach funded by the growth engineered through a compact with finance capital. Another good recent example is the former Labour leader Ed Miliband's 'cost of living' framework, under which Labour drifted into an almost exclusively materialist perspective and was heavily defeated at the 2015 general election. The policy strategy was one of money transfers – such as capping energy prices and rents, abolition of the bedroom tax, higher minimum wages, and capping student fees – essentially fiscal exchanges administered by a central bureaucracy. This intellectual tradition has generally dominated the history of Labour since the 1930s. It is also detectable in the origins of the party, especially in the sectional demands of the unions and their reasons for creating a party to represent labour and the gradualist methods of organizations like the Fabians who came together in 1900 to create the LRC.

It has also helped define the history of Marxism with assumptions of the domination of the economic 'base' over 'superstructure' and of the forces over relations of production driving the overall wellbeing of the masses. Once again, the charge is 'economic reductionism' or 'technological determinism' and associated tendencies to downgrade questions of democracy and power as humans tend to be considered simple carriers of these economic laws; bearers of modes of production. Such a method has helped shape the history of Labour's orthodox hard-left politics, its Leninist character, from the early SDF, which foreshadowed the creation of the party, through to some elements of Bennism in the 1980s and recently reappeared across parts of the Corbyn project.

Across both the left and right, utilitarian thinking has been a critical element shaping party history. It continues to dominate today. Despite mythology and populist depictions of who is political 'friend' and 'enemy', many battles for internal control occur between factional warriors who share more than they often realize, and still do today.

Freedom

If you search for St George's Hill in Surrey you discover a 1,000-acre gated community in Weybridge with average house prices over £5 million for the 400 properties owned by sports stars, entrepreneurs, musicians and entertainers. In 1649 St George's Hill was the site for one of the world's first socialist experiments. The Diggers, a group of political and religious non-conformist dissenters with radical ideas about organizing society and practising religion, emerged as old certainties dissolved following the Civil War, death of the King and establishment of the English Commonwealth.

Their leader Gerrard Winstanley, a bankrupt merchant tailor, embraced a language of liberty and peace and assumed that the end of private property, the 'levelling' of land, coupled with an agrarian lifestyle would bring genuine freedom and complete an unfinished reformation. His manifesto *The True Levellers Standard Advanced* was published by

Giles Calvert, the prominent radical bookseller and source of many of the dissident ideas unleashed through the application of the new printing presses.

Earlier, in late October and early November 1647, the draft written constitution of the Levellers, *An Agreement of the People*, was debated in St Marys Church on the High Street and southern approach to Putney Bridge, in meetings chaired by Oliver Cromwell. It contained five fundamental rights: liberty of conscience over religion, freedom from conscription, a civil war amnesty, equality before the law and constraints on parliament legislating against the wellbeing of the people. It was a draft constitution of the people that rejected discrimination on the grounds of 'tenure, estate, charter, degree, birth or place'. Putney remains a landmark of democratic change. In 1649 England was declared a republic, but one without the Levellers' blessing as their leaders had by then been arrested. In August that year the Diggers were forced to abandon St Georges Hill.

The founding of a new political order including a written constitution, human rights and democratic accountability can be traced back to this period of dissent and political upheaval, many decades before more famous contributions from such luminaries of liberty as Tom Paine and Jean-Jacques Rousseau. The moment passed and English republicanism was exiled abroad, subsequently influencing revolutions in France and America; part of a lost radical English history concerned with questions of freedom and liberty, one barely acknowledged or taught in schools. The roots of this radicalism lie even deeper within English history.

The trial of one Leveller leader, John Lilburne, 'free born John', helped establish the jury as protector of the citizen against the state, trial by jury, arguably the Levellers' greatest achievement. At his trial, Lilburne invoked *Magna Carta* as a symbol of the fundamental laws of England to denounce the legitimacy of the Commonwealth, and in the dock accuse it of treason using the famous seventeenth-century jurist Sir Edward Coke's commentary on *Magna Carta*. He was acquitted to popular acclaim.

Magna Carta emerged from the political upheavals that followed the death of the King, Richard Lionheart, on 6 April 1199 and the succession of his brother John. The outcome of the negotiations at Runnymede in June 1215 arguably constitutes the birthplace of modern democracy.

Specifically, Clauses 39 and 40 stand as the foundations of English law and liberty. The new Charter's phrase 'to no one do we deny' appeared to establish that the citizen has rights and freedoms beyond patterns of ownership. For over 800 years it has remained a symbol of liberty from which justice emerged as an actual process rather than product of royal whim.

Gradually through the sixteenth and seventeenth centuries, the idea of the free man emerged as a key political concern. It was central to the passage of the *Petition of Right* in 1628 setting out individual protections against the state. In the 1630s and 1640s, the pilgrim fathers sought to export the charter. It informed the debates at Putney and Leveller commitment to popular sovereignty, a universal franchise and equality before the law. Nineteenth-century Chartism – with its charter of liberties – was built around an interpretation of *Magna Carta*. With the emergence of Enlightenment and natural law theories, the charter has been used not just in terms of supporting notions of ancient liberty and the defence of common law tradition or parliament, but in opposition to the arbitrary use of power *exercised through these traditions*.[6]

Human rights traced back to *Magna Carta* inspired a generation of post-war leaders. When Eleanor Roosevelt proclaimed the *Universal Declaration of Human Rights* (UDHR), she stated her hope it might 'become the international Magna Carta of all men everywhere',[7] hinting at how the British tradition of liberty is expressed within the UDHR.

This stands as a rich seam within English history regarding questions of freedom and rights. It is a tradition that informs political approaches to justice today. On the political right it is the popular domain of the free market libertarians.[8] On the left are those who seek to advance human rights to remedy economic and social disadvantage, often described in a pejorative way as the preserve of the 'liberal left'.[9]

This tradition of justice is generally understood to be upheld by liberalism, but liberalism itself contains a variety of different, often conflicting, approaches. Questions of democracy and liberty have a proud left-wing heritage traced back through the Levellers and Putney, the exported republicanism of Tom Paine, and Chartism. More recently, the consequence of industrial society and experiences of twentieth-century fascist and Stalinist authoritarian regimes have elevated this approach to protect an essential human dignity.

In the pages that follow we identify three basic inter-related approaches to questions of liberty and freedom that have influenced Labour history. The first approach is focused on questions of *legal equality* and is expressed in the five generations of equalities legislation enacted by successive Labour governments from the 1960s to 2010 and which form the bedrock of the liberal conception of justice within Labour's history. The second approach is centred around questions of *human rights* and is derived from post-war concerns to defend and enhance human freedoms given the effects of totalitarianism and genocide. For example, the post-war UDHR was guided by both Enlightenment and modern social democratic and socialist rights-based thinking as was the 1998 Human Rights Act. The third approach focuses on questions of *constitutional and electoral reform* to challenge the power of the state in the name of liberty and advance citizenship. Initiatives such as reform of the House of Lords, devolution and Freedom of Information under the Blair government reflect this tradition.

These concerns retain a rich history within progressive politics, identifiable in the complex late nineteenth-century relations between the emerging Labour tradition and the Liberal Party. More recently the desire for legal equality drove the pioneering social reforms of the 1960s under the guidance of Roy Jenkins. The Labour Party has a long history of campaigning for constitutional reform. In the 1970s and 1980s, campaigners such as Tony Benn referenced the contribution of the Diggers, Levellers and Chartists when making the case for modern democratic and constitutional renewal. In the 1980s and 1990s, Charter 88 attracted widespread support from across the liberal, social democratic and socialist left. Over the last few years Gordon Brown has urged the party to take up the cause of democratic renewal once again. Brown is consistent in this as in his first week as Prime Minister in July 2007, he argued for a written constitution.

Philosophically, this tradition was given intellectual energy with the publication of John Rawls's ground-breaking *A Theory of Justice* in 1971.[10] His conception of the modern social contract re-established for the left the notion of liberty whilst permitting economic inequality – but only so long as it benefitted the least well off. More generally, such a rights-based approach seeks a non-judgemental state architecture which cultivates the ability of each and every citizen to choose the way they wish to live their lives and actively equips them with the ability to do so. As such it retains a liberal neutrality on what constitutes the good life – that is for each citizen to decide.

The great benefit of this approach is the way it suggests that a utilitarian politics built around allocating resources and material justice is too technocratic and retains a tendency to truncate political understanding of the lives people wish to live. This is of great importance today given that fundamental freedoms are under threat from contemporary capitalism, authoritarian populism and unmediated technology. The danger with it, however, is that it tends to remove moral questions from public discussion because of a belief in liberal procedural justice. A progressive language of rights, liberal opportunity and fairness 'flattens questions of meaning, identity and purpose'.[11]

Virtue

The third approach is more ethical in orientation, concerned with nurturing the human characteristics upon which a good or just society is formed and suggests a more judgemental framework than those that rest on questions of utility or rights.[12] Aristotle remains the classical reference point regarding the virtues that might characterize a just society and the policy and institutional arrangements that enable citizens to live a good life. The field of virtue ethics concentrates on the classic ideals such as honour, duty, wisdom and fortitude to evaluate the reasoning behind moral decision making – as opposed to a mere adherence to rules or the outcome of the action. Aristotle's concern was human flourishing – the practices that help cultivate good character and habits and the state of human life that could only be properly achieved in the city-state community. The idea of the common good associated with this tradition is concerned with personal and mutual flourishing in terms of our talents and vocations, treating people as belonging to families, localities and communities and to shared traditions, interests and faiths neglected by an exclusively legalistic, managerial and technocratic conception of justice and politics.

In the pages that follow we identify three basic inter-related approaches to questions of human virtue that have influenced Labour history. The first tradition is that of *ethical socialism*. This approach infused the early

Labour Party with a non-conformist, anti-materialist religious morality. At the centre of this tradition stood the ILP, which drew on John Ruskin and William Morris for inspiration in their rejection of the indignities of capitalist exploitation. The second tradition, which we describe as *associational*, has throughout Labour history sought to contest statism and instead stress human motivations beyond economics and distributive justice. Questions of fraternity, democracy, solidarity, the building of civic virtue and upholding community life are recurring concerns for this communitarian tradition within the left. It has regularly sought to introduce questions of ethics and democracy into economic debate around, for example, questions of craft regulation of work, economic design, stakeholding and industrial democracy. The third tradition is concerned with *human flourishing* and the measures necessary to build a good society around happiness and life satisfaction, mental and physical health, meaning and purpose, character and virtue.

Within the history of the British left this approach is best represented by what is often described as the early 'religion of socialism'.[13] Influences include dissident, 'non-conformist' Protestant voices – including Methodists, Baptists, Congregationalists, Quakers and Unitarians, assorted churches including the 'Brotherhood Church', the 'Labour Church', later renamed the 'Socialist Church', the 'Ethical Church', Salvation Army and Temperance Church, groups such as the Fellowship of the New Life, alongside visions of 'socialist fellowship' and the moral economy associated with writers such as John Ruskin and William Morris.[14] These later figures sought to challenge the scientific status of economics, and the separation of economic value and utility from questions of human life, and deterministic assumptions regarding modernity and the evolution of socialist society found within much early socialist economic thought.[15] Ruskin's notion of the 'citizens economy', morally underpinned by the idea of universal service and communal life driving a socialist approach to work, labour and social security, captured this movement in the idea of a popular commonwealth.[16]

In the critical last decades of the nineteenth century, the 'religion of socialism' was for many a way of life and often their work took the form of a 'crusade'. The historian Stephen Yeo has explained the way such advocacy often involved forms of conversion, with socialism akin to religious vocations, callings, with activists often termed 'apostles' or 'evangelists' for the cause.[17] Such feelings were intimately related to the brutality of late nineteenth-century capitalism with socialist resistance considered essential to human salvation. Over time such sentiments became institutionally encased, primarily, though not exclusively, within the ILP.

Such 'ethical socialist' traditions are often termed 'romantic'; the product of feelings rather than thoughts and ideas. The effect is to counterpose the 'head' and 'heart' of socialism, a regular reference in party history, with logic and rationality at odds with that of sentiment. Such a method relegates the emotional significance of the Labour cause and underplays how spiritual or ethical socialist traditions are embedded within ancient traditions of thought regarding the promotion of the common good and human virtue. Such stereotypes help us appreciate how ethical traditions have been diluted when consolidated into formal party structures and the calculus of electoral politics. This process helps account for the eclipse of the ILP and the regular 'exile' of ethical elements throughout party history.

The 'religion of socialism' sought to promote a life of virtue, to act with wisdom and compassion, and to cultivate an essential humanity in combatting industrial capitalism. For Ruskin, resistance to *laissez-faire* society informed his artistic criticism. What is of value is not the 'exchange value' contained in both orthodox Marxist and liberal economics. Art represents a politics of resistance to the commodification of life; a continuous struggle, not just against the alienating effects of capitalism but also left-wing utilitarianism and Fabianism in the battle to shape a just society. Socialist change was not simply political and economic – the 'machinery' of socialism, as Morris called it – but heightened consciousness. In the cauldron of 1880s industrialization, it was a politics in search of authentic human life, captured in both religious and secular approaches to fellowship. Socialism was understood as a calling to contest human degradation and retain dignity.

Despite playing a vital role in Labour's prehistory, the significance of this ethical tradition has diminished. It is clearly visible in the leadership of Hardie, MacDonald and Lansbury and the early history of the ILP. We will locate Attlee within this tradition as well as elements within post-war revisionism. This approach intermittently resurfaces in the political character of Aneurin Bevan, Foot and Tony Benn on the left and on the right with John Smith and in the early political identity of Tony Blair. It has recently reappeared in the 'Blue Labour' movement, which seeks to advance associational forms of life beyond the state.

This tradition has played a critical role throughout Labour history. For instance, in informing debate on working-class self-improvement, around questions of democracy and forms of cooperation, of civic renewal and active citizenship, regularly challenging the orthodox statism of utilitarian labour traditions. We can detect it in the work of many key Labour intellectuals, such as Tawney, G.D.H. Cole, Harold Laski and Michael Young. In terms of political economy, we can identify its influence[18] on early Guild Socialism, amongst advocates for industrial democracy, initiatives around workers' control and debates around economic stakeholding. These traditions reappeared in parts of the post-war New Left that pushed back against attempts to truncate socialism into questions of state ownership and economic planning.[19]

Overall, although often imprecise, these ethical or virtue-based traditions of justice originate in the sphere of interpersonal and spiritual relationships and extend into the wider social realm shaping understanding of both community and economy. It offers a politics of the individual rooted in the social goods that give meaning to people's lives: home, family, friendships, good work, locality and communities of belonging. We can identify modern thinkers such as Amartya Sen and Martha Nussbaum in employing virtue ethics to inform their capability approach to international development, or Michael Sandel's approach to ethics and justice, and writers such as Alasdair MacIntyre and Charles Taylor as operating within this tradition.[20]

Labour and Socialism Revisited

This three-part justice schema routes us back into socialist and not just Labour history.[21] Such histories – especially on the radical economistic left – often begin in 1848 with the publication of *The Communist Manifesto*.[22] They thereby underplay the contributions of earlier socialists such as Winstanley or the contribution of the Levellers or early Utopian Socialists such as Charles Fourier and Robert Owen. The 1848 departure point is at the expense of both ethical socialist movements and those anchored around questions of freedom and liberty. Conceptions of justice inform how we interrogate history and how we define socialism. For instance, Crosland's *The Future of Socialism*[23] detailed assorted 'socialisms' yet dodged a definition, suggesting it was about a 'strong' rather than 'liberal' equality. He emphasized the means beyond ownership to address freedom and democracy, planning and growth, indeed beauty; a brilliant combination of distributive, utilitarian economics and radical thinking regarding rights and liberty.[24] Unsurprisingly, in his later work Crosland embraced Rawls.

Tawney, in contrast, defined socialism as resistance to the market and constraints on private profit and identified two approaches: economic and ethical – one driven by socialized ownership, resource distribution and utilitarian welfare maximization to redress poverty, homelessness and the like; the other by human fellowship to contest the indignities of commodification and human dispossession. He suggests a general philosophical fault line within the left, often expressed between scientific rationality and humanism, economism and ethics, stretching back to the seventeenth century.

This divide between ethics and economic utility helps delineate the early history of Labour but neglects questions of liberty and freedom as does one that suggests the best route through Labour history is to compare and contrast the fortunes of the ILP and the Fabian traditions since their creation in 1893 and 1884. Undoubtedly the welfare/ virtue or ILP/Fabian divide provides real insight into Labour politics, especially from the late nineteenth century to the mid-1950s. Yet such a method neglects a third, rights-based approach to justice and Labour history which predates both 1884 and 1848. This also allows for a full appreciation of Crosland's 1956 intervention and later the influence of Rawlsian progressive thinking. This three-part schema moves us beyond the traditional left/right metric whose factions often share similar approaches to justice.

The early division that shaped the origins story of Labour, between utility and virtue, economics and ethics, also defined the history of Marxism and influenced the politics of the Labour left. On one side stands the historical materialism of the Second International. On the other, humanist reactions to contest scientific socialism and the realities of rigid party domination and a bureaucratized, authoritarian politics.[25] The latter reoriented Marxism towards questions of ethics and virtue, aided with the discovery of some of the writings of the young Marx, most notably *The 1844 Manuscripts*.

This division within Marxism took a unique British form, one that helped shape the post-war contours of Labour politics. Specifically, E.P. Thompson's work was part of a distinct political project within the Communist Party to identify a unique English radicalism – a politics of virtue – in the character of William Morris and within the emerging working class itself.[26] Alongside Thompson, Raymond Williams, particularly in *Culture and Society*,[27] defined a political, artistic and cultural tradition from Ruskin, through Morris, to the modern New Left. This tradition, its resistance to *laissez-faire* society, embraced an artistic criticism that asserted 'the art of any country is the exponent of its social and political virtues ... the exponent of its ethical life'.[28] It sought to contest forms of political economy primarily concerned with price and distribution; utility. Morris therefore plays a significant and recurring role, not just in influencing an emerging nineteenth-century working-class politics and formation of the ILP, one that remained significant well into the 1930s amongst influential strands of the party, but also stretching into the post-war era in the form of the New Left.

How these three traditions have influenced the character of the party is the purpose of the rest of the book. The argument is that these three traditions are vital resources for the Labour Party. Labour succeeds when it can draw together these three traditions, as happened under Attlee and Blair. It tends to fail, however, when just one tradition, most often the centralizing utilitarian tradition, dominates the party.

3

Origins

During the late nineteenth century a general divide emerged within British socialism, between ethical and utilitarian traditions of justice. On one side stood William Morris and the secular and religious concerns of the ILP; on the other Fabianism, and various scientific socialist and economistic strands. This basic division would become encased within the emerging Labour Party. Whilst the influence of liberalism remained primarily *external* to the party in the fluctuating fortunes of the Liberal Party, ideological shifts divided liberalism and influenced Labour politics. The political conflicts of the late nineteenth century triggered a neo-classical revolution, where liberal economics withdrew into the scientific realms of utility. Yet the emergence of a 'New Liberalism' dovetailed with some of the ethical concerns of the ILP and helped shape Labour politics as the Liberals collapsed.

Labour historians have often asked if the emergence of the Labour Party was the inevitable consequence of the extension of the voting franchise in 1832, 1867 and 1884, and growth of the industrial working class, with the emergence of the Trades Union Congress (TUC) in 1868 and the rise of general unionism in the late nineteenth century. Or was it more the consequence of unanticipated factors, such as the Taff Vale judgment of the House of Lords, which transformed trade union political involvement, or the events of the First World War and splits within the Liberal Party, which created unforeseen opportunities for a party of labour?

Electoral evidence can be assembled to support the inevitability argument.[1] Labour's election results from 1900 to 1923 suggest a strong trend growth in support (see Appendix C). Labour had two MPs in 1900, 29 in 1906, rising to 42 in 1910, 57 in 1918 before jumping to 142 in 1922 and 191 in late 1923, leading to Labour's first minority government. It dropped briefly in 1924 before rising again to 287 in 1929. In contrast, Liberal MPs numbered some 397 at their highpoint in

1906 before falling to 272 in 1910, 164 in 1918, down to 115 in 1922, rising briefly to 158 in 1923 before plunging to just 40 in 1924. In terms of the distribution of the non-Conservative vote, the two trends appear inversely related and, if you add in the growth in union affiliations to Labour from 1900 to 1924, jumping from 353,000 to well over three million, the historical picture looks clear.

Yet these statistics reveal little of the volatile politics of the late nineteenth century. On the surface, by the mid-1880s the Liberal Party looked to have established itself amongst working-class electors. Following the Third Reform Act, 11 'Lib Lab' MPs were elected, made up of working-class Liberal members, making inroads for the party, especially in mining areas. Yet working-class representatives found it difficult to get selected as Liberal candidates. As we shall see later, Keir Hardie's troubles in Mid Lanark spurred him towards independent labour representation and the emerging socialist movement of the early 1880s.[2]

This movement included the Democratic Federation, founded on 7 June 1881, which became the more militant Social Democratic Federation (SDF) in 1884, the country's first organized socialist party, under the leadership of Henry Hyndman. Following an Executive Council meeting in December 1884, it subsequently split, with a group including William Morris leaving to form the dissident offshoot the Socialist League.

It also contained the Fabian Society, a small body of London intellectuals including Sidney and Beatrice Webb and Bernard Shaw, founded on 4 January 1884, in Osnaburgh St, London. With a logo of a tortoise and named after the 'Delayer', a nickname in honour of a Roman general whose victories over Hannibal were achieved after hard-won acts of attrition, their political purpose remained one of gradual incremental change. In 1889, the Progressive Party composed of Fabians and British Liberals took control of the London County Council; the first council to have substantial socialist influence.[3]

In 1888, the Scottish Labour Party was formed. In July 1889, the Second International was convened in Paris. A few years later Joseph Burgess, the editor of the *Workmen's Times*, initiated a meeting, which included Hardie, on 13 June 1892 at the Democratic Club in London, and established the national Independent Labour Party.

The founding conference of the ILP was held at the Bradford Labour Institute, run by the Labour Church, between 14 and 16 January 1893.[4] Keir Hardie was elected its first chairman and would remain active until his death in 1915. Figures such as Philip Snowden and MacDonald, Labour's first Chancellor and Prime Minister, would emerge through its ranks and into parliament. MacDonald joined in May 1894 and by the end of the decade had become one of its leading figures. George Lansbury would join a decade later.[5] Links with the unions were strong following major disputes at Bryant and May in 1888, the London dock strike of 1889, and at the Bradford Manningham Mills in 1890–1.[6] 1895 saw the ILP reject socialist unity and the economism of the SDF for whom, to quote Bruce Glasier, its 'strange disregard of the religious, moral and aesthetic sentiments of the people is an overwhelming defect',[7] and establish a distinctive radical ethical tradition. In the 1895 election, the ILP put up 28 candidates but won only 44,325 votes.

There is a danger, however, of simply bolting together these organizations to navigate Labour's origins story and neglect a closer inspection of the character of the socialism on display throughout this turbulent period. It was an intense, violent time of political upheaval not easily shoehorned into a Westminster party of labour. The emerging political organizations were part of a quite different socialist imagination compared to what was to come later. While we can formally identify the Fabians as the foundation of a gradualist, utilitarian tradition complemented within Marxism by the SDF, and the ILP as the ethical socialist counterweight, and the Socialist League as the dissident offshoot that transitioned to anarchism, this only explores part of an extraordinary history.

The notion of the 'religion of socialism' captures a distinct period in socialist history and the approach to socialist justice that informed much of the pre-history of the Labour Party. It was an approach captured by the Labour Church pioneered by John Trevor in Manchester; in the Labour Army, Socialist and Brotherhood Churches; in journals such as the Socialist League's *Commonweal* and the *Clarion* newspaper started by Robert Blatchford in December 1891; in the poetry of Edward Carpenter and Morris, including the latter's 'The Pilgrims of Hope' from 1886; in books, literature and pamphlets with titles such as Blatchford's 'The New Religion' and Bruce Glasier's 'The Religion of Socialism'; in

J.L. Joynes's *Socialist Catechism* published weekly in 1884 in *Justice*. It was a language of religiosity that infused the socialism of the period. One that crossed factional and spiritual boundaries whereby:

> The words 'evangelists', 'apostles', 'disciples', 'new birth', 'preachment', 'street preaching' and 'gospel' recurred in the anti-'religious' Morris as much as in the 'religious' Hardie.[8]

Such sentiment was found not just in the ILP but even in the SDF, where Lansbury recalled how in 1892 SDF meetings in Bow resembled 'revivalist meetings', even in parts of the Fabian tradition. Political conversions were often quasi-religious experiences. Socialism for many was an evangelical-like force, one demanding both sacrifice and missionary activity in pursuit of 'making socialists' rather than making policy or electoral machines. The 1885 *Manifesto* of the Socialist League, written by William Morris, declared 'the religion of socialism, the only religion which the Socialist League professes'. For many, Temperance and the socialism of the SDF or Socialist League were not incompatible.

At this stage labourism had not found a particular voice or institutional home, socialism had yet to discover the utilitarian language of the later social engineers or calculators and been captured by the machinery of state welfarism. The politics of labour had yet to be assigned to a political bureaucracy:

> Socialism in that period had not yet become the prisoner of a particular, elaborate party machine – a machine which would come to associate its own well-being with the prospects of socialism.[9]

There existed a sense of fellowship and unity across factions with members moving in and out of the ILP, SDF and Fabians and local branches affiliating to each other's organizations. Internally this was helped by anti-elitist grassroots democratic cultures within these emerging organizations and focus on agency over process, even within the SDF compared to its later Leninist tendencies, or the social engineering of much twentieth-century labour politics. Culturally this was aided by numerous links between political movements and social and recreational activities, sports events, scouts, music and much more.

The First Principle of the Labour Church stated 'That the Labour Movement is a religious movement'. Such sentiment was shared by many across a variety of traditions within a distinct phase of socialism in the 1880s and 1890s. Personal salvation linked to the march of socialism often carried with it a redemptive sense of political and social inevitability, not least due to the weakness of the Liberals before they re-emerged after 1900. This was less to do with the inevitable rise of a Westminster party of labour and more to the upheavals of the age and sense of imminent industrial and social change.

But time passed, and the religion of socialism was overtaken by electoral realism and with it the institutional consolidation of the ethical and economistic traditions. A socialist programme did not emerge from the 1880s and 1890s and emphasis shifted towards electoral politics, finance and the building of the machines. Most significantly the big figures in the ILP – Hardie, Snowden, MacDonald and Glasier – gained bureaucratic ascendency as the century closed and, in alliance with the unions, brought forward the launch of the LRC.

The Labour Representation Committee

In 1899, a Doncaster member of the Amalgamated Society of Railway Servants (ASRS), Thomas R. Steels, moved a motion that called on the TUC to bring together organizations to form a single body to sponsor parliamentary candidates. As a result, the Labour Party was established in the form of the LRC, when 129 delegates from the ILP, SDF, the Fabians and unions representing less than half of the TUC convened at Congregational Memorial Hall, Farringdon St, London on 27 and 28 February 1900. From the beginning Labour was a merger of traditions between the utilitarian priorities of the unions, Fabians and SDF and the ethical socialism of the ILP.

A motion moved by Hardie was passed to 'support a distinct Labour Group in parliament' with their own whips and policy agenda 'which must embrace a readiness to cooperate with any party which for the time being may be engaged in promoting legislation in the direct interests of labour'. This formed the LRC, to coordinate attempts to support MPs sponsored by trade unions and represent the working class. The Committee included two members from the ILP, two from the SDF, one from the Fabians and seven from the unions. It had no single leader; the ILP successfully nominated MacDonald as Secretary. The October 1900 'Khaki' election came too soon for the new party to campaign effectively. Only 15 candidatures were sponsored, but two were successful; Hardie in South Wales and Richard Bell in Derby.[10] In August 1901, the SDF disaffiliated from the LRC.

Taff Vale

Any future success for the LRC could hardly have been anticipated in 1900 not least because of weak membership amongst the unions. Yet the Taff Vale judgment of the House of Lords in July 1901 would alter trade union involvement in British politics for good and see the political character of the early party shift towards gradualism and away from the ILP through the institutional consolidation of the unions.

The unique system of British labour law resulted from the speed and timing of British industrialization. Mass unionism had emerged before any political party of labour. In Britain, unlike countries who industrialized later, the party of labour was not established to sponsor unions through positive individual and collective rights, but the other way around, to keep the law out of industrial relations. Negative immunities from prosecution were preferred over a positive framework of law.[11] The Labour Party was in part, for conservative reasons, created to preserve this separation between labour issues and the law, following a judgment which imperilled both the legal right to strike and financial viability of the unions. As collective bodies they became tortiously liable for inducing workers to breach their contracts of employment when the court awarded £23,000 plus costs against the ASRS rail union.

With the LRC promising to overturn the decision, overnight this boosted the case for independent working-class representation. Union affiliation rose from 353,000 in 1900 to 975,000 in 1906, as the Conservative administration of Arthur Balfour looked captive to industrial and business interests. With increased income and by-election victories that saw David Shackleton, Will Crooks and Arthur Henderson enter parliament, Labour's fortunes improved.

This process was further aided by the covert deal struck between Liberal Chief Whip Herbert Gladstone and MacDonald in 1903 to coordinate anti-Conservative candidates in key seats.[12] The resulting election in 1906 brought 29 LRC candidates into the Commons, which soon increased to 30, and a Liberal landslide.

Labour and Liberalism

In 1906 the Liberals looked all-powerful after 11 years in opposition and appeared intent on attracting continued working-class support with social reforms in support of the poor, unemployed, the sick and old. Moreover, Labour supported the Liberal administration, especially after 1910, and in May 1915 was drawn into the wartime coalition. Yet by the end of the war Lloyd George's government was divided and only sustained by the Conservatives. It is a complex story.

In chapter 2 we noted that approaches to justice that focus on questions of liberty can appeal to political traditions across both left and right. It is now worth developing this point given shifts within British liberalism and its contribution to Labour's history.

Many of liberalism's core propositions, including freedom of speech and from religious domination, trial by jury and the removal of the divine right of monarchs, can be traced back to English traditions of liberty. Yet despite a common heritage, liberalism contains a range of diverse, often contradictory traditions, amongst them classical, new, radical, economic and social iterations.

British liberalism rested initially upon the foundations of Classical Political Economy. With its origins in eighteenth-century enlightenment, this body of work interpreted the stages of human history through the study of alternative modes of subsistence, principally hunting and gathering, pastoralism, agrarian society and commercial relations. Writers such as Adam Smith, John Stuart Mill, David Ricardo and Thomas Malthus helped develop a theory of modern expanded production and the case for self-regulating markets and free trade with political stability achieved courtesy of a 'Trinity Formula' to compensate holders of land, labour and capital to ensure class reconciliation through the just distribution of economic growth.[13] The extension of commerce thereby offered the prospect of an independent economy and open civil society to enhance liberty. Yet the political uncertainties and class conflicts of the 1870s brought with them growing pressures for economic and social reform. In such a climate the assumptions of strict *laissez-faire* political economy offered diminishing returns. Two key reforms occurred within liberalism which would help shape the contours of British politics for the next 150 years. Some elements within liberalism withdrew further into the realms of rational self-interest and the maximization of utility whilst others gravitated towards greater concern for questions of human virtue.

In economics a neo-classical revolution contracted the discipline into an individualized science of society expressed in a strict determination of market prices within a pure exchange system, one that initially isolates then aggregates market transactions determined by crude assumptions regarding human nature, our desires, preferences and actions in pursuit of utility. Yet from the late nineteenth century, within philosophy and politics a quite different reformulation took place primarily through the work of the great English idealist T.H. Green and later L.T. Hobhouse and J.A. Hobson. This reformulation sought to reorientate liberalism away from questions of self-interest and freedom from forms of suffering towards those of character and the ability to act freely within a thriving democracy; of positive liberty. With the later movement, emphasis shifted away from the inherited *laissez-faire* doctrines of Classical Political Economy towards building the social and political institutions to promote moral character and enhance choice and the case for the welfare state, sometimes termed 'new' or 'social' liberalism. These two shifts within liberalism and the tensions they created have played out to the present day within and between the political traditions and parties that represent liberalism, conservatism and socialism and helped shape the Labour story, even before the party was officially created.[14]

In its extreme neo-classical variant, liberalism assumes a model of human behaviour that is rational, acquisitive and ruthlessly self-interested. In the phrase made famous by Bernard Mandeville's poem *The Fable of the Bees*, public benefit is achieved by means of private vice. Since Thomas Hobbes, a central fault line in economic and political thought has been around how we consider the individual. Is it the world of selfish beasts and genes, atomized exchange, and modern liberal economics? Or do we locate the social individual, who cares for others; an approach that informs ideas from Rousseau to Tawney, secular ethical and faith-based socialisms, one that employs a language of generosity and fraternity rather than a disinterested scientism? Its 'fleshed out' form was led by

Green, who rejected the atomistic individualism which represented humans as impermeable, self-contained units enjoying natural rights but owing no corresponding social obligation. Instead, he saw society and the individuals within it as radically interdependent.

This 'New Liberalism' from the early 1880s departed politically from many of the precepts of classical liberalism,[15] specifically in rethinking the role of the state in delivering social welfare. They believed in progressive taxation to compensate for the unequal bargaining power of the marketplace and pay for pensions and other forms of social security. They advocated the common ownership of natural monopolies and vital public services. They viewed property rights as conditional and not absolute, subject as they must be to certain public interest restrictions. They called for the limitation of working hours and new regulations to guarantee health and safety in the workplace. They stood behind the vision of a cooperative commonwealth built on explicitly moral foundations.

Hobhouse described himself as a liberal socialist. Hobson and several other New Liberals went a stage further and joined the Labour Party as the Liberal Party proved to be an incapable vehicle for resolving these tensions within liberalism. He suggested 'New Liberalism' was a kind of 'socialism in liberalism', a phrase subsequently used by Ramsay MacDonald. Green and later Hobhouse and Hobson are all vital figures within the broad tradition of ethical socialism. Their influence over the foremost Labour intellectuals of the early twentieth century – R.H. Tawney, G.D.H Cole and Harold Laski – was both profound and warmly acknowledged. For Hardie, it offered new political alliances in support of the radical elements of the 1906 Liberal government and later a pact with the 'social radicals'. It helps us account for the influence of liberal conceptions of justice on the 1945 Labour government in the creation of the welfare state, the landmark liberal initiatives of the Wilson government in the 1960s and later of the Blair government.

This approach stands for equality as a precondition for liberty. Tawney argued, liberty is 'equality in action',[16] built upon the equality of human dignity and moral worth. In a society based on the principle of fellowship, no group of individuals should be so rich or poor that they are able or forced to live as a class apart. The aim is not to impose uniformity of material condition. It is a society in which differences of wealth and income are contained within limits that allow the individuals to relate to each other in a spirit of mutual regard. The significance of the early 'religion of socialism' gradually diminished as Labour transitioned into an electoral machine, its ethical concerns aligning more with those of the 'new' liberalism as the Liberal Party failed to resolve these tensions within liberalism. The tradition of ethical socialism was gradually adapting to the institutional demands of the party and aligning with radical liberal traditions and diluting its earlier revolutionary approach.

These developments informed some of the later debates under New Labour and the stated desire of key figures to uncover and reconnect with early liberal traditions. The question is: which liberal traditions? In a major speech defining the 'Third Way' and 'social-ism' in 1995, Tony Blair listed both Hobhouse and Hobson as early converts to the cause of New Labour.[17] The inference is that liberalism and socialism cannot be reconciled and that the foundation of the ILP with a distinctively socialist outlook was a historic wrong turning and that the progressive left would have been better off devoting its energies to building an enduring electoral base for a strong and reformed Liberal Party. This conclusion, though never openly stated, was often inferred by Blair. The pioneers of liberal socialism would, of course, have rejected such a misreading of both Liberal and Labour Party history, and the reason many joined the latter was because of the declining potential of the former to advance the case for radical change. These shifts are captured in the career of Keir Hardie.

Keir Hardie

James Keir Hardie was born in Lanarkshire on 15 August 1856, the illegitimate son of a devout Scottish farm servant, Mary Keir. He started work in a bakery aged 8 and down the mine aged 10. He remained a working miner for 13 years. An insatiable reader, by the age of 16 he was consuming Carlyle and Ruskin. At 16 he took the pledge and embraced the Temperance cause. In his early twenties he converted to evangelical Christianity. Both imprinted in him a lifelong personal puritanism and intolerance of dogma be it within the orthodoxies of Scottish Calvinism or SDF Marxism. Yet his faith remained a flexible one – 'a religion of humanity with little doctrinal content, utopian, romantic, outward-looking, democratic and egalitarian'.[18]

Turning 30, Hardie was still an active Liberal supporter. The winter of 1886–7 saw him emerge as a leader of organized labour, becoming secretary of the Ayrshire Miners Union, later the Scottish Miners National Federation, and setting up and editing *The Miner*. Following a standoff with the local Liberal Association, in April 1888 Hardie fought and badly lost the mid-Lanark by-election as an independent labour candidate. In August he helped form the Scottish Labour Party, which 6 years later would merge with the ILP.

In 1892, he was unexpectedly invited to stand as the independent labour candidate for West Ham South. With liberal support he won the seat on 4 July. The next year he was elected chairman of the ILP. He played a decisive role in ensuring the new organization retained a plural internal culture and organizational flexibility whilst steering it away from being labelled the more doctrinaire 'Socialist Labour Party'. He would remain chair until 1900, also performing the role of president between 1894 and 1896. He set up *Labour Leader* in March 1894, which he owned and edited until 1904. He lost his seat in 1895, and, despite his opposition to the Boer War, was subsequently elected for Merthyr Tydfil in September 1900, where he remained until his death 15 years later.

In parliament Hardie steered the LRC into supporting the formation of the Parliamentary Labour Party. In 1906 he was elected chair of the PLP by 15 votes to 14 over David Shackleton. Serious illness in spring of 1907 led Hardie to set forth on a world tour, irritating colleagues. Whilst he was away, Arthur Henderson was elected chair.

Hardie remains the quintessential Labour prophet; the great political agitator on behalf of the secular religion of socialism, one he expressed in distinct spiritual terms: 'Ring out the darkness of the land, ring in the Christ that is to be.' He belonged to a time-specific chapel radicalism of the late-Victorian era, yet is heralded as a timeless champion of an essential socialist creed, although he himself always resisted such doctrinal purity.

His obituary in the *Aberdare Leader* described him as a 'stern, austere prophet' yet he inspired total devotion; on his death he was described as the 'Member for Humanity'.[19] Yet many, especially amongst his parliamentary colleagues, thought him an extremist; impossible, unreliable and ill-disciplined. At times he was isolated and resembled an outcast rather

Keir Hardie
Source: George Grantham Bain Collection, Library of Congress.

than prophet. He disliked Westminster consolidation and remained ill-fitted to the parliamentary grind. As his biographer states:

> For a man of Hardie's poetic, intuitive temperament, this unheroic, constructive labour was not enough. Beyond the day-to-day tactics there was a profound political, moral, and emotional cause to be defined and fought for.[20]

Hardie was a man of contradictions. He was an outsider, a lone and solitary figure. He was never a social conservative, but a dedicated supporter of feminism, and bohemian in his dress. He had a prophetic belief in socialism and was also a mystic who believed in re-incarnation and faith healing. He valued the druids and ideas of returning to nature.

He was never the extremist of caricature but a subtle strategist whose non-conformity helped mould the socialism of an emerging party to the wider political and cultural currents within British society. His passion for women's emancipation and the suffragettes, anti-imperialist struggles and peace movements and colonial nationalism helped align Labour with wider radical movements. Yet his 'dualism of vision'[21] was a source of ongoing tension with Arthur Henderson, MacDonald and Snowden.

By 1903 Hardie had pragmatically come around to accept some form of agreement with the liberals. They had been revitalized under Campbell-Bannerman and appeared more willing to embrace collectivism and social reform, especially in the work of radical Liberals such as Hobson and Hobhouse. Later, when party leader, he worked with Sir Charles Dilke, unofficial chair of the 'social radicals' on the Liberal side, on labour and radical issues. Even at the two elections of 1910, he maintained support for the alliance with the Liberals. Yet by 1912 he had fallen out badly with them, especially Churchill, following the brutal industrial disputes and State response at Tonypandy and Aberdare.

Many of the first generation of Labour leaders, like Keir Hardie himself, had been active in the Liberal Party of Gladstone and broke with it only reluctantly and gradually. Their aim was not to repudiate the liberalism of their youth, but to realize its goals of human freedom and emancipation in the new and more challenging conditions of industrial capitalism. In his non-conformity he held to this task with steely determination. It no doubt shortened his life.

1906–1914

On 15 February 1906, 29 MPs formally adopted the name 'The Labour Party' with Hardie elected as PLP Chairman. From then on Labour was to develop a distinct identity rather than be an adjunct to the Lib-Labs. In the early years, socialists from the ILP provided much of the leadership. Non-conformist and acutely aware of the need for alliances, many had been influenced by radical liberalism. The activist base also came from the ILP as individual membership did not exist until 1918. Yet the tensions between the ethical concerns of the ILP with their ideas of an alternative socialist community and the class sectionalism of the unions would never disappear as affiliations grew, the party constitution evolved and more union members entered parliament.

Did the 1906 election signal the first progressive alliance, and new common ground between 'New Liberalism' and the party of organized labour, uniting in the quest for social reform? It is difficult to make the case in terms of the election itself, which was dominated by questions of Tariff Reform and food prices. Amongst Labour non-conformist ranks there were concerns with Balfour's 1902 Education Act and attempts to integrate denominational schools, shared amongst dissenting Conservative voters who rushed to support Liberal candidates for the same reason. Temperance hostility to licensing reform and the unpopularity of the Boer War were also factors. Labour's priority remained a sectional one of reversing Taff Vale. Overall, it stands less as a progressive realignment than a tactical deal preserving the status quo ante. Within weeks the Lib-Lab truce was over.

The 1906 parliament introduced the Trades Disputes Act, to restore union immunities from civil damages, and the freedom – not the right – to strike and organize. From 1905 to 1908 under Campbell-Bannerman the Liberals reunited and government priorities reorientated towards social reform.[22] Asquith as Chancellor introduced non-contributory old-age pensions. Yet the government faced serious challenges from Ulster Unionism, from escalating industrial unrest, from the suffragettes and from a more assertive Labour voice. The social reform upon which Lloyd George and Winston Churchill embarked in 1908 – particularly national insurance and unemployment insurance – did not go far enough for Labour given the scale of inequalities that disfigured Edwardian Britain.

Liberal principles of freedom of speech, freedom of conscience and equality before the law, all codified in law in the nineteenth century, left unaltered the structural inequalities of Britain. The initiative of 'New Liberalism', from welfare and tax reform to democratic changes to the Lords and monarchy, although welcome, proved insufficient. Labour encouraged and supported progressive reforms, over workers compensation, the Mines Act, compulsory medical inspections in schools and limited health and unemployment insurance initiatives. Yet the Liberals remained unwilling to challenge fundamental inequalities in wealth and income and the dominance of economic and social elites.

Whilst the Liberals held together over Irish Home Rule and the reform of the House of Lords, the tensions within liberalism were further exposed in escalating industrial conflict after 1910. The Liberals also fell short following another significant labour law judgment from the railway industry, which challenged the ASRS financial levy backing Labour. In December 1909 the House of Lords backed the Osborne judgment ruling trades unions could no longer donate money to fund the election campaigns and wages of Labour MPs, as such funds were deemed *ultra vires*. The Liberals stood unwilling to repeal this decision although they did introduce a wage for Members of Parliament. Falling short of repeal, the 1913 Trade Union Act allowed for secret ballots to determine political funds following pressure from the unions. It revealed splits within the Liberal administration and the whole process consolidated the overall shift of unions affiliating behind Labour following the miners switch from the Liberals to Labour in 1909. New political funds further consolidated the process of independent working-class representation.

At the January 1910 election Labour secured 40 of the 78 seats it contested and in December 42 of 56. Despite some by-election defeats from 1911 to 1914, the overall situation was solid but not remarkable, with steady progress at municipal level and major advances in terms of union support. Through the Edwardian years Labour showed incremental advances, building a distinct character and critique of the Liberals, who retained significant internal tensions of their own.

The First World War

Given Labour's solid but unremarkable progress up to 1914, some argue it was possible the party could have been absorbed by the Liberals. What propelled Labour into becoming a prospective party of government was the circumstances of the First World War and the prospects for post-war expansion it brought. Yet the immediate impact of the war suggested the party might split rather than prosper from the conflict when MacDonald resigned his post as chair of the PLP, in opposition to the war, in line with the views of the Socialist International, with the ILP backing his stance. MacDonald's replacement Arthur Henderson then joined the Asquith government. Fears of a split were overcome, and the party majority accepted a wartime political truce, one which would demonstrate that Labour could effectively administer and hold ministerial office.[23] Asquith sought union support to expand munitions and brought Henderson in both to advise on labour matters and to act as President of the Board of Education and later Paymaster General.

The Liberal Party soon had its own difficulties. In May 1915, Asquith was forced to make a coalition with the Conservatives and include Labour. Due to infighting he gave way to Lloyd George in December 1916 with Henderson now entering the inner war cabinet. The resentment that followed triggered a Commons battle in 1918 with defeat for Asquith and a major rupture within the Liberal Party. George Barnes from the engineers union replaced Henderson as Labour's cabinet representative following disagreements over attending an International Socialist Conference in Geneva. John Hodge of the steel workers became Minister of Labour.

The extension of the franchise with the Fourth Reform Bill in 1918, and changes to elections expenses also appeared to work in Labour's favour. The Franchise Representation Act 1918 extended the vote to all men over 21, and women over 30. At the 1918 election, Labour put up 388 candidates compared to 56 in December 1910, yet won only 57 seats. In the 'coupon election', held immediately after the Armistice with Germany, Lloyd George sent letters of endorsement to coalition-supporting candidates resulting in major losses for the non-endorsed Independent Liberal faction, including Asquith, leading to a coalition landslide.

Although the subject of some disagreement amongst its MPs, Labour under William Adamson remained independent, greatly increasing its vote share and exceeding the votes cast for either Liberal faction, although only gaining a net 15 seats and losing key figures such as MacDonald, Snowden, Fred Jowett and Henderson. Yet the tally of 57 MPs was not a true depiction of the strategic position and the overall strength of the labour movement, a product of the party's 'underlying unity', which enabled it to exploit many of the opportunities offered by the war,[24] opportunities which, despite phases of retreat, by 1922 saw Labour emerge as the official opposition to the Conservative government at the expense of the Liberals.

Talk of unity and overall strength can underplay how Labour was changing. In opposing the war, not without disagreement, the influence of the ILP was significantly reduced whilst bolstering the role of the unions within the apparatus of the party, as well as within an expanded state and across wider society. Union membership increased by two and half million during the war. The PLP had become dominated by the unions as key ILP figures were defeated. It marked a distinct shift in the character of the party with the rise of the utilitarian, sectional concerns of organized labour at the expense of the ethical traditions. MacDonald was himself beginning to separate away from the ILP activists. Having resigned he embraced the anti-war radicals and left-wing liberals to establish the Union of Democratic Control rather than align with the militant resistance of many from the grassroots. Emerging as an inspiring idealist, once elected back to parliament in 1922, he stood as a natural antidote to the maladministration of the Lloyd George coalition and quickly became leader of the party he would come to dominate throughout the rest of the decade,[25] yet gradually isolating from the ILP in ways he would later repeat with the Labour Party.

One final point of note. Keir Hardie died on 26 September 1915 in Cumnock, an old 59. His passing went largely unnoticed due to the dramas of the First World War. It was not a good death. Hardie's last year broke both his spirit and body. Two days before the country entered the war, Hardie had marched in support of a General Strike against the conflict and a day before registered his opposition in parliament, while other Labour colleagues showed a different solidarity by singing the national anthem in the voting lobbies. His mental state eroded further after a peace meeting at Aberdare Market Hall in his constituency was broken up, and where Hardie, according to the local paper, was 'howled down'. A jingoistic mob included the pro-war union leader C.B. Stanton, soon to be Hardie's successor in Merthyr, who was seen waving a gun in the air. For Hardie, it was a profoundly troubling period. He was to admit it brought him appreciation of Christ's own suffering in the garden of Gethsemane.[26]

Waning physiological health and a broken spirit following relentless personal attacks helped induce a mild stroke in early 1915. His final public appearance was at the ILP annual conference in Norwich in April. Periods in Caterham sanatorium and further mental and physical deterioration followed. He eventually withdrew into a deep coma and passed on 26 September. The final cause of death was registered as pneumonia. Hardie was cremated in Maryhill, Glasgow.

Days later a memorial service followed at St Andrews Hall in the city with the main address given by MacDonald and a rendition of 'The Red Flag'.

Clause IV[27]

One reason why the party did not split in 1914 was the creation of the War Emergency Workers' National Committee (WNC) set up in August to defend working-class living standards through the course of the conflict. It brought together a very wide range of union, Labour and socialist organizations, and both pro- and anti-war figures including MacDonald, Hyndman and Sidney Webb under the chairmanship of Henderson. Whilst conflict remained, such as over conscription and entry into the coalition, the committee helped ensure 'a series of crises at the top of the Labour movement were overcome without irreparable damage'.[28] Towards the end of the war the committee developed a more radical policy edge regarding nationalization, tax and wealth inequalities as the economic reach of the wartime state dramatically expanded as did organized labour's role within it, consolidating the utilitarian character of the party and the overall drift towards statism. In January 1916, the Party Conference established a committee to tackle post-war issues. This more muscular view of the state in economic affairs, and arguably the need to signpost a peaceful domestic journey to socialism following the Bolsheviks taking power in Russia in November 1917, provided extra impetus behind the review of the party constitution, something already in motion because of the changing franchise.

It is difficult to characterize this new constitution and specifically Clause IV (or as it was at the time Three (d)) as marking a decisive shift to the left, and a precise statement of a definitive socialist creed, however. Over recent years the party had in reality been moving to the right, with the unions consolidating their grip of the structures and leadership, and the socialist influence of the ILP diminishing along with any residual progressive lib-labbery. The socialism on offer was of a very different variety to that of the early religion, although the actual wording remained sufficiently vague to suggest it could be shared across a variety of traditions and maintain the common ground established within the WNC.

Webb, in a somewhat unlikely alliance with Henderson, did much of the drafting, and his involvement, given his hostility to the 'sentimentality' of the ILP – despite having joined it in 1912 in a different climate – spoke to the ideological changes within the evolving party and shifting policy fashions. It had become more mechanical and statist, concerned with the 'machinery' of socialism that always troubled William Morris. But rather than heralding the birth of socialism, it was very much a 'flag of convenience'[29] to provide distance from the Liberals and unify the Labour movement. Clause IV was nonetheless a significant utilitarian foothold in party history. The party's purpose appeared less concerned with 'making socialists' and with human liberty, more with material distribution through state control. Although at the time Clause IV failed to excite much interest, the revised constitution also introduced individual membership. Up until this point the ILP had provided the majority of activists. It also ensured a strong union majority on the National Executive Committee (NEC) with 13 of the 23 seats assigned to the unions and the ability to vote for the other ten, a sure sign of the direction of travel.

In 1922 Labour more than doubled its number of MPs, with key figures such as Jowett, Snowden and Henderson and not just MacDonald returning. By the time of the late 1923 election, Labour was in a strong position and gained a narrow lead over the Liberals. Yet it was hardly a natural evolution. The war had dramatically affected the Liberals, compounding earlier tensions within liberalism. Labour had consolidated its position amongst the working class aided by the widening franchise. It was building a policy agenda distinct from the Liberals, but one that rested uneasily with its early ethical character. Labour was transitioning away from the ILP, ethical socialism and the old religion as it institutionally grew, and following the experience of war embraced statism. Hardie was long dead and, whether for good or bad, the party was moving out of his shadow.

4

Minorities
(1924–1931)

The 1920s saw two minority Labour governments in 1924 and 1929. Labour made steady progress throughout the decade, yet it ended disastrously with the party collapsing from 287 MPs in 1929 to just 52 two years later.[1] The trauma of 1931 would transform the character of the party. The two minority governments suggested the party had grown too quickly and lacked a coherent policy programme. Whilst utilitarianism had asserted control, it had failed to develop an agenda to deliver distributional justice. Labour was found wanting.

The ILP generation of Hardie, MacDonald and Lansbury – three devout 'apostles of the old faith'[2] – established a Labour identity drawn from William Morris and Christian socialist traditions; the ILP retained both alongside significant Marxist influences. Yet by the 1930s Labour would turn away from its prophets towards younger figures such as Hugh Gaitskell, Douglas Jay and Evan Durbin under the general guidance of Hugh Dalton. It signalled a takeover by the utilitarian middle-class Fabians and defeat for the party intellectuals such as Cole and Tawney. These events were the consequence of the policy failures of the first two Labour governments and the traumas of 1931 that shattered assumptions regarding the inevitability of socialism.

Later, it would be on Lansbury's watch as party leader that the ILP decided to secede from the Labour Party at a special conference on 30 June–1 July 1932 in Jowett Hall, Bradford, where it had been founded some 39 years earlier. The ILP grew from the bottom up – 'from those shadowy parts known as the provinces', to quote E.P. Thompson. Its image was one of bohemianism: 'braving apathy and hostility, buoyed up by optimism, concerned not with the minutiae of political dealings but the broad uncomplicated advocacy of ethical principles'.[3] Yet by 1931 it had descended into the 'heart of Labour's agony', to quote David Howell.[4] The story of the demise of the ILP expresses the declining status of the old religion and of ethical socialism played out throughout Labour's first experiences of power and the personal complexity of its first Prime Minister, Ramsay MacDonald.

Ramsay MacDonald

Whilst Keir Hardie has been sanctified by Labour, James Ramsay MacDonald is often portrayed as a sell-out to the cause, the party's first Prime Minister who succumbed to a 'bankers' ramp' in August 1931.[5] From the left treachery is a word regularly used; from the right inadequacy or incompetence. Yet if he had died in the 1920s, MacDonald like Hardie would be revered and celebrated as a true Labour pioneer, brilliant orator, astute organizer and tactician, and major intellectual force.[6] He helped build Labour but also nearly destroyed it.

MacDonald was born on 12 October 1866 in Lossiemouth, Scotland, the illegitimate son of an agricultural labourer, John MacDonald, and housemaid, Anne Ramsay. He left school at 15 to work on a farm, then later as a school assistant. Moving to Bristol he joined the Democratic Federation, the forerunner to the SDF, later relocating to London and studying at what is now Birkbeck College. In 1888 he started work as private secretary to Thomas Lough, who was later elected a Liberal MP. He remained active in Fabian, Radical and labour politics in London and, having failed to secure the Liberal nomination for Southampton, joined the ILP in 1894. As their Southampton candidate he was heavily defeated at the 1895 election. He became part of the ILP executive, the National Administrative Council. At the 1900 election he lost again, this time in Leicester. Later that year he was appointed the first secretary of the LRC, a position he held for 12 years. In 1906 he was successfully returned as MP for Leicester, rising to become party treasurer in 1911 and 1912 and Chair of the PLP between 1911 and 1914 and leader from 1922 to 1931.

We forget more than we remember about MacDonald. We forget his successful negotiations with the Liberals that helped ensure Labour's 29-seat breakthrough in 1906 and his contribution as a key party intellectual. In a dozen books he helped provide a positivist Darwinian vision of Labour's purpose, one that would naturally evolve beyond the limitations of liberalism within an expanding economy and society. He articulated the case for a muscular state politics on behalf of a national

Ramsay MacDonald
Source: Harris & Ewing Photographs, Library of Congress.

community rather than any sectional interest and helped steer Labour away from both the absolutism of the SDF and militancy of syndicalism. He was a man whose principled, dignified opposition to the First World War and defence of liberal internationalism propelled him into the leadership, but not before it cost him the chairmanship of the PLP and his seat in parliament from 1918 to 1922. Like Hardie, the stance brought with it terrible personal persecution, including great anguish after his name and birth details were published in *John Bull* magazine in September 1915. Yet he was to emerge as arguably the most significant politician in Britain throughout the 1920s, a decade which saw Labour prosper at the expense of the Liberals. The divisions within the Liberals and the extension of the suffrage were critical but not sufficient. Labour had to secure and retain liberal voters and reach beyond its core class constituency, which in no small part was down to MacDonald's strategic and organizational abilities. He was 'a decent and likeable man'[7] who for the most part led his party with considerable skill and tenacity. Yet he remained a conflicted personality, prone to introspection and self-pity, in part a product of acute loneliness and isolation following the tragic early death of his wife Margaret in 1911. They married in 1896 and had six children together.

By the early 1920s the party was both radical and safe – 'a party of government which had not ceased to be a party of protest'.[8] Arguably his full contribution was only revealed decades later 'with the wide-ranging, heterogeneous Labour coalition that won the 1945 election: the lineal descendant of the Liberal coalition of 1906'.[9] The tragedy of MacDonald's career is captured at this moment of historic achievement; his contribution largely removed, the consequence of calamitous decisions made for honourable reasons. In effect MacDonald's brand of ILP politics rested uneasily with the sectionalism of the unions and 'with the pressures of office, a conception of socialism founded on the welfare of the community could shade into a conservative character-ization of the national interest'.[10]

Path to Victory

Between 1918 and 1929, Labour gradually enhanced its position. At the 'Coupon' election of 1918, Labour won 57 seats but lost some of its key figures. In terms of the number of MPs the result was disappointing yet the underlying strategic position of the party was healthy. In the years that followed, Labour developed its organization in the country under the direction of Egerton Wake, the National Agent, including the intro-duction of new women's sections following the extension of the franchise. The NEC rationalized its work under four sub-committees and with the TUC acquired the *Daily Herald*.[11] The unions continued to dominate the annual Conference with Ernest Bevin at the Transport and General Workers' Union (TGWU) remaining a key influence. Also important was their role on the NEC and in the parliamentary party under the auspices of the Joint Council of Labour, the key PLP, TUC and Labour Party joint committee, later renamed the National Council of Labour in 1934. Despite this dominance the party/union relationship was not without tension. The decade would see significant disagreement within the movement over the retention and use of the Emergency Powers Act, the failure to abolish the 1927 Trades Dispute Act and, towards the end of the decade, the response of the second Labour government to mass unemployment and austerity.

The 1922 election result suggested a major political realignment. Following the 'Spanish Flu' pandemic that killed nearly a quarter of a million people and against a backdrop of strikes and austerity, Britain went to the polls on 15 November 1922. The Conservatives led by Bonar Law won a healthy majority. Britain had been governed by a Conservative–Liberal coalition led by Lloyd George committed to public spending cuts, known as the 'Geddes Axe'. The 1922 election saw Labour overtake but not totally replace the Liberals, who remained split between the National Liberal faction of Lloyd George and Asquith's Independent Liberals.

Labour's leader at the 1922 election, its first English one, J.R. Clynes, founding member of both the ILP and LRC, would soon be gone. Labour moved from 57 to 142 seats and saw the return of radical figures such as MacDonald, Snowden, Jowett and Lansbury as well as new ILP MPs such as James Maxton, John Wheatley and Emmanuel Shinwell. In November, from the left, MacDonald beat Clynes to the post of party chair by 61 votes to 56, an event that would change the course of party history. The position of PLP chair and leader effectively became the same and the following year an apparent shift to the left was maintained in PLP elections that saw victories for senior ILP figures and a move away from the unions. Such appearances were deceptive, however. By the early 1920s Labour was in reality re-emerging as a more cautious gradualist party, one that emphasized its respectability and was reaching out to middle-class and liberal voters at the expense of both the party of Gladstone and the radical traditions of Hardie and the ILP.[12]

The Tories lost 35 seats in 1922, Asquith's Liberals won 62 seats in total, and the National Liberals 53. Overnight Labour had replaced the Liberals as the main opposition party based on its support amongst a growing working-class electorate. Within a year Bonar Law would be dead from cancer and replaced by Baldwin, who would swiftly renege on his predecessor's pledges over free trade. This about turn led him to seek a fresh mandate in 1923. The 6 December election saw a significant swing against protectionism, with the Tories losing nearly 100 seats.

It remained the largest party, however, with 258 Conservative MPs returned against 191 for Labour and 158 for the Liberals. The result saw significant Labour gains, although the results were inconsistent, with no seats secured in Birmingham and only one in Liverpool. The balance of power was now held by the free trader Asquith. In anticipation of coming events, soon after polling day, MacDonald, hostile to coalition with the Liberals, discussed the possibility of a minority Labour administration with the PLP executive, NEC and General Council, who endorsed his approach.

On Tuesday 8 January 1924, on the day the Soviet newspaper *Pravda* reported Leon Trotsky ill, a sign of his possible removal within the Communist hierarchy, and Lenin dead from a stroke, the Commons passed a motion of no confidence in Baldwin's government by 328 votes to 256. That evening at the party's packed Victory Rally in the Royal Albert Hall, Ramsay MacDonald announced Labour would accept office as soon as invited to do so, although he warned it would be taking over a 'bankrupt estate'. W. Massingham brilliantly surveyed the event for the *Nation*[13] and the sense of expectation amongst the membership. But he also depicts a tension that would help define the next 100 years of Labour's history – tension between Labour's desire to build a new society and the gradualism that was capturing the organization:

> To the thousands of young men and women – the average age struck one as between 20 and 30 – who poured into the Albert Hall, the event came as an almost solemn act of dedication rather than a flaming signal of party triumph. The British Labour Party resembles the Catholic Church at least in two particulars. It has faith and an organisation, and it is the union of these two characteristics that produces the effect of disciplined enthusiasm of which these central assemblies are evidence. The order of the Albert Hall meeting was perfect, evolved as it was out of the simple and impressive ritual of the Labour demonstration and the close harmony of its poetry and aspirations with the temper of the audience ... The singing, mostly of hymn tunes and led by a trained choir from the orchestra, was set to the three or four fine English poems by Morris and Carpenter, whose familiar rhythm makes the marching music of the party and spiritualises their vision of a new social order ... Here and everywhere was the evidence of a spirit not of a party so much as a religion, which it means to apply, in full confidence, to the art of government.

In anticipation of a coming new dawn the religion of socialism had reappeared. The ethical, spiritual wing associated with the ILP is clearly identifiable – with its desire for a new 'social order' inspired by William Morris and Edward Carpenter. Yet it is being subtly confronted by MacDonald in a call for moderation and a solemn pledge to run the country along sound economic lines. Massingham continues:

> This tone of mingled buoyancy and seriousness, with its suggestions of a young evangelistic church in bloom of its days of faith, was not the only remarkable feature of the Albert Hall meeting. There was something more notable still and that was the harmony between leaders and followers. Mr MacDonald came to say a difficult word to an idealistic audience. The word was moderation … Impatient idealism might have revolted, and had it done so, the life of the Labour government, if it had ever begun, would have dwindled in a short and inglorious episode. But the response was perfect. The enthusiasm of the meeting was restrained and enhanced; and it was evident that the new government, basing itself not on class war, but on the cooperation and even the religious instincts of the whole nation, would have behind it the wonderful movement, which brought it into being.

The report didn't focus on the less idealistic sectional, distributional concerns of the unions, although that same day 60,000 rail workers went on strike protesting a recent reduction in wages ordered by the National Wage Board. Massingham highlights the need to reconcile the religion of socialism with the practical realities and demands of government; the desire for a new social order alongside the necessity of moderation and reassurance. David Marquand has noted how MacDonald that night managed 'to tap the vein of emotional, utopian socialism which played such a large part in the Labour movement, and yet to make it clear that the Labour Party would take office in a severely pragmatic spirit'.[14] The harmony both writers identified would not last. This tension at Labour's heart, between an ethical desire for justice and pragmatic, incremental ways to achieve measures of distributive equality, would remain unresolved and percolate throughout the next century. It was certainly visible at the Victory Rally in Kensington days before MacDonald kissed the hand of the King, and since that night has remained ever present.

Despite the ethical and spiritual desires of the membership, and the apparent leftward tilt within the PLP since 1922, the leadership was heading in a different direction. On 12 December over dinner at the home of Sidney and Beatrice Webb at 41 Grosvenor Road, the 'Big 5' of MacDonald, Snowden, Arthur Henderson, Clynes and J.H. Thomas – to quote MacDonald – were 'unanimous that moderation and honesty were our safety'.[15] As it approached government, Labour was not just shifting to the right but away from the ethical concerns of the membership and embracing the 'inevitability of gradualness'.

At midday on 22 January, MacDonald went to the palace to be sworn in to the Privy Council and listen to the King complain about the singing of the 'Red Flag' and the 'Marseillaise' at the Albert Hall event days earlier. Later that day he accepted the King's commission, arriving in full court dress to kiss the hand of the monarch as Prime Minister. The day before he had privately noted 'the load will be heavy & I am so much alone'.[16] He was not wrong. Against a regular drumbeat of betrayal, the first Labour government was to be a brittle, underwhelming affair.[17] It achieved little, yet retained deep antagonisms between its three leading figures – MacDonald, Snowden and Henderson. Within a year it would drift to defeat amidst charges of incompetence over the 'Campbell Case'. Yet from MacDonald's perspective, it contained some significant successes in demonstrating Labour could establish a competent government without recourse to the Liberal Party. Seven and a half years later, these personal and political tensions would crack wide open with the formation of a 'National' government after a run on the currency and an austerity package that would split the labour movement; events which Sidney Webb would famously suggest involved a conspiracy with the King.

The First Labour Government

The first Labour government lasted from January to November 1924.[18] The desire for respectability and to demonstrate a capacity to govern preoccupied MacDonald whilst the Conservative papers obsessed over the domestic Bolshevik threat. There were no pioneering reforms, in part due to the government's minority status and reliance on the Liberals, but also because of a desire to demonstrate moderation. The 1918 programme was not a significant influence on the administration, with policies such as nationalization, the 'capital levy' and public works programmes played down or ignored altogether. John Wheatley's Housing Act was the most significant legislative intervention, which by 1933 would help subsidize some 521,700 rented homes at controlled rents. Constraints on landlord repossessions and rent rises were also important measures as were repair and modernization funds for government dwellings. Of note in international affairs was the August 1924 agreement on peace and reparations signed in London between Germany and the Allies.

There were a few more limited successes. Slight improvements were made to pensions and unemployment benefits, although little of note to combat unemployment, and children's allowance doubled. The duration of unemployment benefits was extended to 41 weeks, although a 'genuinely seeking work' clause drew criticism from within the labour movement. Local authorities were empowered to raise the school-leaving age to 15 and to limit class sizes. Minimum wages for agricultural workers were restored and miner's silicosis was included for workmen's compensation. Various measures were introduced to improve mine safety. Spending restrictions imposed on the Poplar Board of Guardians were removed. Child welfare and maternity services were extended as was support for war widows and orphans. Throughout, the government made the case for balanced budgets, the gold standard and, as it had at the election, support for free trade.

After ten months the government collapsed following a red scare and alleged communist threat. the communist J.R. Campbell, the assistant editor of the *Workers' Weekly*, had been arrested on charges of incitement by the Attorney General after publishing an article calling on troops not to fire on strikers. The government then withdrew the prosecution, with their political opponents detecting a 'Red' hidden hand influencing the leadership. Asquith called for a committee of enquiry, which MacDonald refused, instead declaring the vote a confidence issue. The large majority in favour led to the resignation of the government. This was followed four days before polling day with the publication of the Zinoviev letter in the *Daily Mail*, a forgery purportedly written by the head of the Comintern, requesting supporters prepare for imminent revolution and implicating Labour in the plot.[19]

The Conservatives were returned to power under Baldwin with a majority of over 200, although most of these gains were at the expense of the Liberals, who lost over 100 seats. Labour increased its vote share despite losing 40 seats. MacDonald had achieved his main objective, with Labour consolidating its position as the main rival to the Tories, and demonstrated it was a serious party fit for government, one which would be returned to office within five years. Apparently an impregnable leader, in office MacDonald had become a remote one who found it difficult to delegate and retained strained, difficult relations with senior colleagues. Of most significance was the limited policy resources the party could draw on, especially in confronting unemployment, themes that would reappear later in the decade.

Interregnum

In opposition, internal tensions reappeared. There was disquiet in the PLP at what had appeared to be cack-handed management of the 'Campbell Case' and in the way MacDonald dealt with the Zinoviev letter. Lansbury was nominated for the chair of the PLP yet later withdrew. The unions had concerns regarding Labour's record in government, with Bevin especially frustrated with MacDonald. These tensions would be brought to a head in 1926 over the General Strike.

Miners' wages had continued to be threatened as mine owners passed on falling prices given the global glut of coal stocks and strong pound after Britain re-entered the Gold Standard. Baldwin intervened in 1925 with a nine-month government coal subsidy to stabilize miners' wages and a Royal Commission into the sector under Sir Herbert Samuel. Following the Commission's report, which proposed ending the subsidy, the owners announced wage cuts and increased hours. The miners' response was 'Not a penny off the pay, not a minute on the day'. With the breakdown in negotiations, the TUC called a General Strike for 11.59 pm on Monday 3 May to force the government to intervene. The armed forces and volunteer strike-breakers were used to maintain basic services alongside special constables and organized militias to maintain order on the streets. After 9 days the TUC was forced to back down. The Trades Disputes Act of 1927 subsequently placed new legal constraints on industrial action and forced workers to individually 'opt in' to paying the political levy to the financial detriment of Labour.[20]

Since before the war MacDonald had been an opponent of the General Strike weapon, insisting on the parliamentary route to engineer social and economic change through nationalization of the sector, and had been quarrelling with the union leadership. In public he backed the action; in private he became increasingly anxious. Yet with the defeat of the left, the strike, although difficult for Labour, helped strengthen his leadership hold over the PLP. The party was moving further in its embrace of gradualism, with the left increasingly estranged, reflected in the changing composition and direction of the ILP. In 1926 James Maxton was elected as its chair and started to push a more muscular policy agenda, including a living wage informed by theories of underconsumption and inadequate demand. The ILP was itself becoming more economistic and reorientating away from the ethical socialist tradition. Later in 1928, in partnership with ILP member and ex-communist A.J. Cook, Secretary of the Miners Federation, and claiming the legacy of Keir Hardie and spirit of the early pioneers, the Cook–Maxton manifesto rejected the gradualism of the leadership and threatened the secession of the left from the party unless it embraced a more aggressive socialist platform. The campaign failed and by weakening the position of the ILP once more strengthened the hand of MacDonald and the leadership.

The reality was that any radical alternatives to statism and utilitarianism were in retreat. The influence of thinkers such as Cole, Laski and Tawney was in decline.[21] All three were forced to come to terms with the direction of travel in the party under MacDonald to retain any significant influence. The policy agenda of the party became vague, culminating in the 1928 party programme *Labour and the Nation* overseen by Tawney, who, as we shall see, would bitterly regret this period of party history. At the May 1929 election Labour would emerge for the first time as the party with the most MPs. Despite the effects of the General Strike and tensions amongst the key players, the leadership of MacDonald was dominant and the ILP a residual force. Yet the vagueness of the policy agenda meant the PLP and the utilitarian traditions in control of the party had failed to cohere around a concrete plan for government.

The Second Labour Government

George V reappointed MacDonald Prime Minister on 5 June 1929. Labour had won 287 seats, the Tories 260 and Liberals 59. Once more the new Prime Minister was reliant on Liberal support to form a minority government, one that under-represented the left of his party but included the first woman cabinet minister, Margaret Bondfield, as Minister for Labour.

Housing policies again topped the list of notable achievements. Arthur Greenwood's 1930 Housing Act provided subsidies for slum clearance, resulting in the demolition of 245,000 dwellings by 1939, and the construction of 700,000 new homes. It also allowed local authorities to set up differential rent schemes for their tenants. The Coal Mines Act sought to remedy the causes of the General Strike with the introduction of a 7½-hour daily shift. Owners were guaranteed minimum coal prices through compulsory production quotas and a Mines Reorganisation Commission was established to encourage amalgamations. In other radical initiatives the Land Utilisation Bill of 1931 would have given ministers sweeping powers to purchase land nationwide but was whittled away in the Lords.

Grants for public works schemes were introduced but proved inadequate given the scale of the challenge. Minor changes in benefits for the unemployed and amendment of the 'genuinely seeking work' qualifications were introduced. The number of people on transitional benefits rose from 120,000 in 1929 to more than 500,000 in 1931. The Pensions Act 1929 granted pensions to over 500,000 old people and widows previously excluded. A Fair Wage Clause was applied to all employees on road passenger services, and regulated the working hours of drivers. Wage inspectors in the agricultural sector were expanded and disability compensation for asbestos introduced as well as uniform safety standards for cargo ships. New regulations on Sunday working came into force alongside special regulations for the prevention of accidents in the shipbuilding industry and protections for workers in the cement industry and tanneries.

The 1929 Local Government Act abolished the workhouse test and replaced the Poor Law with Public Assistance Committees for the relief of the destitute, while Poor Law hospitals came under the control of local authorities, who were also given more control over local and regional planning. Support for war veterans and their family members was expanded and teachers' numbers increased by some 3,000.

Yet the October 1929 Wall Street Crash and Great Depression derailed the government soon after coming to power. When Labour took office, unemployment stood at 1.16 million. In January 1930, 1.5 million people were out of work, in June 2 million and by December it had topped 2.5 million and would later peak at over 2.8 million. Neither J.H. Thomas nor Margaret Bondfield provided any adequate response. Labour was caught in a policy vice, seeking a balanced budget to maintain the currency on the Gold Standard, yet wanting to offer aid to the poor and unemployed as revenues declined. The macroeconomic orthodoxy that gradualism embraced – free trade, balanced budgets and a stable currency – viewed with scepticism the case for major public works, whilst the vagueness of pre-election policy development provided limited resources for the party to draw on. The outcome was over-reliance on the Bank of England to resolve the crisis and inertia on the part of the government.

Junior minister and former Conservative Oswald Mosley, MP for Smethwick, frustrated by the fiscally conservative Snowden, with the aid of Lansbury put forward a memorandum in January 1930 calling for the public control of banking, public works and import controls, and higher pensions and allowances to encourage earlier retirement from industry. When this was rejected, in May 1930 Mosley resigned and, although he badly mishandled a PLP motion critical of the government, the saga demonstrated growing concerns amongst MPs over government performance. Later that year he issued the 'Mosley Manifesto', a mix of corporatism and Keynesianism, with the support of 17 Labour MPs. In February 1931 he formed the New Party, and the following year the British Union of Fascists.

In response to the deficit, Bondfield introduced legislation to remove 'anomalies' in unemployment benefit, aimed at stamping out apparent 'abuses' of the unemployment insurance system, further damaging the reputation of the government amongst Labour supporters. By early 1931 a budget crisis appeared inevitable. Following a Liberal motion, a committee headed by Sir George May was appointed to review the public finances. On 30 July, May recommended wage reductions and public spending cuts to balance a projected £120 million shortfall, made up of £24 million tax rises and £96 million expenditure cuts.

The dispute fatally split the government. The cabinet repeatedly failed to agree spending cuts or tariffs. Deadlock caused investors to take fright, with a flight of capital and gold destabilizing the economy.

On 21 August the cabinet agreed a package of £56 million cuts without resignations, although days earlier the TUC had registered its opposition to all cuts. The package was deemed insufficient by opposition parties so cabinet was recalled to discuss further cuts, which could not be agreed, although permission was granted to discuss a 10 per cent reduction in unemployment benefit with bankers in New York to secure the loans necessary to maintain the currency – creating the legend of the 'bankers' ramp' of party mythology. With a positive response from New York the final split occurred after four hours of cabinet discussion over whether to accept the 10 per cent reduction. Nine members opposed the reduction and eleven supported it. The eleven included MacDonald, Snowden, Bondfield, Morrison and Webb. The nine included Henderson, Clynes and Lansbury. It was not a simple left versus right split nor one between those with and without a union background.

With his cabinet and movement split and with a hung parliament, MacDonald initially thought to take the party into opposition. On 24 August 1931 the government formally resigned. Yet to widespread astonishment MacDonald, the great Labour pioneer, on the urging of the King and opposition parties, no doubt cynically wanting a Labour figure to oversee budget cuts, led a small number of senior colleagues, notably the evangelical socialist Snowden and trade unionist J.H. Thomas, in forming the 'National' Government with the Conservatives and a small group of Liberals. MacDonald and his supporters were then expelled from the Labour Party and formed the National Labour Organisation. Labour, now led by Henderson, and a few Liberals went into opposition.

In opposition, Labour came out against expenditure cuts, irrespective of the £56 million agreed in cabinet. The political culture of loyalty within the PLP cultivated by MacDonald now acted against him, minimizing further defections through the desire for solidarity, although few MPs would survive the coming deluge. Over time, Labour revisionism ensured culpability for the crisis and the erosion of social protections in advance of fiscal orthodoxy was laid at the feet of MacDonald, and the betrayal narrative took shape, including by those who had supported him in cabinet.[22] The sense of confusion palpable in August was chipped away and the myths created. This usefully disguised the policy limitations within Labour and its own orthodoxy, the consequence of gradualism. The reality was that all members of the cabinet economic committee and the wider cabinet accepted the need for a balanced budget; there were few intellectual resources and no radical economic strategy to turn to. The differences that did exist were over scale not principle.

By the time of the autumn Party Conference, the Gold Standard had been suspended, the MPs that had followed MacDonald had been ejected and an election appeared imminent. The political rhetoric against the government intensified to sharpen the identity of the party. In his fraternal address to the Conference, the TUC President and backbench Labour MP Arthur Hayday referred to recent departed members of the PLP as 'political blacklegs'.[23]

Parliament was dissolved on 7 October. The 1931 election resulted in a landslide for the National Government; Labour won only 52 seats, 235 fewer than in 1929. MacDonald would continue as Prime Minister of the Conservative-dominated National Government until 1935.

Mythology

In the parliamentary party the left were isolated and the ILP would soon break away; a few years later the Socialist League would be forced down a similar road. The events of 1931 would forever be replayed within the factional struggles for supremacy and the traitors, MacDonald and Snowden, became regular features in party mythology. The events of 1969 over *In Place of Strife* would be reminiscent of 1931, with Callaghan playing the role of Henderson, although this time the government held together. The party would never be the same again. Policy limitations would be recognized and confronted and push the party even further away from the ethical traditions that helped create it. The Darwinian certainty surrounding the party driven by a belief in progress and inevitable socialist change, the forward march of Labour, would be fundamentally challenged by the disaster of 1931. As David Howell has written: 'The rise of Labour to the status of largest parliamentary party in 1929 had been accompanied by a rhetoric of ethical socialism and progress that characterized the party as an ecumenical expression of enlightenment.'[24] That would be eroded and the events of 1931 would be forever stamped on the genotype of the party although regularly obscured through myth and denial.

Labour's second minority administration appeared to hold a stronger position than the first. Yet within six months it had been hit by a Wall

Street Crash and global recession that soon saw unemployment triple. MacDonald's greatest error was to reject Keynes's advice on 5 August 1931, who privately advocated a British New Deal to combat deflation and mass unemployment before Roosevelt had even been elected US President. Keynes advocated a new currency unit and an expansionary internationalist agenda, telling MacDonald austerity would deliver 'a most gross perversion of social justice', instead urging devaluation and public works.[25]

The demonization of MacDonald following the events of 1931 has allowed Labour's own mixed response to the crisis to be obscured. MacDonald played a weak hand badly but there were few easy answers, with parts of the left anticipating the end of capitalism, and parts of the right embracing authoritarianism and the collapse of democracy. Undoubtedly, he found it psychologically difficult to refuse the King, encumbered by a sense of national duty and a communitarian outlook in unprecedented times before the era of New Deal politics.

MacDonald remains a complex figure. Unlike Hardie he was never the agitator, rather an early, consistent advocate of the progressive alliance and a utopian Edwardian liberal pacifist, as well as brilliant organizer.

MacDonald died of heart failure at 7.45 on the evening of 7 November 1937. He was a broken man. The last year and a half of his life had been intensely painful – professionally he had shrunk into an 'an almost forgotten figure, cruelly aware of his diminishing effectiveness, full of grievances against his colleagues and the world, and with no real influence on events'. Often snubbed within government and yet ridiculed and abused by opponents, with no 'patronage, no future, and hardly any following'.[26]

He had lost his seat at Seaham Harbour at the November 1935 election to an old comrade, Manny Shinwell, who 13 years earlier had proposed him for the party leadership. He was subsequently elected member for the Combined Scottish university two months later. Approaching his 70th birthday, his sight and overall health were in decline. In August 1936 he spent a fortnight in a nursing home following a minor operation and was advised he needed a full six-month rest and recuperation to reclaim physical and mental balance. The decline was palpable. The political destruction of his old friend and comrade J.R. Thomas over leaked budget secrets intensified a sense of 'helpless agony' surrounding him.[27] The courageous opponent of the First World War was now isolated within the cabinet over events in Spain and the drift towards fascism, personally upholding a bleak assessment of an imperilled democracy. He agreed to leave office at the same time as Baldwin. On 27 May, eleven years after kissing the hand of George V on becoming Labour's first Prime Minister, he had his final audience with the King. A day later he ceased his role as government minister. Later that year at a dinner held by Hugh and Helen Roberton with old ILP colleagues in Glasgow, MacDonald insisted that he had always been and remained a socialist. Many of the embarrassed ex-comrades present had not spoken to him since the events of 1931.[28] MacDonald left Liverpool on 5 November with his daughter Sheila for a period of rest in South America on the liner *Reina del Pacifico*. Some forty-eight hours later he was dead. A public funeral was held at Westminster Abbey on 25 November before a private cremation in Golders Green, with his ashes then taken and buried in his wife Margaret's grave overlooking the Moray Firth.

The verdict of Shinwell, the man who proposed him for leader and later humiliated him at the ballot box, is a useful corrective to much Labour mythology:

> To dismiss MacDonald as a traitor to Labour is nonsense. His contribution in the early years was of incalculable value. His qualities as a protagonist of Socialism were of a rare standard. There has probably never been an orator with such natural magnetism combined with impeccable technique in speaking in the party's history. Before the First World War his reputation in international Labour circles brooked no comparison. Keir Hardie, idolized by the theorists of the movement, did not have the appeal to European and American Socialists that MacDonald had.[29]

R.H. Tawney

One of the most important political diagnoses of the events of 1931 was supplied by R.H. Tawney.[30] In his most significant academic work, *Religion and the Rise of Capitalism*,[31] Tawney explored the relationship between Protestantism and economic development in the sixteenth and seventeenth centuries. He argued that the division between commercial relations and social morality brought about by the reformation meant the subordination of Christian ethics in the pursuit of the accumulation of wealth. It is generally understood that Tawney's political thought was derived from his religious beliefs and the incompatibility of capitalism and Christian principle. As such he is often cited as the leading proponent of ethical socialism born of religious conviction. What is more significant, however, is how Tawney's ideas and interventions changed as Labour itself changed. Both moved away from the religion of socialism and embraced gradualism. Tawney would then produce one of the most blistering responses to the events of 1931 and the gradualism both he and the party had embraced as Labour pivoted to the left.

Undoubtedly Tawney's political beliefs were derived from his Christian faith. In his private diaries written between 1912 and 1914 but unpublished in his lifetime, he asserted that political concepts such as equality and his critique of capitalism were dependent on the belief in a Christian God. Yet this position was gradually abandoned and replaced with more secular arguments in favour of socialism and a more practical engagement with Labour demonstrated by his authorship of *Labour and the Nation* in 1928. The changing emphasis is reflected in his two influential books *The Acquisitive Society* and *Equality*.[32] The former criticized the selfish individualism of modern society on moral grounds; the latter outlined the practical case for an egalitarian society.

Tawney's shifting concerns provide insight into the changing dynamics within Labour prior to 1931 and how the party erupted in its aftermath. Through an early engagement with Toynbee Hall, the East End settlement movement and the Workers Education Association, Tawney became attracted to the ideas of guild socialism. The National Guilds League, created in 1915, advocated a theory of democracy that rejected democratic representative government in preference for a brokered consensus between a variety of functional groups – political, vocational, religious and philanthropic. Tawney joined the League and the theory influenced *The Acquisitive Society*, published in 1921. Yet the post-war re-establishment of both parliamentarianism and independent trade unionism, with the latter's embrace of free collective bargaining rather than industrial democracy, saw the decline of guild socialism, and early advocates such as Tawney and G.D.H. Cole would turn towards parliamentary reform and gradualism in the 1920s.[33] In his private diaries before the war, Tawney wrote how Fabians 'tidy the room, but open no windows to the soul',[34] yet he would later serve on the executive of the

Fabians from 1921 to 1933 and in the late 1920s oversee the year-long process that culminated in the gradualist 1928 party programme. By 1934, reflecting a wider leftward shift in Labour, he emerged as a savage critic of gradualism. Later still, in the 1950s he would come to endorse revisionism.

In 1934 Tawney published a short essay, 'The Choice Before the Labour Party', dusted down ever since by those frustrated with Labour's achievements. The article was provoked by the events of 1931 – 'the landscape after the earthquake' – and, despite his extraordinary intellectual and spiritual output, was one of his first interventions into internal Labour controversies. He challenges those who look for the causes of political disaster in outside events. 'It is the author, the unintending and pitiable author, of its own misfortunes.'

Within Labour mythology the essay is often considered an attack on MacDonald. Yet the significance of the essay is that it rejects the demand to identify any individual traitor or culprit which deflects from any deeper assessment of the party's limitations. Rather than an act of political transference to blame a leader's limitations for an inability to deliver socialism, Tawney's focus is purpose and not person. He ridicules Webb and the 'laments by ex-ministers of "conspiracy", which stabbed them in the back – as though a Titan, all energy and ardour, had been felled at his forge'.

In contrast, he suggests the Labour government 'ended by forgetting the reason for its existence. It has to now rediscover it.' The symbolic quality of socialism, its rhetoric had from the outset obscured a lack of definition revealed at the moment of crisis when it reverted to the orthodoxies of the bankers and surrendered its social programmes. The essay would mark a major challenge to gradualism. Tawney identifies two types of authentic socialism: the economic and ethical, who both share 'common intellectual convictions'. In his earlier work he had argued that such socialist convictions were the product of distinct religious concerns, best reflected in the Christian Church, but here appears to relax this definition. Labour has failed to define its brand of socialism leading to doctrinal confusion and policy incoherence – 'a glittering forest of trees, with presents for everyone' – and an overall inability to advance the cause.

The objective is a classless society with both ethical and technocratic brands of socialism valid methods to achieve this goal. Given Tawney's central status within the history of ethical socialism, this intellectual equivalence between the two strands of socialism reflects his growing acceptance of Fabian utilitarianism from the late 1920s and the declining status of the ILP. His hostility to both the 'private socialism' of union sectionalism and dialectical materialism of Marxist intellectuals remains resolute, however. His embrace of the economic route signals the wider reformation underway in the party as Labour reorientated away from the religion of socialism.

By the end of the 1930s the party had moved away from the old religion yet was unclear where it was heading. Labour had failed to build a robust policy framework to underpin its entry into government. According to Tawney it had survived on a mixture of rhetoric and determinism, and been reliant on the machinery of sectional interests. In the aftermath of the crisis, it was now retreating into blame and mythology rather than rebuilding by returning to questions of fundamental purpose. Two such models were open to it: the ethical and the utilitarian.

For Tawney the events of 1931 were the occasion and not the cause of the debacle of the Labour Party; it requires sincerity and not scapegoats. 1931 was a logical consequence of 1924: 'it sprang from within, not without'. Found wanting was not two years but a decade of Labour politics. To focus on individuals is to exaggerate their importance – 'to expel a person is not to exorcise a spirit'. Tawney's critique was echoed by Keynes, who assumed intellectual orthodoxy precluded Labour from ever becoming an economically radical party. From Keynes's liberal standpoint, Labour was too dominated by sectional interests and ideologically timid, leading MacDonald to reject his private advice over the May Committee report and the failure to stand up to the bankers in 1931.

The glamour of the word socialism has concealed the state of the movement. Clarity was now required in terms of the essentials: the kind of society it desired, the resistance to achieving it and methods and machinery to establish it. To date British socialism has rested on the machinery at the expense of the purpose.

Within this is an acknowledgement of the failings of socialist inevitability. In this sense British socialism had become as arid as Marxian socialism – 'whole battalions were shepherded into it, much as the troops of Feng-Yu-Hsiang, "the Christian general" were baptised with a hose'. The Labour government had come to power too easily, in ways that veiled socialism in 'radiant ambiguity' and forgot the reason for its existence: it 'demanded too little and offered too much'.

For Tawney, 'the function of the party is not to offer the largest possible number of carrots to the largest number of donkeys'. It requires definition and purpose and cannot 'relapse into the "philistinism of the May economy" report'; one that considers only capitalist economic interests as important. He offers a hostile verdict on those who conceived of socialism as inevitable and gradualism the method to achieve distributional justice without the accompanying policy rigour born of an understanding of purpose.

Labour had held office in two minority governments but faced disaster. Could it learn and rebuild?

5

Thirties
(1931–1939)

The 1930s, described by W.H. Auden as 'a low dishonest decade',[1] was turbulent for Labour and for democracy itself. Following the events of 1931 Labour required purpose and rigour but would have to discover it in a decade upended by economic depression and political extremism culminating in war. On the right many yearned for the past and the restoration of elite power. On the left leading radical intellectuals such as Auden, Stephen Spender, the Webbs and Laski looked east for inspiration, towards Soviet communism. Britain appeared politically bereft. Much of the political class consumed abstract fantasies fuelled by either nostalgic nationalism or the scientific utility of technological socialism.

Within literary modernism many conceived of the modern world as a betrayal. T.S. Eliot requested a spiritual reawakening through tradition, echoed by the literary critic F.R. Leavis in his rejection of a squalid modernity. The literary world also witnessed a socialist turn, despairing at a General Strike and 1930s crash, attached to blind belief in immanent upheaval and a necessary terrible reckoning. To writers such as George Orwell, this dishonest denial of the dangers of violence and authoritarianism exposed a righteous socialist superiority.[2]

For Labour the events of 1931 were traumatic. The leadership deserted its members and at the October election over two million voters shifted allegiance from the party. Labour emerged with just 46 MPs together with six unendorsed, supportive others. Henderson was gone as were Clynes, Greenwood, Herbert Morrison and Dalton. Three significant figures from the left survived: Lansbury, Attlee and Stafford Cripps. The National Government won 554 seats, of which 470 were held by Tories. The vague policy agenda of the party had been exposed by the trauma of 1931. The leadership appeared inert. The utopian dreams attached to Labour as the party of socialist inevitability had been shattered. Party fortunes would fluctuate throughout the decade. Initially the party would turn to the left and yet experienced a further split in July 1932 when the ILP opted to disaffiliate by 241 votes to 142. For a short time its role was taken up by the Socialist League, led by Cripps. In 1937 it proposed a Popular Front coalition with the Communist Party and the NEC moved to close it down. Yet despite a difficult decade where the hopes of the 1920s had evaporated, Labour would remain ahead of the Liberals and within a few years recover significant ground through resolute working-class support.

In this volatile environment, political continuity was provided by two unlikely figures, George Lansbury and Clement Attlee, accidental leaders immersed in the ethical traditions of the East London ILP. Both remain misunderstood figures. The fundamental decency and moral convictions of Lansbury helped hold the party together at a moment of great crisis. Instead of being destroyed in the wreckage of 1931, Lansbury helped ensure the party could be handed on to others to successfully lead. By 1935 it would prove impossible for him to remain as leader due to the same moral convictions that were so necessary for party unity earlier in the decade.

As the 1930s progressed, it was difficult to imagine Labour ever again being led by a 'prophet' from the ethical socialist tradition. Yet the unlikely figure of Attlee would invoke a form of leadership equipped to do just that, successfully consolidating the party and, after being significantly strengthened by the war, propelling Labour towards a landslide. Attlee would mask his radicalism in a 'rib cage of tradition'[3] and reconcile his personal passions and character to the task of governance. Attlee would unite the three traditions of justice and in doing so he would transform a nation.

Yet any future success required change, especially over policy, and the 1930s would see the emergence of an extraordinary cohort of young economists and planners in reaction to the limitations of the minority governments and harsh realities of office. This group, under the sponsorship of Dalton and urged on by the unions, especially Walter Citrine and Bevin, would help reconstitute the party. Statism and utilitarianism would come to define Labour through the decade at the expense of the early visionaries of a new socialist commonwealth, despite brief flirtations with the guild tradition and workers control in the early 1930s.

Lansbury and Attlee

Over a turbulent decade a thread of continuity was maintained by Labour's two leaders, Lansbury and Attlee. Lansbury, the quintessential ethical socialist, divides opinion. 'No brain to speak of' sneered Beatrice Webb, yet according to A.J.P. Taylor he was the 'the most lovable figure in British politics' and Attlee's brother Tom described him as 'almost a Gandhi'.[4] He once said 'socialism without religious enthusiasm … will become as selfish and soulless as any other movement that has cursed the world'.[5] His moral principles led to two resignations, from his seat in parliament and from the party leadership, and left him in Brixton as leader of the Poplar Rates Rebellion and Pentonville following militant rhetoric when campaigning for women's suffrage.

Lansbury was briefly MP for Bow and Bromley from 1910 to 1912. On 25 June 1912, he was suspended from parliament having attacked Asquith over the torture of women prisoners. He later resigned his seat, fought a by-election over women's rights and lost. As Labour's first Mayor of Poplar, he led the Rates Rebellion in 1921 and the following year returned to parliament after a rates revision was won. In 1927 he was elected Chairman of the PLP. In the second Labour government he was First Commissioner of Works. He survived the 1931 election and again became Chairman of the PLP. In 1932 Henderson stood down from the leadership in the country and Lansbury was elected.

Lansbury became leader because there appeared to be no other choice. He was the only surviving pioneer. Henderson was absent from parliament until 1933. Lansbury remained defiant about Labour's future. Despite the collapse in Labour's seat numbers to just 52, he correctly realized that with 6.5 million votes, and similar vote share to 1923 when Labour had won 158 seats, there were grounds for optimism given the unique circumstances of 1929–31 and the formation of the National Government. His biographer notes that given the depth of disillusion and sense of betrayal 'there could have been no better leader for the Labour Party at the collapse of its political fortunes in 1931 than George Lansbury – a universally popular choice, and a source of immediate inspiration amongst the ranks.'[6]

With his personal brand of honesty and humility, he offered a different type of collective leadership. With Attlee and Cripps, Lansbury

George Lansbury
Source: George Grantham Bain Collection, Library of Congress.

formed a 'socialist triumvirate' in the commons with all three sharing the office assigned to the leader behind the Speaker's chair. They feared further defections and could do little to stop the departure of the ILP in 1932 given the way the left had been in open revolt throughout much of the second Labour government. Although the Labour opposition was numerically outnumbered by roughly 12 to 1, they resisted any idea of a pact or alliance with the Liberals. Gradually, through 1931–5, Labour's position strengthened, reflected in ten by-election gains and healthy municipal election results. Lansbury deployed elements of the old religion to help rebuild morale. In a series of articles in *Clarion*, which later came together in his book *My England*, he talked of how 'Our Movement is in urgent need of being born again'[7] and how the next Labour government would 'reconstruct the whole life of the nation'.[8]

Lansbury's essential decency and collegiate leadership helped stabilize the party at a moment of acute crisis. George Thomas said 'He not only saved the soul of the party, he saved the party. We could have sunk into oblivion and the Liberals could have been reborn'. The PLP, according to Raymond Postgate, 'was reeling from the double shock of treachery and defeat. It wanted someone who could restore its confidence in human decency'. Desertion had destroyed the PLP. In Lansbury they 'found someone whom they loved and who loved them with no touch of patronage'.[9]

As leader Lansbury suffered a series of personal blows between 1933 and 1935. On 23 March 1933, his wife Bessie died. In December, in Gainsborough he fell and fractured his thigh. He felt close to death and was hospitalized for over 6 months and away from work for nine, with Attlee appointed interim leader. In hospital, a renewal of his faith occurred, believing he had been spared by God to continue his pacifist work and resist the drive to war. Confrontations with the axis of Dalton, Bevin and Walter Citrine became more frequent as Labour re-examined foreign policy with renewed emphasis on military force. He suffered loneliness and melancholia as his physical separation in a hospital bed complemented his political isolation within the Party he led. He suffered an overwhelming loss when his son Edgar died from inoperable cancer on 28 May 1935. It was followed by a profound crisis of conscience in the weeks leading up to the Party Conference as he accepted the irreconcilable relationship between his Christian pacifism and the responsibilities of party leadership. After a number of thwarted attempts to depart, it culminated in resignation, days after a brutal, unpleasant attack from Bevin on the Conference floor, as giant hailstones smashed into the roof of the Brighton Centre. Here Bevin likened the actions of Lansbury and other pacifist dissidents to those of MacDonald four years earlier.

Lansbury's successor, Clement Attlee, began his association with East End Labour politics in October 1905 through Haileybury House, a charity in Stepney run by his old school. Two years later he was appointed the club manager. In 1909 he worked to popularize *The Minority Report on the Future of the Poor Laws*, drafted by Royal Commission members Lansbury and Beatrice Webb, which helped pave the way for the future welfare state. The following year he accepted the secretaryship of Toynbee Hall in Whitechapel.

On being officially discharged after the war on 16 January 1919, Labour's future leader caught the tube to the East End and later that year Major Attlee became the youngest ever Mayor of Stepney. Two years later he supported Lansbury and the Poplar Rates Rebellion before being elected MP for Limehouse in 1922. He backed MacDonald over Clynes for leader and became his Parliamentary Private Secretary (PPS).

In the first Labour government Attlee served as Under Secretary of State for War. His appointment to the Simon Commission to investigate self-rule for India meant no immediate role in the second Labour government. In May 1930 he replaced Mosley as Chancellor of the Duchy of Lancaster and in 1931 became Postmaster General. In his autobiography he described MacDonald's actions that summer as 'the greatest betrayal in the political history of this country'.[10] At the 1931 election Attlee held on by 551 votes following the formation of the National Government to become deputy to Lansbury, and following the latter's resignation in 1935, defeated Greenwood and Morrison for the leadership.

Little discussed are the political continuities between the two men. The man who held Attlee's hand when he died, his manservant Alfred Laker, noted that he 'had a depth of feeling he took care to keep hidden'. Frank Field has described it as the construction of a political death mask. Attlee succeeded where the ILP could not because his political passions were consciously locked down within a 'rib-cage of tradition'.[11] Attlee was anchored within the English idealism of the late nineteenth and early twentieth centuries and its rejection of empiricism and utilitarianism through the influence of academics such as Ernest Barker and the writings of T.H. Green. This helped secularize the Christianity ethic within Attlee and 'marked him indelibly with a confidence so that he could attach absolute meanings to such concepts as duty, responsibility, loyalty and courage',[12] which was reinforced by the philosophy of social progress he studied at the London School of Economics (LSE) under E.J. Urwick, a student of Green.

His brother Laurence first took Attlee to the Haileybury Club in Durham Road, Stepney, in October 1905. Yet it was another brother Tom – disciple of the Christian socialist F.D. Maurice, pacifist colleague of Lansbury, and avid reader of Ruskin and Morris – that proved to be critical in the making of the socialist. He wrote that

Clement Attlee
Source: Winterbergen, Fotocollectie Anefo, Dutch National Archives.

through Tom 'I too began to understand their social gospel'. By early 1908 it led him to the ILP. Attlee joined with 15 others to form the Stepney branch of the ILP in January 1908 after an East End wharf keeper, Tommy Williams, came to Haileybury House to denounce the Charity Organisation Society and the inhumanity of the workhouse. A few streets away, Lansbury had made a similar journey four years earlier. As Attlee described it: 'Williams proclaimed his socialist faith and I, listening, said, "I am a socialist too"'.[13] He had been active in the Fabians but found them underwhelming, writing that 'The Fabian school of socialism, while strong in dealing with facts, was always rather weak in dealing with persons. It considered more the organisation of things than the life of the people'.

Complications: Labour and Patriotism

Whilst the transition from Lansbury to Attlee ensured a certain East End ILP political continuity within the Labour leadership, it also marked a significant reorientation over questions of patriotism and foreign policy. These two allies within the ethical Labour tradition would take very different positions over questions of rearmament, foreign policy and the defence of the national community. Like Hardie and MacDonald, Lansbury had stood resolute against the First World War, whereas Attlee served with the 6th South Lancashire Regiment and was the last but one off the beach at Gallipoli. Having been wounded at El Hannah, he served the final months of the war on the Western Front. This divergence within the left was one replicated within his own family with his pacifist brother Tom – an anti-war 'absolutist'. In his autobiography Attlee wrote:

> The difference of view in the party was well illustrated in our family. My brother Tom was a confirmed conscientious objector and went to prison. I thought it my duty to fight. We ended the war as near neighbours in Wandsworth – I in hospital and he in gaol – but with no breach in our mutual affection.[14]

Like Henderson and many others, Attlee was 'socialist pro-war', challenging the 'might is right' doctrine; 'In different ways we are on the same side', he privately wrote to Tom. As Leader of the Opposition Attlee orchestrated the retreat from Labour pacifism. It was a difficult personal and political journey. In the early 1930s pacifism remained significant within the party. Attlee had been active in the No More War movement in the 1920s and it was not until 1935 that he became fully convinced of the case for rearmament, breaking with Lansbury and Cripps in supporting action against Italy over Abyssinia. Yet at the 1935 election Labour remained ambiguous on rearmament. It had consistently voted against the defence estimates, and Attlee refused to change position on this in 1936, although most MPs were by now in support of rearmament. Labour remained in support of the League of Nations yet against rearmament at home. Attlee refused to simply drive policy changes through the party, partly due to family loyalties to Tom and respect for Lansbury and the many comrades from the ILP. Although by November 1937, helped by events in Spain where significant parts of the left rallied in support of the Republican forces, Labour was pushing back against the government in their defence expenditure and contingency planning and reframing the debate around appeasement. In October 1938, Attlee denounced Chamberlain over the Munich Agreement accepting the German annexation of the Sudetenland. Labour only later joined the government in May 1940, the month Lansbury died, once Chamberlain had been replaced by Churchill, and Attlee would play a vital role in helping resist widespread Conservative calls for a negotiated peace with Hitler.

In contrast, during the final years leading up to the Second World War, Lansbury continued to preach the gospel of peace as chair of the No More War movement, the War Resisters' International and President of the Peace Pledge Union. For him 'the peace question was a matter of conscience, similar to religion and temperance'.[15] He toured the country in support of the pacifist cause, making the case for a world summit through the League of Nations and challenging the doctrine of a justifiable 'Holy War'. In 1937 he was in Belgium and France and on 19 April met Hitler in Berlin for two and a half hours, and later that year visited Mussolini in Rome. He welcomed the Munich Agreement of September 1938 but was left devastated by Britain's entry into the war. Health issues returned. In early 1940, suffering from bronchitis, he was advised to take a complete rest. On his return to work he collapsed. A recurring heart condition and inoperable stomach cancer – the same disease that had taken his son – finally brought down the 81-year-old on 7 May 1940.

Whilst Lansbury represented the long-standing pacifist religious tradition within the Party, and Attlee the strain of Edwardian idealism influential in Labour's origins story, there were other notable strands of thinking regarding questions of war and peace.

A long-standing rationalist position within Labour viewed patriotism as essentially a pathological condition. Its origins, according to Miles Taylor,[16] can be traced back to the late nineteenth century and the disconcerting 'new' imperialism evident after the failed Jameson Raid of 1895, contributing to the Second Boer War. The left recoiled as this patriotic 'jingoism' bled into the ballot box at the 'Khaki' election of 1900. Hobson's *The Psychology of Jingoism* sought explanation in the essential irrationality of the sentiment;[17] considered 'a primitive lust' fuelled by a cynical press, one which exposed a brittle democracy evidenced by the decline of the Liberal Party. In the Edwardian era, much of the left consequently lost faith in any progressive enlightened notion of patriotism.

This perspective informed parts of the inter-war pacifist movement within the ILP, Labour and the Communist parties, and aligned with other religious pacifist sentiments. In 1934, the ILP favoured an international general strike and its successor the Socialist League total unilateralism, before both later teamed up in support of a United Front.

The fear of the pathological capacity of the masses tended to consolidate elitist, centralist political cultures on the left. Put simply, the masses needed leadership as the working man's primal instincts crowded out their rationality. As Taylor notes, 'lacking any critical faculty he was liable to go along with a wave of mass opinion like jingoism, rather than determine his own views, unless educated to an appropriate level of political awareness'. It also tended to identify the origins of fascism in the same irrational forces that fed jingoism at home.

Things began to change in the late 1930s given the drumbeat of war. But looming conflict was not the only force reshaping the left's approach to the defence of the nation. Slowly an alternative, more positive vision of the democratic community emerged compared to much of the inter-war left; one built on the active participation of the citizens and the associational elements of the ethical socialist tradition.

The Mass Observation surveys of 1937–40 challenged the docile view of the masses susceptible to fascism. A renewed emphasis on the peculiarities of the English culture and heterogeneity of the people gradually emerged, which, in the words of Orwell, sought to 'reconcile patriotism with intelligence'. A loose group of writers, photographers, filmmakers and artists, including Orwell, J.B. Priestly, Barbara Jones, Laurie Lee, Dylan Thomas, Bill Brandt, among others, throughout the inter-war years resisted the abstractions and certainties of the time to build a politics 'out of the everyday, the ordinary, to imagine a good society',[18] one that found expression in Orwell's 'reflection on the mundane', Priestley's role as 'chronicler of everyday experience' in an England of suburbia and New Towns. War propelled these ideas forward. The everyday concerns of the people were the key resource necessary to prevail in any looming conflict and cohered around the idea of 'the people's war' – developed by Priestly in his *Postscripts* radio talks. Patriotism was seen less as an animal lust within the susceptible mob to be led by the knowledgeable few, but rather was suggestive of a democratic revival and more open political culture built around the British people and their virtues, such as with the civic virtue expressed in the patriotism of the 'Home Guard'.

In the pre-war period Attlee could align his party with such sentiment, in part because they were an echo of earlier traditions on the left. Writers such as Paul Ward[19] have demonstrated such democratic beliefs had informed much earlier ethical socialist ideas of national identity captured in the contributions of Ruskin and Morris and the radical conservatism of Robert Blatchford.[20] Alongside Attlee after 1935 stood Ernest Bevin – labourer at 11, lorry driver, dockers' leader and key figure in the founding of the TGWU – from a very different tradition but central to Labour's vision of an emerging national story. Later as wartime Minister of Labour, he would anchor the organized working class into the fight against appeasement and for the war effort, vital tributaries leading to the landslide of 1945.

This realignment within Labour under Attlee, with elements of labourism joining forces with associational ethical party traditions in helping shape the party's foreign policy, is, however, only one part of Labour's consolidation in the 1930s. In *Labour's War*,[21] Stephen Brooke places a different emphasis in his account of the 1945 victory. He argues it can be traced back to the lack of systematic policy work when the ILP prophets and utopians led Labour, leaving the party terribly exposed in 1931. This failure was overcome in the 1930s after a new generation of economists and planners helped reformulate policy with a rigour never seen before within Labour helping pave the way to 1945.

Intellectual Reorientation

In reaction to the events of 1931, Labour shifted to the left. At the 1932 Conference Somerville Hastings of the Socialist Medical Association (SMA) moved a resolution calling for the establishment of a State Medical Service and in 1934 the annual Conference unanimously accepted an official document on a National Health Service largely prepared by SMA members. In 1932 Conference agreed to nationalize the joint stock banks. In 1933, in *Socialism and the Condition of the People*, it supported nationalizing the banks and the steel industry. In 1934, the party adopted *For Socialism and Peace*, which committed to the nationalization of land, banking, coal, iron and steel, transport, power and water supply, as well as the setting up of a National Investment Board to plan industrial development, although the left offered the document only a cautious welcome. These commitments reappeared in Dalton's *Practical Socialism for Britain* in 1935. However, this tilt to the left in the early 1930s was in reality a 'piecemeal and qualified shift'.[22] For instance, by 1937, commitments to steel nationalization had been removed from *Labour's Immediate Programme*.[23] At the 1937 Conference the party rejected the Popular Front route favoured by the Communist Party and the left from 1935. In May that year, it had forced the Socialist League to end its activities or face expulsion. In January 1939, both Cripps and Bevan were expelled. More significant than any apparent left turn was a decade-long reorientation within Labour towards deliverable concrete policies in contrast to the vagueness of the late 1920s programmes.

Much early socialist thought was infused with teleological assumptions of inevitable socialist change and ideas of Darwinian social evolution. MacDonald, for instance, subscribed to a positivist developmental model of socialism which anticipated society evolving though higher stages of human development. From a more orthodox Marxist perspective, the SDF echoed Lenin's belief that accelerated technological change would deliver socialism. Both Ruskin and Morris rejected such optimistic readings of human evolution and accommodations with capitalism and the links between modernity and any frictionless transition to socialism. This emphasis on political struggle against the commodifications intrinsic to industrial capitalism and Ruskin's notion of the 'citizens economy' with an ethic of universal public service to alleviate want found widespread support across the early labour movement, especially within the ILP, guild socialist and syndicalist traditions. Even within the Fabian tradition, G.D.H. Cole rejected the evolutionary approach. The events of the First World War also challenged such optimistic approaches to socialist change, reflected in the renewed emphasis on political struggle in the 1918 Constitution and the *New Social Order* document. This reorientation gathered pace following the bitter experiences of the General Strike and collapse of the second Labour government. Cumulatively, Labour embraced a more antagonistic approach to political change, markedly less confident about the inevitable evolution of socialist society.

Deterministic assumptions of socialist inevitability had meant a lack of systematic policy work, reflected in the limited options available to Labour once in office. As Tawney had argued with hindsight in 1934, socialism had evolved rhetorically rather than through building an agenda for enduring change. Gradualism's embrace of balanced budgets and macroeconomic stability rested on similar grounds, setting a stable backdrop for social evolution and progress to occur. Such certainties were derailed by the events of 1931. The desire for fiscal orthodoxy had prevailed over the defence of social protections and the advance of socialism. Across both the left and right, renewed emphasis was placed on economic policy development to fill the policy vacuums revealed in office. Across both the left and right, the 1930s saw the consolidation of utilitarian thinking over economic policy.

A subtle economic reckoning took place within Labour during the 1930s with both left and right coalescing around questions of utility and departing from ethics. It was one that drew less on the insights and ideas of the moral or citizens economy and the rejection of utility as the organizing principle of society traced back to Ruskin and Morris, and more on questions of economic and social efficiency through planning. Inspiration came in part from the experiences of state economic management in the war, ideas subsequently discarded by post-war austerity following global shocks cruelly revealed in the limitations of the minority Labour administrations. On the left, significant policy renewal included the ILP Living Wage proposals of 1926 underpinned by pre-Keynesian theories of deficit demand and underconsumption[24] and proposals for a National Industrial Authority to drive a corporatist economy. Similar ideas had been advanced by G.D.H. Cole with his proposed National Economic Council. The Socialist League, set up by Cole, Laski, Cripps, Attlee and others in 1932 after a merger of the guild socialist Society for Socialist Inquiry and Propaganda (SSIP) and remaining ILP members who stayed with Labour after its secession, also embraced a radical policy platform. They advanced the case for five-year plans based around nationalization, including the banking sector. Yet apart from Bevin as honorary chairman, the League attracted little union support. Organized labour's approach to planning tended to focus instead on job creation through public works packages, an echo of US New Deal programmes. The unions remained uneasy about the central planning advocated by the League and retained their long-term preference for voluntarism, autonomous bargaining and traditions of collective *laissez-faire*.

The approach of the Socialist League was rivalled by the public corporation model of common ownership pushed by Herbert Morrison and the more pragmatic approach of the New Fabian Research Group, part of an emerging network of groups revising Labour's economic thinking feeding into Dalton's powerful Finance and Trade Sub-Committee, set up by the NEC in 1931. This included a 'Cole Group' based at Oxford under the guidance of G.D.H. Cole, which attracted figures such as James Meade and Hugh Gaitskell, the so-called XYZ group of financial journalists and academics including Douglas Jay, and the Fabian Research Group, which included Gaitskell and Evan Durbin. They all shared an interest in questions of planning and a general dislike for the centralism of the Webbs and retained mixed views of Keynes. Critically, however, in contrast to gradualism's early embrace of economic orthodoxy to deliver inevitable social evolution, these revisionists sought to secure similar social outcomes but through planning and economic reform rather than the laws of history. They embraced a more modest National Investment Board as a tool for steering a mixed economy alongside an interest in Keynesian regulation and reflation to drive investment, rather than more radical talk of five-year plans and the state administration of industry. In 1937 Dalton placed Durbin, Jay and Gaitskell onto his NEC Sub-Committee.

Overall, the events of 1931 inspired a variety of interventions that shared a common emphasis on the role of state power in directing policy rather than the evolutionary assumptions of earlier socialist thought. Significant differences existed, especially with the New Fabians who were more strongly attached to the role of market forces, preferences that would reappear decades later in the arguments of 1950s revisionists, 1980s modernizers and advocates of New Labour. Embedded within these different 1930s approaches were alternative assumptions about the democratic health of the country. Within the Socialist League, an early home for left wingers such as Aneurin Bevan and Barbara Castle, née Betts, many such as Laski regarded democracy itself to be in decline. Such positions informed demands for a Popular Front with the communists and the argument for dictatorial emergency powers, leading to figures such as Attlee distancing themselves given the rise of authoritarianism across the continent. In contrast, within the revisionism of the New Fabian group, Evan Durbin, in *The Politics of Democratic Socialism*, emphasized the role of parliamentary democracy and political pluralism in nurturing a country's 'psychological health', whereas excessive political purity and authoritarianism suggested sublimated fear, guilt and social aggression.

Durbin remains an underappreciated figure in Labour history, particularly his work in collaboration with psychologist John Bowlby, the early pioneer of attachment theory who, as we shall see, would come to play a vital role in post-war Labour social policy and the revival in revisionist associational forms of ethical socialism. Durbin would draw on psychology rather than economics in making the case for civic renewal and democratic pluralism. Tragically, on 3 September 1948, aged 42, Durbin died from drowning whilst trying to rescue his daughter and another child on Strangles Beach near Bude in Cornwall with his friend Bowlby close by.[25]

The war years would see the influence of this group of young economists grow. Gaitskell became an advisor to Dalton at the Board of Trade. Jay and Durbin along with a young Harold Wilson also moved into government service and Meade went to the Economic Section of the Cabinet Office where he would play a key role in the 1944 full employment White Paper. Later in 1945 Gaitskell, Durbin and Wilson would all enter parliament, as would Jay following a period as private secretary to Attlee.

Years of Consolidation

In the 1930s Labour recalibrated its purpose in response to the events of 1931 and the party's parliamentary collapse. By-election and local election victories were early signs of recovery. Relative success continued at the November 1935 election shortly after the departure of Lansbury, and saw the return of leaders such as Clynes, Dalton and Morrison. Labour secured 154 seats and 38 per cent of the vote, although the government still retained 429 seats and the Tories 387. Organizationally the decade would see membership more than double and NEC reforms that granted more power to the Constituency Labour Parties (CLPs) and greater control over the selection of their representatives.

With Attlee as leader, aided by Dalton and Bevin, Labour would challenge appeasement and develop a muscular foreign policy in tune with the times. But it was in the field of ideas and policy that Labour made its most significant changes given the limited resources available to it in the summer of 1931. In local government, especially after 1934 with the capture of the London County Council (LCC) under Morrison, Labour was building a distinct framework for civic administration. By the end of the 1930s, the party was running sixty local authorities pulling together its own agenda for housing, education, public health services, and in the services transferred to them in 1929 from the Boards of Guardians. In Glasgow slum clearance resulted in 200,000 new homes between 1934 and 1939. In London Labour unified the transport system, embarked on active slum clearance and council housing, introduced a municipal health service foreshadowing the NHS, and brought forward major education reforms.

Nationally despite an initial turn to the left, the unions remained a cautious force in the party. The doctrine of the 'inevitability of gradualness' was being contested but in ways that resisted the demands of the Socialist League and instead embraced a generation of young economists of the XYZ group and New Fabians with detailed plans for nationalization, domestic policy and planning, reflected in the 1937 document *Labour's Immediate Programme*, which would anchor the programme of the 1945 government.

The personality of Attlee, guided by the axis of Dalton, Bevin and Citrine, would help blend together the ethical and utilitarian late nineteenth-century traditions of the early ILP and Fabian Society and bolt the organized working class within this coalition. The planners provided rigour and ballast. But economics was itself part of a deeper story of national renewal and reorientation from Empire. In his 1933 essay on 'National Self Sufficiency', Keynes had confronted the 'decadent international but individualistic capitalism' that caused the Wall Street Crash.[26] 'It is not just, it is not virtuous – and it doesn't deliver the goods', he said, in words appealing to the patriotic young economists within Labour. In its place he advocated an English cultural renaissance with his economic theory grounded in the idea of a new economic community. The appropriation of certain parts of Keynesianism by Labour's young planners aligned with the leadership of the Edwardian idealist Attlee and combined by 1938 to provide robust opposition to appeasement and the ideology of *laissez-faire*. Throughout the 1930s, utilitarian thinking had been renewed and updated and yet the ethical traditions remained visible, in part due to the political continuities supplied by Attlee's leadership.

Jerusalem
(1939–1951)

By 1939 Labour's electoral prospects had undoubtedly improved, although a political landslide or even election victory looked well beyond reach. The same concern existed over policy. Throughout the decade significant advances were made to build an agenda to achieve socialist change. Yet the party remained vague about the practical means to achieve its political goals. For example, in 1934 there was little evidence it could achieve the nationalization plans envisaged in *For Socialism and Peace*. Arguably, if it had been victorious at the 1935 election, government policy would not have significantly differed from the MacDonald era.[1]

International events would once more come to the aid of the party, in the form of the Second World War. As was the case from 1914 to 1918, wartime mobilization legitimized enhanced state power in ways inconceivable in the years preceding the conflict. After 1945 Labour was the beneficiary of a vast range of legal, economic and administrative powers secured with popular cross-class consent. The party's theorists might henceforth achieve their political goals through democratic means given new regulation over incomes and property, the supply of manpower and information. The conflict established a practical framework to help enact party commitments over public ownership, redistributive taxation, planning and socialized public services without recourse to soviet methods. It also brought widespread recognition of the failures of post-First World War reconstruction and a popular desire not to return to pre-war normality. Future change might be achieved without class conflict and antagonistic sectional demands because of the popularity of the Beveridge Plan[2] and with it the prospects for universal 'levelling up' building on the shared sacrifice of the war effort.

The demands of the conflict coupled with post-war austerity and an emerging Cold War reinforced the case for pragmatic political management and practical governance. The scale of victory in 1945 meant Labour represented an increasingly wide coalition of interests, geographies and classes; one that would not easily cohere around one specific political identity. Despite this, however, it remains a widely held, orthodox view of Attlee's government that questions of political purpose were resolved by the dominance of Fabian expertise; that the war would see the consolidation of a top-down approach to public administration, of statism and labourism, and the post-war Labour government would be dominated by the utilitarian economics that had captured the party in the 1930s. It was a view accepted in some unlikely quarters. For instance, by 1949 a relaxed Tawney, when compared with the angry combatant of 1934, could foresee only two real problems facing Labour: becoming too utilitarian and economistic and that social democracy might too readily pander to popular taste; people had to learn to use their growing freedoms.[3] It was a theme echoed from a different perspective by Douglas Jay in his famous phrase 'the gentleman in Whitehall really does know better what is good for the people than the people know themselves.'[4]

We will suggest a slightly different, unorthodox interpretation of the 1945 government. Labour's path to victory in 1945 would reveal little in the way of any underlying public philosophy; Labour remained a coalition of traditions. The late 1930s saw the sectional demands of the unions under the skilful guidance of Bevin align with a generation of economists to advance utilitarian elements within the party, yet Attlee represented continuity with the old ILP and ethical traditions of the past. The war helped Labour insert itself into the story of the nation rather than being considered simply as a sectional class representative and shape the politics of post-war reconstruction through its control of the domestic policy agenda. Yet crucially Attlee would also manage to align his plans for welfare reform with post-war ideas for new economic, social and human rights in the pursuit of liberty and democratic freedom. Cumulatively, whilst his government is exalted for using the central state to nationalize major sectors of the economy and build a welfare state, its success can also be accounted for by the way it successfully reconciled competing traditions of justice within the post-war administration. For the first time in Labour's history the three traditions of justice had creatively aligned.

Wartime Coalition

War was declared by Neville Chamberlain on 3 September 1939, in a move supported by the Labour opposition. An 'electoral truce' was established between the political parties, although Attlee resisted any suggestion of joining a coalition led by Chamberlain, who was by then a broken man. By the spring of 1940 the 'phoney war' came to an end with Hitler invading Norway and Denmark. On 8 May, Attlee told the PLP it was time to break the truce and bring forward a no-confidence vote. Although the government prevailed, 134 of its own MPs rebelled. On 10 May, Germany invaded France, Belgium, the Netherlands and Luxembourg as Labour assembled in Bournemouth for its Conference. The NEC agreed to enter a coalition but not one led by Chamberlain, in effect removing the Prime Minister. Chamberlain was forced to resign and Churchill, in an echo of the First World War, brought the other main parties into a unity government. Although many in Labour's ranks disliked Churchill for his anti-union record, recalling the use of troops in the Tonypandy riots of 1910, the Conference heavily rejected attempts to rule out serving in any administration he would lead.

Some have suggested that entry into the wartime coalition brought in a third Labour government,[5] arguably one more successful than the first two minority administrations given the way it effectively took control over the home front, implementing wide-ranging social and economic reforms. It certainly demonstrated a renewed competence as Labour brought rigour and order to government operations and the functioning of parliament, as well as the drive for reconstruction. Just as in 1914, the war helped propel the party forward, although in comparison Labour was a more united and disciplined force in 1939 given the clear fascist threat of Hitler, whose domestic actions included the attack on unions and imprisonment of social democratic leaders.

In total, 16 Labour ministers were appointed to the government, a figure that would rise to 27 by 1945, with Labour given control of the domestic policy agenda. Clement Attlee became Lord Privy Seal and chair of the Food and Home Policy Committee and, with Arthur Greenwood, entered a War Cabinet of five. In 1943, Attlee effectively became the country's first Deputy Prime Minister as well as Lord

President of the Council. In May 1940, Bevin, who weeks earlier had been dropped into the Wandsworth Central parliamentary seat, became Minister of Labour and National Service, entering the War Cabinet in October, the same month Morrison was appointed Home Secretary, having previously served as Minister for Supply. A.V. Alexander resumed the role he had held in the previous Labour government as First Lord of the Admiralty. Dalton became Minister of Economic Affairs, later President of the Board of Trade. Cripps was made Ambassador to the USSR and, in February 1942, joined the War Cabinet as Lord Privy Seal. From the ranks of brilliant young economists, Wilson, Jay and Gaitskell were all appointed as civil servants. Although the Exchequer remained in Conservative hands, a firm understanding was established with Labour regarding the equitable distribution of tax burdens and support for rising incomes. The top rate of income tax reached 98 per cent in 1949, and real wages increased by 18 per cent between 1938 and 1947.

Within weeks of Labour entering the wartime coalition, British forces were enclosed on Dunkirk beaches. Churchill, vulnerable following the collapse of France, appeared old and isolated amongst his Conservative colleagues as invasion looked imminent. Between 26 and 28 May, War Cabinet disagreements intensified as Chamberlain and Halifax pushed for a negotiated peace with Hitler. Attlee, ably backed up by Greenwood,[6] showed extraordinary resolve in supporting Churchill, ensuring his survival and eventual success in the full cabinet meeting held late on 28 May, thereby derailing the last attempts at British appeasement from within the Conservative ranks.[7]

From the beginning of the conflict, in documents such as *Labour War Aims* in 1939 and *Labour's Home Policy* in 1940, the party maintained a keen focus on rebuilding the country after the war, ensuring it reached beyond advocating on behalf of any sectional interests. May 1941 saw the formation of a special NEC committee on post-war reconstruction, which oversaw thirteen sub-committees to drive policy development forward, culminating in the 1945 manifesto *Let Us Face the Future*. Consistent themes included the retention of wartime planning and controls to ensure full employment and reconstruction, widespread nationalization, social security and education reform alongside somewhat vague commitments to a national health service.

Morrison, as he had shown in London, proved to be a highly impressive minister who effectively oversaw civic defence, repairs and regeneration following the blitz. He embraced penal reform, expansion of the probation service and improved workers' compensation and industrial injuries protections to include miners' pneumoconiosis and cotton workers' byssinosis, and established a National Fire Service. Alongside him, Dalton advanced an effective regional policy to help deprived areas.

In June 1941, following the suggestions of the TUC, Arthur Greenwood as Minister Without Portfolio set up the Interdepartmental Committee on Social Insurance and Allied Services to investigate the state of Britain's social welfare programmes, and appointed Beveridge chairman of the committee. The 1942 Report helped lay the foundations for the post-war British welfare state. Labour saw its early introduction as vital whilst Churchill prevaricated. In a February 1943 parliamentary division over support for its implementation, 97 Labour MPs rebelled, led by ex-miner James Griffiths, MP for Llanelli and future Minister for National Insurance, and 30 abstained leaving just 23 Labour MPs, including 22 ministers, to support the whip and back the government. The rebellion helped align Labour with growing support for social reform and a summer 1943 Gallup poll placed the party 11 points ahead of the Conservatives.[8] In 1943 the government established its own reconstruction committee, which would develop both the 1944 Education Act following a close collaboration between Labour's James Chuter Ede and Rab Butler, and the same year the White Paper on Full Employment, which Bevin moved to adopt in parliament.

Bevin proved to be an extraordinary force within the government. He raised the wages of low-paid workers, including miners, railwaymen and agricultural labourers, and extended company medical and welfare provision. Essential Work Orders guaranteed basic employment rights and Ministry of Labour Training Centres helped boost productive capacity. Whilst Order 1305 banned strikes and lockouts in favour of arbitration, Bevin throughout favoured a more cooperative, tripartite route. A National Joint Advisory Council with equal worker and employer representation was introduced in 1939 to help in the regulation of industry followed by the Joint Consultative Committee a year later.

Forty-six new Joint Industrial Councils were introduced to foster cooperative employment relations and Bevin extended Wages Boards, so that by the end of the war 15.5 million workers were covered by their minimum wage provisions. Union density rose from 32 per cent in 1939 to a wartime high of over 40 per cent partly because of full employment but also the positive environment nurtured by Bevin. A Catering Wages Commission was established to oversee wages and working conditions in restaurants and hotels. Compared to the First World War, profiteering was effectively controlled and rent controls and food subsidies helped peg back inflation.

By 1945 Labour was seen as the party of social reform and distinct from the Tories who had retreated from a February 1944 White Paper commitment to a free system of national health. Economically, at the December 1944 Conference, Labour again pledged support for widespread nationalization. Labour's policy agenda aligned to the wartime statecraft and appeared ready to reset the social order post conflict.

Internal tensions were ever present within the party, however, especially in the manoeuvrings of Laski and Morrison. Despite the fact that the PLP remained relatively quiet and the unions strongly supportive of the leadership, Attlee would encounter internal divisions and face criticism over compromises with the Conservatives and inferences of 'MacDonaldism' from the likes of Bevan, readmitted in 1939, who along with Shinwell would articulate the left's arguments against the coalition in parliament, and Laski.[9] At local level several parties were forced to disband over communist entryism. Yet staffing changes pointed to a renewed professionalism and energy at the centre, including Morgan Phillips being appointed Party Secretary in 1944 and Michael Young head of research. Union affiliations increased, bolstering the financial health of the party, and from 1942, with momentum behind Beveridge and the case for social reform, individual membership grew significantly. Labour had a good war, proving effective in government, aligned with growing pressures for change and greatly benefitting from the expanded role of the state to render intelligible its 1930s policy work and transition towards socialism. In 1944, the NEC argued for an immediate election at the end of the conflict to be fought along party lines.

Building Jerusalem

Following the German surrender and the end of the war in Europe in May 1945, Labour resolved not to repeat the 1918 Liberal error and withdrew from the coalition to contest the election. Churchill was appointed head of a caretaker administration and quickly dissolved parliament on 5 June with polling day scheduled for 5 July, a move which also had the effect of checking any move by Morrison against Attlee. The eventual result, delayed by three weeks to allow for overseas vote counting, saw Labour secure 393 seats, a net gain of 239, with 48 per cent of the poll and a majority of 145, compared to 210 Conservative seats and 39.9 per cent. Labour had polled especially well across the Midlands and London, gaining significant middle-class support to sit alongside a solid working-class base.

Labour had a strong leadership team, albeit an ageing one, with the average age of the first majority Labour cabinet in the mid-sixties. The 1930s era of appeasement and mass unemployment had damaged the Tories. Labour appeared the party best equipped to advance the social reforms suggested by Beveridge aided by the rediscovered administrative credibility supplied by the war. Morrison was appointed Lord President of the Council with a remit covering domestic strategy. Bevin was Foreign Secretary and Dalton Chancellor, with Cripps at Trade and Greenwood Lord Privy Seal. Cripps later became Chancellor after Dalton was forced to resign following leaked budget details.[10] The left in cabinet was represented by Bevan, covering health as well as housing, Ellen Wilkinson, the only woman, as Education Secretary and Shinwell as Minister for Fuel and Power.

The prospect of an immediate economic crisis shook the new administration following the unilateral American announcement to end lend-lease aid on 19 August 1945. The US Congress first agreed the Lend-Lease Act in March 1941 authorizing the President the ability to lend or lease military equipment and provide aid in defence of the United States. Britain would subsequently benefit from tens of billions of dollars of generous loans throughout the war which helped stabilize the UK economy as export revenues plummeted. It came to an abrupt halt at the end of the conflict, partly a consequence of right-wing American reaction to the prospect of upholding British socialism. Following negotiations for new loans to avoid economic collapse led for the UK by Keynes, the December follow-up agreement contained challenging new terms, including that sterling should be convertible to the dollar and access to British markets – conditions that would trigger a run on sterling and a balance of payments crisis following the introduction of 'convertibility' in 1947.

Despite these significant economic uncertainties, the government swiftly moved to introduce a comprehensive welfare state including socialized health care and a wide-ranging nationalization programme whereby over 20 per cent of the economy was brought under state control.

In 1946, the government moved to nationalize the Bank of England and civil aviation, the next year inland transportation including railways, road haulage and canals, as well as coal and cable and wireless. Gas and electricity followed in 1948 with iron and steel being completed in 1951. After an initial burst of activity, the programme gradually wound down, with the final element, iron and steel, proving to be possibly the most difficult sector, in part due to opposition from Morrison but also a lack of support from the steelworkers union. Nationalizing the sector had remained controversial throughout the 1930s and was only reluctantly included in the manifesto following interventions from the Keep Left group of MPs at the 1944 Conference, and in government it was pushed through in part to appease an increasingly frustrated Bevan. Despite its socialist *bona fides* and status within the 1918 constitution, the nationalization programme lacked clear political purpose and the public corporation model failed to restructure and align the respective state sectors within any overarching socialist plan. There was no attempt to embrace industrial democracy despite the history of guild socialism and consultative machinery of wartime, with the unions appearing content to adhere to the long-standing principles of voluntarism and collective *laissez-faire*. Morrison could appear hostile and Attlee agnostic. Although it is of note that the 1951 manifesto would promise to 'associate workers' with the future running of public services suggesting a subtle embrace of industrial democracy and a wider rethink of Labour's approach to public ownership.

In terms of developing the welfare state, in 1946 Jim Griffiths introduced the legislation designed to extend the scope of the 1911

National Insurance Act and establish a comprehensive system of social security along similar lines to that advanced by Beveridge four years earlier, funded from weekly national insurance contributions of all those of working age excluding married women.[11] It included sickness and unemployment benefits, pensions, family allowances and widows support, and was implemented in 1948.

The National Health Service Act 1946, also introduced in 1948, went further than the health reorganizations suggested by Beveridge, or indeed vague earlier party commitments especially in terms of its reach, whereby hospitals and GPs were brought under the umbrella of the state, all paid out of general taxation. The legislation had been challenged by Morrison because of its omission from the manifesto and provoked a long-standing battle with the British Medical Association (BMA) over part-salaried GPs, before their eventual introduction.

Alongside these changes the government implemented the 1944 Coalition Education Act, raising the school leaving age to 15; comprehensive schooling would only come in 1965. In 1946, Labour finally repealed the Trades Disputes Act of 1927. On housing, despite a relatively slow start, by the end of the parliament it was completing 200,000 new council homes per year. The 1948 Industrial Injuries Act provided new compensation for workplace accidents. Little advance was made in terms of constitutional reform, however, beyond the removal of university seats in parliament and plural voting, although the blocking powers of the Lords was slightly constrained. The 1945 government remained wedded to the constitutional status quo, reflecting the long-held Labour view that the state remained the key institution to advance social progress and regulate the market, rejecting calls from guild socialist or syndicalist alternatives.[12]

It was not all plain sailing. 1947 was an especially difficult year. Marshall Aid support following the renegotiated US loans had allowed the government to drive forward its reform agenda as exports recovered. However, the wretched winter of 1946/7 and fuel and food shortages saw unemployment climb whilst escalating US prices and the July onset of convertibility saw sterling slide and a balance of payments crisis develop. After just five weeks, convertibility was suspended. Dalton was subsequently replaced by Cripps and another sterling crisis forced a devaluation in September 1949. Meanwhile the escalating costs of the

NHS saw Morrison and Cripps start to push for prescription charges. In the short term the row was resolved following the disappointing 1950 election with the move of Bevan to the Ministry of Labour. Things then deteriorated further.

Defence expenditure became an increasingly divisive issue, reaching 14 per cent of GDP in 1951 as the Korean War placed strains on public finances following the outbreak in atrocities in June 1950 and the involvement of British troops from August. Gaitskell as Chancellor introduced prescription charges for NHS dentures and spectacles, causing Bevan, along with Wilson and John Freeman, to resign. These resignations helped cohere an emerging left wing as all three quickly joined the Keep Left group. Whilst relations with the PLP had been generally good since 1945, partly because the unions remained strongly supportive and partly the result of a well-organized process of policy consultation, after the 1950 election loyalty corroded. The future fault lines between the emerging 'Bevanites' and the 'Revisionists', which we discuss in the next chapter, were being drawn around the stalled programme of nationalization, defence expenditure, industrial relations and the funding of public services, foreshadowing the factional political battles of the coming years.

Left-wing criticism was also directed at foreign policy. The resistance of Harry Truman to sharing any nuclear capability and concerns about isolationism led Attlee and six cabinet ministers to decide in January 1947 to secretly develop Britain's independent nuclear deterrent. Despite the abrupt end of Lend-Lease and Attlee and Bevin's fear of a repeat of US inter-war international withdrawal, relations improved, and, despite an initial reluctance, the United States agreed to the formation of NATO, in turn discarding any residual Labour leadership associations with peace and disarmament. Early post-war attempts at building on wartime cooperation with the USSR came to little, however, and relations deteriorated following the communist coup in Czechoslovakia in March 1948 and Berlin blockade that summer, pushing the US towards finally accepting the case for a new alliance, especially after the communist victory in China a year later. Labour would in turn, albeit reluctantly, back the US over the Korean War, angering significant parts of the party. Labour established an interim government and oversaw troop withdrawal and granted independence to India in August 1947 and withdrew from Palestine the following year. Yet both were difficult. The former brought with it partition and extraordinary bloodshed and the latter significant violence.

Attlee led two Labour governments. The first, ending in February 1950, was one of the great reforming administrations of the twentieth century, establishing the contours of a post-war welfare state and a foreign policy framework that would endure for decades. But in the end the government ran out of energy and vitality, with many of its key figures ageing, some dying, having been in power for approaching a decade. The manifesto of 1950 sought consolidation rather than change – its author Michael Young would later describe it as a 'pretty tawdry affair' – and Labour lost 78 seats despite leading the Tories in terms of vote share by 46.1 per cent to 43.5 per cent. Attlee's second government lacked purpose and quickly disintegrated as financial and industrial difficulties mounted alongside a growing and increasingly alienated Labour left. Cripps, dying of cancer, was replaced by Gaitskell but not Bevan, thereby angering the left and eventually leading to the prescription charge resignations. Bevin, also very ill, was moved to Lord Privy Seal in March 1951 and replaced by Morrison. He would be dead a month later. Even then, Labour only narrowly lost the 25 October 1951 election, by 295 seats to 321, and after receiving a larger share of the popular vote than the Conservatives and its highest vote ever numerically after once more running a defensive campaign.

Questions of Economic and Social Progress

Assessing the record of the Attlee governments, the historian Andrew Thorpe has reflected on why we might be critical of their approach to nationalization.[13] He points out how many sectors were taken over on grounds of efficiency and their unattractiveness to private investors, thereby creating a rod for Labour's back when the same inefficiencies could later be sourced to socialist economics. He also notes how the public corporation model, where the industry in question remained free from political interference and run on business lines, ensured a lack of integration across sectors; a strange approach from an administration attracted to the virtues of economic planning. Moreover, there was little interest in questions of industrial democracy, on one level understandable

given the difficult economic environment the government had to respon-
sibly navigate, which acted as a disincentive to innovate. Overall, these
features helped ensure limited worker commitment to the practice of
public ownership.

Thorpe then makes a vital connection between these limitations
and questions of justice within the history of Labour. He suggests
such innovation and political creativity over industrial design and
worker democracy were rejected as they would also challenge the 'by
now almost all-pervasive Whig interpretation of Labour history; that
is, the view that Labour was moving ever onward and upward'. We
have previously suggested that the early Darwinian ideas of social
evolution that underpinned Labour's gradualism offered diminishing
political returns following the First World War and the experience of
two minority Labour administrations. Yet Thorpe suggests Labour's first
majority victory rehabilitated such thinking and self-belief, revealed in
the books celebrating the party's fiftieth birthday. He suggests it also
informed a process of *natural selection* in terms of Labour's purpose.
Early guild socialism and its critique of statism might best be understood
as a 'mutant strain of British socialism', now extinct through inherent
weaknesses, 'as much immediate relevance as Clarion Cycling Clubs
or Labour Churches … and Keir Hardie's cap' rather than seeing these
approaches as competing visions of socialist justice. Criticism of nationalization was therefore reactionary. For strands of dominant Labour
thought, just as in the 1920s, the gateway to socialism was through the
growth engineered by the capitalist enterprise. Gradualism had learnt
lessons from 1931 and rejected the strict *laissez-faire* macroeconomics of
earlier years, but the capitalist firm remained a political black box despite
the 1930s policy reorientation towards economic planning.

The commitment to state ownership and planning, the hallmark of
both the orthodox Marxism and Fabianism dominant within this period
of labour history, and with it the rejection of 'mutant' early socialisms,
reoriented much of the left towards a preoccupation with the levers and
systems of central government. Other more liberal, ethical and pluralist
elements within the left canon emphasizing 'associational forms of life
above the state'[14] had become marginal concerns at the moment of
Labour's greatest triumph. Classical Fabianism had prevailed, technological determinism had never really gone away, despite the ethical

convictions of its leader Attlee. Early concerns with human flourishing and the promotion of human virtue, captured in the idea of 'making socialists' and working-class self-organization, were now relics from the time of Labour's political conception, discarded as history unfolded and socialism advanced. Yet, as we shall see, this would change in the years to come both within Marxism and more mainstream party thinking as the working class were reinserted back into their own history. But for now, British democracy and British socialism appeared to have been centralized and it was a process that stretched well beyond questions of natural selection related to economics and nationalization. Utilitarianism had won; statism, labourism and welfarism had prevailed as socialist thought had itself evolved.

On 16 February 1943, William Beveridge listened to parliamentarians discuss his report that sought to establish a 'comprehensive policy of social progress', before travelling to deliver the annual Eugenics Society Lecture in memory of Francis Galton at the Mansion House. Eugenics had been the brainchild of Galton, Darwin's cousin, in response to his theory of natural selection and been taken up as a programme of political action by Darwin's son Leonard.

In this way the writer Chris Renwick has anchored the creation of the welfare state within the nineteenth-century natural sciences.[15] He argues that post-war reforms to social insurance, health, education, planning and local government need to be understood in terms of philosophical concerns regarding progress and human rationality that informed generations of thinkers and practitioners across all political parties for over a hundred years. Renwick's study offers us a history of applied utilitarianism from the 1830s to the 1940s. Sidney and Beatrice Webb were enthusiastic supporters of the eugenics movement, which implied the poor were genetically inferior and that poverty was inherited. The eugenicists aimed to replace natural scientific selection with planned social selection, and statism was a precondition for this socialization of breeding. In July 1912, at the Hotel Cecil on the Strand, the First International Eugenics Conference took place with Balfour and Churchill both present. Labour pioneer and later MP Will Crooks was a strong advocate as was Bernard Shaw and H.G. Wells, sharing similar concerns with the 'social residium'. Eugenics was for many seen as central to social advancement and linked to notions of human evolution and progress fashionable within the first half of the twentieth century, with opposition drawn almost exclusively from religious sources, especially Catholic ones.[16] The Eugenics Society reached its peak during the 1930s. A 1931 *New Statesman* editorial embraced what it regarded as the legitimate claims of eugenics. Keynes served on the society's governing council and was its director from 1937 to 1944. The editor of *Eugenics Review* was Richard Titmuss, later dubbed 'the high priest of the welfare state'.

Yet the Second World War changed everything and exposed the inhumanity of applied eugenics and the sinister realities of this form of social scientific enquiry, most graphically in genocide and the realities of the death camps.[17] The war morally compromised the eugenics movement and helped revitalize humanist political concerns for questions of human liberty, freedom and justice in ways that would help shape the next 75 years of Labour history and challenge the domination of statism and utilitarianism on the left.

Liberty and Human Rights

Attlee is often considered a centralizer and statist. Yet his approach was more thoughtful and nuanced. He backed the Poplar rebels in the 1920s in contrast to Morrison, who later oversaw the nationalization programme. In his writings he attacked statism within Labour and was involved in ILP policy making with an emphasis on industrial democracy, the living wage and devolving power. Francis Packenham stated that 'Attlee didn't care a damn for nationalization'[18] although as leader he felt obliged to implement the party manifesto. It is a view echoed by his biographer John Bew who states that nationalization – the 'bread and butter of socialist economists – did not particularly exercise his attention'.[19] But questions of human dignity and welfare reform certainly did, going back to his days supporting Lansbury and the Minority Report.

Attlee's contribution is often diminished. It starts with the suggestion of the 'accidental leader' by those who did not survive 1931. The party was to be led by a 'little mouse', said Dalton. It is shaped by the portrait of a technocrat, one perceived to lack warmth and vision; colourless, taciturn, who oversaw a cabinet of great talents. Yet he himself helped cultivate this caricature to help carve out a political persona to disguise his idealism, indeed romanticism. His rejection of empiricism and utilitarianism was signalled in the journey from the Fabians to the ILP.

He was a man revered by the likes of Shinwell and Fenner Brockway. According to Donald Soper, Attlee retained 'inward serenity ... a moral and intellectual quietness ... born of conviction'. Francis Packenham talked of 'the most selfless politician of the first rank ... but the most ethical PM in the whole of British history' – a person who trained himself to withdraw and underwhelm to manage acute shyness but also as an act of conscious political disguise in pursuit of his socialism.

One of the most fearful fates of human dispossession was that of the Paupers Grave. Reclaiming the dignity of the person at the point of death was an early ethical socialist concern given the dehumanizing effects of capitalism and the workhouse. Peter Hennessey, Frank Field and John Bew, in their thoughtful writings on Attlee,[20] all cite a conversation with Jim Griffiths, his welfare minister, whilst steering the national insurance reforms through the commons. He asked Griffiths if he could move the clause to introduce the death grant, an immensely revealing moment as Prime Ministers do not move bill clauses or bills. Throughout, Attlee gave unstinting support to Griffiths against those who sought to dilute his post-war welfare policies. Attlee was consistent and resolute in his approach to working-class respectability; welfare essentially an ethical not transactional question or one concerned with an underclass or any notion of 'social residium' popular amongst eugenicists.

Attlee believed his welfare reform agenda was distinct from orthodox utilitarian approaches to welfarism. He believed it was the way 'to introduce a British "New Deal" – a new contract between state and citizen',[21] built around long-held ideas of citizenship and commonwealth that had inspired him before the First World War and its immediate aftermath. His ideas owed very little to continental models of socialism. Rather they were influenced more in the spirit rather than legislative detail of FDR's 1930s New Deal, especially over social policy, insurance and welfare. Attlee was subtly contesting the statism and utilitarianism considered by many to be the hallmark of his own government and re-connecting Labour with long-standing concerns on the left for questions of freedom, liberty and social virtue.

On 13 November 1945 in a speech to the US Congress,[22] Attlee said, 'We, in the Labour Party, declare that we are in line with those who fought for Magna Carta, habeas corpus, with the Pilgrim Fathers and with the signatories of the Declaration of Independence'. He spoke of 'a world as orderly as a well run town, with citizens diverse in character but co-operating for the common good'. T.H. Marshall's 1949 Cambridge lectures claimed Labour's welfare reforms had universalized social rights in a similar way that mid-eighteenth-century battles over *habeas corpus* had universalized legal rights.[23] Through their approach to social reform, Attlee's government had expressed a significant humanist shift in thinking occurring across the post-war left inspired by the experiences of authoritarianism and genocide. It was a shift that would subsequently become entrenched within the Labour Party over the next 70 years with layers of legislation in pursuit of legal equality and the wider embrace of human rights.

Britain's oldest human rights campaign, Liberty, previously The National Council for Civil Liberties (NCCL), was formed following violent clashes between police and hunger marchers in October 1932. The journalist Ronald Kidd became the organization's first Secretary and the novelist E.M. Forster the first President. H.G. Wells, Laski and Attlee were founder members. Its first meeting was held on 22 February 1934 in the crypt of St Martin-in-the-Field church on Trafalgar Square. In a letter announcing the formation of the group published in *The Times* and *The Guardian* two days later, it cited 'the general and alarming tendency to encroachment on the liberty of the citizen' as the reason for its establishment. Such motivations were very much within the spirit and tradition of the Levellers and the Chartists, to defend what they understood to be 'ancient English liberties', the right to peaceful dissent and the 'whole spirit of British freedom'. Early supporters included George Bernard Shaw, Orwell and Priestley. Their first campaign was against the criminalization of pacifist or anti-war literature under what was known as the 'Sedition Bill', where the NCCL succeeded in watering down the proposed legislation.

However, within the early Labour Party questions of liberty and human rights never really came to the fore until the Second World War, where they emerged as part of a wider reorientation across France, the US and the UK. In 1940, one of the initial members of the NCCL, H.G Wells, wrote *The Rights of Man; Or, What Are We Fighting For?*, which included a *Declaration of Rights* that he traced back to *Magna Carta*.[24] Here he suggested a range of new economic and social rights which, when combined with traditional liberties, could after the conflict become 'the fundamental law of mankind throughout the world'.[25]

Wells sent a copy to his friend the US President Franklin D. Roosevelt (FDR) and they corresponded over the contents. Months later, in January 1941, FDR concluded his State of the Union address with his 'four essential freedoms' – freedoms of speech and worship and from want and fear, themes he would return to throughout the rest of his life. Later in August that year, the first general statement of peace aims, the *Atlantic Charter*, included a reference to 'improved labour standards, economic advancement and social security' insisted on by Bevin. At the third St James's Conference in London in January 1942 the allies agreed to widen this reference and include amongst their war aims to 'preserve human rights and justice'. Reference to the 'four freedoms' would reappear in 1948 in the *Preamble* to the *Universal Declaration of Human Rights* (UDHR).

On 11 January 1944 in his State of the Union Address, FDR unveiled plans for a Second Bill of Rights. He argued that the 'political rights' guaranteed by the US Constitution and Bill of Rights had 'proved inadequate to assure us equality in the pursuit of happiness'. He proposed a new framework 'under which a new basis of security and prosperity can be established for all – regardless of station, race, or creed'.

The New Deal programmes of the 1930s reflected FDR's early political commitment to economic and social reform to confront a domestic fascist threat. Years later, the war effort and desire to 'win the peace' propelled forwards a Second Bill of Rights to take this early agenda in more radical directions by establishing eight fundamental economic and social entitlements 'encoded and guaranteed by federal law'. These were the right to work, to a home, to security in retirement and from sickness, disability and unemployment, alongside the right to public education and healthcare. The search for a new global order underpinned this agenda. The generous terms of the 1941 Lend-Lease Act, alongside strong domestic growth, consolidated US post-war power. From this position of strength FDR sought to provide security from a wide range of social risks as a fundamental right, a condition of freedom, by reimagining the very purpose of post-war politics in order to remove the international threats posed by fascism and tyranny. Four years later, and after his death in April 1945, this agenda helped shape the UDHR.

It was FDR's widow, Eleanor Roosevelt, as chairperson of the drafting committee, who worked to ensure economic and social rights were prominent in the Declaration so that questions of human dignity were not dependent on the vagaries of capitalism but central to a new world order; part of a wider post-war generational struggle to civilize and regulate the market. The UDHR was adopted by forty-eight governments on 10 December 1948. This is the context within which Attlee understood the actions of his government in terms of a British New Deal, as a new economic and social rights covenant between citizen and state, a point well understood by T.H. Marshall.

Until the UDHR was adopted, virtually *any* criticism – let alone interference – by one government over the treatment of the citizens of another was considered a breach of the principle of national sovereignty. As such, human rights abuses were deemed as lawful if they complied with a country's domestic laws; beyond remedy and international justice. The origins of the Declaration – as its Preamble states – lay in the 'barbarous acts which *outraged* the conscience of mankind'. Renewed interest in human rights was not part of a general evolution in 'natural' on 'inalienable' rights, the product of reason and deduction. Following genocide and fascism such enlightened thinking was unfashionable; an overriding belief in rationality and progress offered little when faced with such barbarity. The UDHR was an attempt to *challenge* such thinking and reassert the ethical case for human rights to safeguard democracy, indeed humanity, rather than a sense of enlightened social evolution.

A key figure in the drafting process, Rene Cassin, the Jewish resistance activist and legal advisor to De Gaulle, and later president of the European Court of Human Rights, had fled to London early in the war. There he launched the Free France Commission, whose work included attempts at drafting an *International Declaration of the Human Rights and Duties of Man and Citizen*, building on the French 1789 Declaration. Cassin was in turn heavily influenced by Wells's booklet as well as the Beveridge Report of 1942 with its focus on social and economic rights, and less concerned with individualistic enlightenment notions of freedom. These and other such interventions, such as Cambridge academic Hersch Lauterpacht's 1945 *International Bill of Rights of Man*, informed the drafting of the Declaration. These exiles also argued for a revised international architecture grounded on human rights to replace the failed League of Nations and at the Tehran Conference in 1943 the allies agreed to replace it with the United Nations, incorporating the previously unrepresented United States. The first session of the UN General Assembly was held in January 1946 in Westminster Central Hall where in his address Attlee reiterated the new themes of international human rights with talk of his desire to help 'create a world governed by justice and the moral law'.

The Convention quite consciously sought to revive the principles of justice inherited from *Magna Carta*. The drafters built a text they believed would enhance individual protection from state tyranny and abuse, foster peaceful international relations on the basis of equal treatment of citizens and promote understanding of the inherent dignity and equal worth of 'all members of the human family'. The thirty articles of the Declaration gave equal weight to civil and political liberties *alongside* economic, social and cultural rights. Nearly two decades after the Declaration's initial introduction, two legally binding international covenants were adopted by the UN; one on civil and political rights, the other on economic, social and cultural rights.[26] Together with the UDHR, these were labelled the *international bill of rights*. The UDHR has served as the model for many domestic bills of rights including much later, under New Labour, the UK's Human Rights Act.

This post-war rearticulation of human rights would reshape Labour history and re-establish questions of freedom and liberty in future debates regarding the purpose of the party. These renewed concerns emerged from the challenges of extremism in Europe revealed in the weaknesses of Weimar and in the US with the domestic fascist movement in the years preceding the first years of the New Deal. They revealed the brittle character of a Western democracy too underpowered in the face of tyranny, ruthless authoritarians and assorted strongmen. Soviet communism offered few solutions either. The era sought to reclaim traditions of liberty deep within English history with the first idea of a Bill of Rights in 1689 and the 'Great Charter of Freedoms', or *Magna Carta*, of 1215; Eleanor Roosevelt suggested the UDHR 'may well become the international Magna Carta for all men everywhere'. This was the backdrop to Attlee's British New Deal, an agenda for establishing new economic and social rights for citizens and reclaiming for the left ideas of freedom and liberty, rather than the orthodox statist, utilitarian interpretation of his government's agenda.

Endnote

Three types of criticism tend to be aimed at the 1945–51 Labour government. From the left, writers such as Ralph Miliband regretted how the revolutionary potential disappeared through a consensual consolidation of the work of the wartime coalition and incorporation of liberals such as Keynes and Beveridge. Such a consensus would in the 1950s be satirically described by *The Economist* as 'Butskellism', political shorthand denoting a merger of the policy agenda of Gaitskell and Conservative Rab Butler. There was little appetite for reforming the state or undertaking significant constitutional reform. From the right, authors such as Correlli Barnett and Keith Middlemas have offered a parallel dislike for the creeping post-war corporatism Labour helped established; one that would remain unbroken until the late 1970s.[27] Both arguments would gain political prominence in the decades ahead and influence Labour's future story. So would a third form of criticism, from more liberal, pluralist and ethical traditions within and outside Labour, frustrated in the way a government became encased within a bureaucratic utilitarianism. This third critique would reappear in the years ahead in a variety of different guises.

In the 1950s these frustrations would shape attempts to fuse questions of utility and ethics through forms of social engineering advanced by a new generation of academic economists, sociologists, statisticians and social policy experts. They would also reappear in parts of an emerging New Left in part reacting to the authoritarianism of the Communist Party. In markedly different ways they would also be revealed in the work of writers such as Priestley and Orwell who had helped shape the democratic civic patriotism of the late 1930s. This group believed Labour after 1945 rejected their insights in preference for a relentless modernism. Driven by material concerns, the government 'appeared invested with hubris', once again consumed by grand abstraction and little desire to change the way of politics.[28] For them, socialism remained captive to determinism, certainty and impossible utopias, forgetting what was important in the everyday, captured by Orwell in his pessimistic writings from the mid-1940s until an early death in 1951, notably *Animal Farm* and *1984* and Dylan Thomas's *Under Milk Wood*, his 'utopia of the everyday'. Such a politics briefly surfaced in the 1951 Festival of Britain – a celebration of the parochial without empire, glory, heroic hubris or monarchy. It was clearly on display in the 'Lion and the Unicorn' pavilion on the South Bank – a story of national character, including *Magna Carta* and Tolpuddle Martyrs, wrapped in an 'instinct for liberty'.

All these reactions to Labour's greatest government would help shape the future Labour story. But it is possible that all these critiques missed something. From very different perspectives they all accept the widely held interpretation of the Attlee government as statist, technocratic and utilitarian. They share the orthodox depiction of Attlee as the uninspiring administrator who lacked vision, rather than the East End ILP ethical pioneer and idealist. Yet on closer inspection Attlee was a complex politician and arguably the greatest Prime Minister of the last century due to the way he subtly reunited the three competing visions of justice that have shaped Labour history. His personal idealism and commitment to the ethical concerns of the ILP is often ignored. As leader it operated alongside his oversight of significant policy development within the party in the late 1930s, the experience of war time and his leadership of an extraordinary cadre of Labour cabinet ministers. It all came together and built the welfare state. It was a welfare state that for Attlee established a British New Deal of economic and social rights and re-embraced long-standing left-wing concerns for freedom and liberty. In this way Clement Attlee was a most outstanding and extremely unorthodox politician. Under his understated leadership Labour transformed the nation through successfully uniting the three traditions of justice that define the party's history.

7

Waste
(1951–1964)

Despite the 1951 defeat, many within Labour's ranks remained confident the result amounted to little more than a temporary setback given the widespread belief in the inevitability of socialist change. Yet Labour would spend 13 traumatic years in opposition.[1] A new era of post-war affluence, heightened leisure opportunities and mass consumption would underpin a series of impressive Conservative victories and Labour's declining electoral performance. These political realities ensured that deeply embedded ideas of social evolution and electoral success were swiftly discarded and replaced with a widespread concern that Labour might never win again. The years following the 1951 defeat saw Labour pivot away from confident assumptions of evolutionary change and socialist reform to confront its own mortality and ask the *death question*: could Labour survive?

The period would also see fundamental ideological splits within the party, with lasting consequences. Attlee contested his final election in 1955 and retired shortly after the defeat. Under his replacement, Hugh Gaitskell, Labour briefly appeared more united. Yet after another defeat in 1959 the infighting resumed, particularly over nuclear weapons, entry into the European Economic Community (EEC), nationalization and Clause IV of the party constitution; issues that would divide the party for decades to come.

Yet years of defeat and social change also brought significant intellectual reassessment within Labour and the wider left, serving to blur factional divides and challenge the utilitarian character of much of the party. After the 1951 defeat, divisions cracked open between the revisionist Gaitskellites and left Bevanites, echoing traditional party tensions. Gaitskell had risen to prominence in the 1930s as one of Dalton's middle-class acolytes whose approach to economic planning had augmented the traditional gradualism of the utilitarian right.[2] Bevan, in contrast, emerged from Celtic working-class, non-conformist mining traditions, a romantic ILP tribune railing against such gradualist tendencies through the Socialist League and the pages of *Tribune*.

Yet the division between Gaitskellites and Bevanites is only one part of the story. The period would see renewed concern for questions of freedom and liberty on the left which would become more significant in the 1960s. These would influence the brilliant economist Tony Crosland's attempts to fundamentally rethink the case for socialism. The Labour revisionism in the 1950s and 1960s, advocated by the likes of Crosland, Roy Jenkins, Douglas Jay and contributions within *Socialist Commentary*, rejected the orthodoxy of nationalization, replaced with a renewed focus on questions of liberty and equality within a mixed economy. Yet different shades of revisionism would also emerge; subtle but significant variations within the overall revisionist project. These would include the ethical concerns of writers and activists such as Michael Young and Phyllis and Michael Wilmott gaining prominence with the growth of sociology, and within the study of industrial relations with figures such as Hugh Clegg and Allan Flanders.

Across the radical left, years of Cold War, blockade and East European occupation would weaken the traction of orthodox Marxism and see the emergence of a New Left aligned with international concerns for human rights, and help renew interest in questions of freedom and virtue. The changing complexion of revision on the Labour right and emergence of the New Left would help to reshape Labour politics up to and beyond the era of New Labour. Therefore, beneath the headline factional tensions, Labour's underlying political philosophy was being reshaped. The death question brought forward an era of political revisionism across the left, although little of this would be on display in 1964 with the victory of the economist Harold Wilson following the sudden death of Gaitskell a year earlier.

Factionalism

The tensions that disfigured the 1950 government quickly resurfaced in opposition. An ageing Attlee stayed on to stop Morrison's ascent to the leadership. Attlee believed the party should be run from the left, and on the question of his successor quietly backed Bevan over Gaitskell, a preference that reflected the understated radicalism of the departing leader. Harold Wilson was of the belief that Attlee would have been able to keep Bevan in the cabinet in 1951 if he had not been in hospital and had resisted the clamour to expel the Bevanites in 1952. Years later Attlee disagreed with Gaitskell's crusade on Clause IV and found Wilson's government to lack radical fire.

Numerically in 1951, the left was growing within a more rancorous parliamentary party. The election saw Jennie Lee return to a PLP which, since 1945, now included Ian Mikardo, Michael Foot, Richard Crossman and Barbara Castle, and since 1950 Fenner Brockway. The Bevanites drew heavily from the dissenting 1940s Keep Left group, expanded after the 1951 resignations following Gaitskell's cuts, and aided by the *Tribune* newspaper under the editorial direction of Foot. They remained strong advocates of public ownership and public sector efficiency in preference to Keynesianism, preserving the intellectual influence of Laski regarding tax, savings and physical planning after his early death aged just 56 in March 1950. In March 1952, 57 Labour MPs voted against German rearmament in defiance of the party whip, after which the PLP standing orders were reimposed for the first time in six years. At the 1952 Conference, the wider party also looked to be shifting left. The NEC CLP section elections saw six of the seven places go to the Bevanites, with the casualties including Hugh Dalton. That same year the Conference resolutely re-endorsed nationalization and Bevan was re-elected onto the Shadow Cabinet. The leader of the left would remain in Labour's top team for just two years, however, before once more resigning, this time over the recurring issue of German rearmament, replaced by his one-time comrade Wilson. Bevan then contested the party Treasurer post against Gaitskell and lost heavily.

In early 1955, Bevan was threatened with another expulsion after he and 62 colleagues abstained over support for nuclear weapons production. It resulted in a Shadow Cabinet and narrow PLP vote in support of the removal of the whip. He was warned by the NEC over his behaviour. Despite the clamour of the right, the executive resisted calls for his expulsion, in part because of Attlee's desire to retain what little remained of party unity.

The internal tensions of the early 1950s were not just between the Bevanite left and centre right of the party, however. To add to the general sense of unease, the unions in their defence of nationalization and labourism were resistant to the demands of the emerging 'revisionist' right, yet also remained hostile to the expanding voice of the left in the party.

To add to Labour's difficulties, between 1951 and 1955, under an ageing Churchill, the Conservative government proved more agile than many had expected. In part this was due to what they didn't do. They conceded the basic features of the welfare state, ensuring they could no longer be easily defined by Labour as the party of pre-war depression and mass unemployment. Their growing confidence was buttressed by the lifting of rationing, an improving economic environment and expanding post-war affluence, all helping to enhance their relative position given Labour's internal difficulties and lack of leadership.

The rise of affluence and consumer choice would also feed back into the internal tensions within Labour and offer support for the arguments of those 'revisionists' wishing to contest and revise the party programme, especially regarding nationalization.[3] 1952 had seen the publication of two texts that began to demarcate the factional tensions within the party, Bevan's *In Place of Fear* and the *New Fabian Essays* edited by early Keep Left advocate Crossman.[4] From July 1949 through to October 1950, G.D.H. Cole convened five 'Problems Ahead' meetings held at Buscot Park near Oxford, which culminated in the book of essays. Participants included Cole's wife Margaret along with Crosland, Denis Healey, Roy Jenkins, Wilson, Young, Clegg and Flanders, as well as some notable figures from the left, including Mikardo. The emerging divisions between left and right contained significant policy differences but also personal animus and class antagonism, clearly on display in 1954 with Bevan's barely concealed depiction of Gaitskell as a 'desiccated calculating machine'.

Churchill eventually retired in April 1955 and was replaced by Anthony Eden, who grasped the moment and quickly dissolved parliament. As in 1950 and 1951, Labour's manifesto was essentially an act of political consolidation regarding renationalization, pledging to return both road haulage and steel into the public sector, but also included some tentative suggestions regarding industrial democracy, moves towards a more comprehensive approach to education and an embrace of equal pay. On polling day, the Tories secured 345 seats on 49.7 per cent of the vote compared to Labour on 277 seats, 18 fewer than in 1951, and 46.4

per cent of the vote. Labour looked visibly stale. The result signalled the need for change. On 7 December, the party's longest-serving leader Clement Attlee announced his resignation aged 72. Although the right of the party split, Gaitskell won the succession battle on the first ballot, securing 157 votes compared to 70 for Bevan and 40 for Morrison. Bevan then lost to Jim Griffiths for the deputy position. In the years that followed, Bevan changed tack and journeyed back inside.

The leader of the left became Shadow Colonial Secretary and in October 1956 party Treasurer. A month later he was Shadow Foreign Secretary after finishing third in the Shadow Cabinet elections. Both he and Gaitskell prospered throughout the 1956 Suez crisis and events that led to Eden's resignation in January 1957. At that year's annual Conference, to the dismay of many old comrades, Bevan famously spoke against disarmament, describing unilateralism as 'an emotional spasm' and warning of the consequence of going 'naked into the conference chamber'. It was a week that saw the defeat of the left and

Hugh Gaitskell
Source: COI Official Photograph, National Portrait Gallery.

the growing dominance of the revisionists, the Gaitskellites, with the unions playing a vital role in helping to consolidate their control of the party.[5]

The Gaitskellites undoubtedly retained greater political and policy coherence than the Bevanites, being generally multilateralist and unified in regarding nationalization as a means to certain political ends rather than the end itself. They argued that with the changed environment of the welfare state, full employment and strong independent unions, socialism could now be advanced in a mixed economy and counter the tendency towards capitalist crises by way of regulation and Keynesian stimulus. Tony Crosland's 1956 *The Future of Socialism* was both a revisionist answer to orthodox Marxism and simultaneously an assault on the foundations of market economics – neo-classical theory. It was an intellectual cornerstone for a social democracy built on an interventionist nation state and class reconciliation through growth. Class antagonism had not disappeared but shifted towards questions of 'education, style of life and occupational status'. Consequently, the left should prioritize the quest for social equality and 'personal freedom, happiness and cultural endeavour' and greater consumer opportunities, very much at odds with the approach of the Bevanites, critical of private property and owner-ship.[6] In effect, Crosland had brilliantly reset the inevitability argument dominant in Labour throughout the first half of the century for the post-war era, but with recourse to social policy and educational reform rather than nationalization.

A year after the publication of *The Future of Socialism*, the Labour Conference passed *Industry and Society: Labour's Policy on Future Public Ownership*, which advanced the case of alternative forms of common ownership, echoing many of the themes advanced by Crosland. Yet the party would suffer another heavy defeat in 1959 as the Conservatives under Macmillan quickly recovered ground post-Suez. Despite a profes-sional election campaign coordinated by a young Tony Benn, Labour returned just 258 MPs compared to the Tories 365. The defeat was especially difficult for the leadership as the manifesto reflected their revisionist policy reorientation, with limited nationalization plans beyond road haulage and steel, and because it followed promised tax cuts unveiled by Gaitskell late in the campaign.[7] Following the defeat, the tensions between the left, the unions and revisionists quickly reappeared over the leader's desire to rewrite Clause IV of the party constitution. The ex-Chancellor Gaitskell and his allies focused on nationalization policy in their diagnosis of the defeat. The party had to change direction given the scale of the electoral rejection, and the party constitution offered them a vivid symbol of the change necessary to revise Labour's purpose, reorientate away from statism and establish a more agile politics embracing the social and economic changes of the time.[8]

In their January 1960 revisionist tract *Must Labour Lose?*, Mark Abrams and Richard Rose explicitly confronted Labour's *death question*[9] suggesting that Labour appeared to be on the wrong side of history in terms of the decline of heavy industry and wider social changes, including the consumer preferences of an expanding middle class. Yet following opposition from both the left and the unions at the 1959 Conference, Gaitskell was forced to withdraw attempts to alter Clause IV. Although in a compromise move it was decided it should be comple-mented with an NEC statement of party principles. Whilst the 1960 Conference document *Labour in the Sixties* maintained the strongly revisionist direction of the party under Gaitskell, the leadership suffered a further economic setback when the assembled delegates voted to extend public ownership. To add to his difficulties, two years after the formation of the Campaign for Nuclear Disarmament (CND), the same Conference adopted a unilateralist stance leading Gaitskell to pledge to 'fight, fight and fight again to save the party I love'. The vote was reversed at the following year's event.

By 1960, the year Bevan died from cancer aged just 62, both Labour and Gaitskell appeared to have stalled. In November the leader faced a challenge from Wilson, who polled a healthy 81 votes from the PLP. By the late 1950s the Bevanites had been defeated, both by the actions of Bevan himself as Shadow Foreign Secretary and due to the strength of the leadership's revisionism. Yet the revisionist project had itself suffered policy reversals and been overturned over the party constitution. Both factional flanks looked to have run out of energy and the party appeared beleaguered following three ever larger election defeats. In 1961 the issue of Common Market entry further split the party, although not on the strictly factional lines of the 1950s. Macmillan had launched a bid for entry in July 1961. Partly to maintain unity, but also due to a pro-commonwealth euro-scepticism detectable within revisionist ranks from the 1930s, Gaitskell in 1962 rejected the Prime Minister's terms which 'means the end of a thousand years of history', angering many within the revisionist ranks.

Despite these internal tensions and setbacks, by 1961 Labour had started to improve in the polls as the economy stalled. The following July, Macmillan overacted and culled his cabinet in the 'Night of the Long Knives', and by year end Gaitskell looked to be in a strong position on top of what appeared to be an increasingly united party. Yet by January 1963 he too would be dead, and aged just 56 would enter party mythology as one of Labour's lost leaders. Harold Wilson then defeated George Brown and Jim Callaghan to secure the leadership.

Wilson was a Keep Left member turned economic modernizer; a cunning politician who by 1964 had accepted many of the revisionist positions yet still favoured central planning and active state intervention. Unlike Crosland, he did not believe that the structural weaknesses of

Harold Wilson
Source: Eric Koch, Fotocollectie Anefo, Dutch National Archives.

the UK economy had been resolved. In October 1963, he embraced the cause of growth. It would be engineered through a National Plan in order to release the forces of the 'white heart of the technological revolution', advance social and economic progress and also protect citizens and communities. As Wilson built his case, the government's problems intensified. The French rejected the UK application to join the EEC in January 1963. Later that summer the Tories were rocked by a sex scandal involving the Secretary of State for War John Profumo. By October Macmillan had gone, replaced by the aristocratic Alec Douglas-Home, who by renouncing his title helped cement Wilson's credentials as a man of the people and the force of his meritocratic arguments.

The October 1964 election saw Labour returned to government after 13 years but with a majority of just five, after a campaign fought by Wilson on a generally revisionist agenda. Yet the core economic rationale remained embedded within traditional Labour gradualism, albeit with an additional Keynesian and technological veneer. Once more, Labour was reliant on capitalist growth to secure inevitable socialist change and it would be the lack of economic growth that would derail Wilson in the years ahead. But before reviewing the Wilson years, it is worth briefly considering some other intellectual currents percolating across the left that would become influential in the decades to come.

Shades of Revisionism

By 1960 the Bevanites were defeated, although the Gaitskellites lacked momentum following setbacks over policy and the climbdown over Clause IV. Despite being labelled by Wilson the 'wasted years', the period saw significant discussions take place over the nature of socialism and new political movements emerge across the left adjusting to the culture of affluence and mass consumption, responding in different ways to the defeats of 1951, 1955 and 1959. Crosland offered a particular revision of socialism which engaged with questions of freedom as well as economics but there were other notable interventions. Three in particular would be significant for Labour, all rethinking the case for socialism by returning to the left's ethical traditions and questions of liberty and justice.

Industrial Pluralism

On the right, after a 1947 relaunch, the journal *Socialist Commentary* served as the focus for revisionist thinking under the editorship of Rita Hinden. Between 1953 and 1955, Gaitskell served as parliamentary chair of the *Friends of Socialist Commentary*. Hinden and other contributors also established the *Socialist Union* think tank in March 1951 with the support of party secretary Morgan Phillips. The industrial relations academic Allan Flanders acted as chairman of both. In the 1930s Flanders had been the chair of *Socialist Vanguard*, the group from which *Socialist Commentary* emerged. *Socialist Union* published three key revisionist pamphlets in the 1950s. *The Statement of Principles* came out in 1952, *Socialism and Foreign Policy* in 1953 and *Twentieth Century Socialism* in 1956, the same year as Crosland's *The Future of Socialism*. The first and third were co-authored by Flanders. In the 1960s, Flanders became a leading member of the Campaign for Democratic Socialism (CDS) formed to defend Gaitskell and revisionism. Yet, in contrast to Crosland's model of distributive justice, Flanders sought a revival of ethical socialism within revisionism.[10]

Flanders, a neglected figure in Labour history,[11] stood at the intersection of two worlds: an industrial relations community influential within the Labour governments of the 1960s and 1970s and the evolution of post-war social democracy. He pulled these twin concerns together into an applied industrial pluralism. Influenced by guild socialism, it sought to institutionalize the industrial working class into the functioning of the post-war economy. Guild socialism, with echoes of William Morris's approach to human creativity, worked to support enhanced industrial democracy through guild regulation of the labour process.[12] These ideas, looking back for inspiration to the Middle Ages, were expressed in the pages of the early Christian Socialist publication *The New Age*, having been pioneered in Arthur Penty's 1906 *Restoration of the Guild System*.

G.D.H. Cole would become the most influential advocate of this tradition. In 1915, he formed the National Guilds League and between 1917 and 1920 authored four books on the subject. Cole's contribution, and the wider ideas regarding democratic workers control, inspired a diverse group of writers including Tawney, Karl Polanyi and figures from the New Left such as Stuart Hall.[13] Its formal significance declined after the first few decades of the twentieth century, yet the guild tradition would remain a key reference point for various libertarian, democratic and anti-statist socialist and social democratic interventions over the next 100 years, concerned with questions of fraternity and associational relations beyond the state.[14] Practitioners who drew inspiration included Laski, Walter Milne-Bailey within the TUC Research Department, Michael Young within Labour's research department, as well as Flanders and fellow industrial relations academic Hugh Clegg. The 'utopian pluralism'[15] of Flanders's and Clegg's studies of labour relations and advocacy of employment rights and the extension of collective bargaining brought insights from the guild tradition into the labour relations reforms of the 1960s and 1970s. They were early advocates of what we might today call economic stakeholding.

Both Clegg and Flanders transitioned from pre-war radicalism to post-war revisionism.[16] Their wartime experience of left- and right-wing totalitarianism and of institutional democratic collapse placed in them a renewed emphasis on pluralist balance within industry and political, legal and social regulation of employment relations in the post-war era. Flanders intellectually shaped post-war industrial pluralism,[17] but before the war had been a full-time revolutionary follower of the German ethical socialist and philosopher Leonard Nelson. In the 1930s, he graduated towards a more mainstream Labour politics as the fascist threat intensified. He was recruited to the TUC as a researcher to support a team of economists that included Cole, Durbin, then personal assistant to Attlee, and Joan Robinson. Subsequently he was deployed by Ernest Bevin to aid post-war German reconstruction. In March 1949, he was offered a lectureship at Oxford where he would emerge as a key figure in the labour relations reforms of the Wilson government. At Nuffield College and Warwick University until his early death in 1973, Flanders evoked the language of Morris and the spirit of fraternity and fellowship in criticizing a trade unionism built around a 'narrow materialism' and distinguished his ethical socialist method from what he considered to be Crosland's utilitarian concerns for distributive justice.[18] Through the contribution of figures such as Flanders, some of the early guild socialist tradition would reappear in post-war corporatism. Later the Blair government would signal an early interest in economic stakeholding and industrial democracy when it launched a review of company law.

But those pushing the case for reform were to be disappointed when the underlying supremacy of shareholder interests went unchallenged and furious that hard-won reporting requirements on how companies were serving non-shareholder interests were unceremoniously ditched in front of an approving CBI audience in 2005.

Post-war Sociology

The contribution of Michael Young to Labour's post-war intellectual renewal provides further insight into the various shades of revisionist thought seeking to influence post-war socialism. Young was the author of the 1945 manifesto and the party's director of research until 1950, and his career demonstrates 'the way ethical and humanist traditions of British socialism were expressed and reinforced through social science and social research in the mid-twentieth century'.[19] Young, a student of Laski at the LSE, was heavily influenced by John Bowlby, Evan Durbin's friend and political ally. Bowlby, another figure active in the New Fabian Research Bureau, was the pioneer of human attachment theory and Deputy Director of the Tavistock Clinic, and from 1950 a mental health consultant to the World Health Organization. His research focus was on the study of loss and suffering experienced by young people from real events, rather than the fashionable, unconscious theories that dominated the psychoanalytic community. Bowlby's insights helped influence notions of social responsibility and a renewal of democratic socialist thinking regarding work, community and politics.[20] This humanist approach sought to contest Labour economism using applied social policy. A more sociological approach to equality would be advanced by a cohort of younger researchers, one that was less convinced than Crosland that improving access to education would pull down class barriers, and focus on how poverty had survived the distributionism of Labour's universalist welfare state.

Young became increasingly critical of the 1945 manifesto he authored and the overall government planning apparatus. In 1948, he wrote a pamphlet *Small Man, Big World* calling for Labour to embrace an active democracy and the radical devolution of power to people in their neighbourhoods and workplaces. Democracy, Young argued, satisfies two of our fundamental needs: to love or to contribute to the good of others, and to be loved or to receive the affection and respect of others. Democracy, he argued, gave everyone the opportunity to contribute to the wellbeing of others and to earn their respect. He wrote, in anticipation of another victory in 1950, that: 'The main step for Labour's second 5 years is for the people to run the new and the old institutions of our society, participating at all levels as active members – workers, consumers, citizens – of an active democracy'.[21]

He would, however, come to regard the 1950 manifesto as a 'pretty tawdry thing' given its preoccupation with questions of economic utility.[22] In Cole's 'Problems Ahead' sessions, Young presented *The British Socialist Way of Life*, suggesting a renewed emphasis on fraternity, including industrial democracy rather than traditional nationalization; of solidarity, community and family. It was not well received. His frustration found expression in his last submission to the party's research committee, *For Richer, For Poorer*, subtitled 'essays on family, community and socialism', which foreshadowed his later work from 1953 at the Institute for Community Studies (ICS), now better known as the Young Foundation. In 1957, with fellow Labour Research Department alumnus Peter Willmott, Young published *Family and Kinship in East London*, upholding the virtues of extended working-class families and culture as informal systems of social assistance, themes echoed in Richard Hoggart's 1957 *The Uses of Literacy*.[23]

Young admitted he sought 'to reform the Labour Party through sociology', as the state remained preoccupied with the symptoms rather than causes of social distress and deprivation and was plainly ignorant of the lives of ordinary people. The ICS board included social scientists such as Richard Titmuss, Bowlby himself and Barbara Wootton, with Peter Willmott as research officer. The Institute challenged, in the words of Peter Townsend, the giant evils and 'abstract "wants", "squalors" and "diseases"' views of Beveridge with an alternative approach to poverty and Labour politics based around social conventions and the resilience provided by community life. It embraced questions of fraternity rather than simple distributive justice, of human motivations stretching beyond economics whilst pushing back against the Victorian moralism of Beveridge.[24]

Through the applied use of the emerging social sciences, Young sought to reconcile the ethical and Fabian traditions through a scientific understanding of human wellbeing and relationships to put family and community at the centre of socialist renewal.[25] It rejected the economism, statism and utilitarianism of much of the traditional left. Young would seek to institutionally encase this rich communitarianism in an organizational chain which included Labour's own research department, the LSE, the ICS and, as we shall see, the new Social Science Research Council. Recurring themes would include the alienating possibilities of modernization, industrialization and urbanization, the role of the small group or association and the conflict between communal belonging and the market economy, and the ethical challenges of mass consumption. Young would eventually leave Labour in 1981 in response to the rise of the left to help form the SDP, but in the 1950s many of his concerns were shared across a more radical New Left.

The New Left

As noted earlier, Attlee stood down in 1955 and a year later Crosland published *The Future of Socialism*. In 1956, Khrushchev gave his secret speech to the Twentieth Congress of the Communist Party, Hungary was invaded, and the Suez crisis erupted after the Israeli invasion of Egypt. Yet many on the left perceived the Bevanites to lack energy. The agenda on which they contested revisionism defended the past and traditional nationalization. Within this environment a New Left emerged, one motivated by international events and emerging social trends, but hostile to the twin orthodoxies of Bevanism and a Stalinist Communist Party culture disinterested in democratic renewal. The first period of the New Left offered a surprising political bridge in the history of Labour. It provided a route back to the traditions of Morris, Ruskin and the early ILP, yet played a key role in shaping a Labour left in the late 1960s associated with Michael Foot, and later in the 1970s and 1980s with Tony Benn. Later still, after further splits in the Communist Party, elements of the New Left continued to influence Labour's municipal renewal and modernization under both Kinnock and Blair through their diagnosis of Thatcherism and the influence of the magazine *Marxism Today*.

In July 1956, the first edition of *The Reasoner* was published, founded by the historians E.P. Thompson and John Saville.[26] Two more editions were produced that year as the tanks rolled into Budapest and Communist Party tensions erupted over revelations of Stalinist abuses and the realities of democratic centralism. Both founders left the Communist Party and launched *The New Reasoner*. In tandem in Oxford, following the Suez debacle, the *Universities and Left Review* emerged from Cole's politics seminars and left-wing elements within the Labour Party, seeking to promote 'free open, critical debate'. The two journals merged in 1960 to form *The New Left Review* with an editorial board that included Thompson and Raymond Williams alongside the journal's first editor Stuart Hall. Their wish was to stimulate a socialist humanism, in part drawn from English libertarian radical traditions and the early pioneers of socialism; traditions which they argued had been surrendered within a bipartisan 'Butskellism'. In 1962 a 'Second New Left' emerged following an internal takeover with a new editorial board led by Perry Anderson. Subsequently, the journal sought to embed itself within broader, more abstract theoretical currents within Western Marxism and develop a distinct internationalist perspective.

There remained an ongoing ambiguity over whether the first New Left was an intellectual or political movement and over its relationship to Labour. The local New Left clubs were diverse, often including many party members and activists. Generally, the New Left favoured a 'one foot in, one foot out' approach, although its most robust critique of Labour, supplied by Ralph Miliband in a series of articles culminating in his 1961 book *Parliamentary Socialism*, rejected the possibility of any genuine socialist politics given Labour's dogmatic commitment to the parliamentary system. Tensions also existed between what some termed 'culturalists' like Williams and humanists such as Thompson, alongside wider geographical and generational differences regarding the role of the traditional labour movement.

From the first issue of *The Reasoner*, Thompson sought to defend a working class that was 'present at its own making'[27] and attacked left-wing orthodoxies that denied class agency and sidelined the moral and ethical components of human activity. He challenged the abstract universalism of both liberalism and socialist thought in favour of the romantic, anti-capitalist political and literary traditions of Morris, Ruskin and Carlyle. Yet for many in the New Left, such an approach was too removed from the complexities and politics of the contemporary formation. Williams, in contrast, sought to diagnose the complex modern domination of the working class through new forms of communication and manipulation. Material advances threatened Labour yet offered the prospect of mass indentured consumption under modern capitalism. On this basis Williams, whilst also grounded in nineteenth-century literature, offered a powerful contemporary critique of the limitations of both revisionism and Labour orthodoxy.

The New Left sought to engage with Crosland over the economic and social necessity of 'modernization' – a term later deployed by both Wilson and Blair. Some argued that *The Future of Socialism* sought to challenge orthodoxy and rethink the case for socialism given the changing character of British society in ways not dissimilar to their own.[28] They shared with revisionists a rejection of Morrisonian nationalization, the belief in planning as a socialist panacea and a rejection of labourism and statism. They appeared to share a mutual interest in associational forms of economic organization, industrial democracy and the democratization of the public sector, and with the role of the consumer and modern youth culture. From very different positions on the left, they both looked to respond to the age of affluence, consumerism and Conservative ascendancy, sharing the concern that Labour might be irrevocably weakened as its traditional political constituencies fractured and died.

Wilson would call the period from 1951 to 1964 the 'wilderness years'. They are often considered through the factional prism of Bevanites and Gaitskellites and their disagreements over economic policy and questions of distributive justice, with one concerned with public ownership and the other equality and Keynesianism. Crosland offered a specific elegant economic solution which introduced questions of freedom into a radical revision of socialism. Yet the picture was a more complicated one than often described. The historian Ben Jackson has suggested the key political fault lines within the 1950s left were less about divisions between left and right factions, Bevanites and Gaitkellites, fundamentalists and revisionists, but rather between elements within both revisionism and the radical left concerned with distributive economistic goals, and those inspired more by questions of fraternity, democracy and solidarity.[29] The latter group were all seeking to rethink the purpose of socialism given concerns about the future death of Labour following the post-war social and economic transformations. New debates emerged over questions of freedom and virtue informing revisionist thinking across both the left and right, including parts of the New Left, radical sociologists such as Titmuss, Townsend and Young, and the industrial pluralists.[30]

8

Strife
(1964–1979)

Labour would hold power for eleven years between 1964 and 1979, after which it would remain in opposition for eighteen, leading many to once again confront the death question and ask if the party might ever win again. The factors that help account for this near two-decade residency in the political wilderness are regularly traced back to the economic difficulties and industrial strife experienced by Labour governments in the 1960s and 1970s. Often cited are the party's domination by the trade unions and failure to engineer economic growth. Despite notable achievements, the Labour administrations of 1964–70 and 1974–9 had to navigate challenging economic conditions which blew both governments off course and brought with them significant industrial relations tensions over *In Place of Strife* and the *Winter of Discontent*. The economic model Labour entered office with in 1964, developed by Crosland and others in the preceding years, quickly ran into trouble. Yet Labour was not alone. The intervening Heath government of 1970 was also upended by a difficult economic climate and labour disputes over the 1971 Industrial Relations Act, the miners' strike and three-day week. The years between 1964 and 1979 would also see the advance of the left within Labour aligned with wider liberation movements and in response to the economic failings of the government. Labourism and traditional statism were in retreat.

The Wilson and Callaghan governments tend to be considered as political failures. Yet they contained notable achievements, especially in the development of forms of legal equality, which demonstrated that liberal approaches to socialist justice were now firmly established at the centre of the party, challenging utilitarian orthodoxies.

Upswing and Second Landslide

An economic downturn and a series of scandals, most notoriously the Profumo Affair, derailed the Tories in the early 1960s. Labour's revival saw Wilson achieve a five-seat majority in 1964, which, following a by-election reversal, quickly became four. The majority was extended to 97 on 31 March 1966, in an election where Labour secured 48 per cent of the vote and the Tories 41.4 per cent. It marked a second landslide and an impressive revival in fortunes given the concerns of leading revisionists just a few years earlier about the party's electoral prospects. Yet by the decade's end, Labour's position had once more deteriorated.

Wilson's skills at party management saw him balance a generally revisionist cabinet with figures from across the movement including Crossman, Castle and the Trade Unionist Frank Cousins. Ten of his first cabinet had served in government before and Wilson had access to a group of able young junior ministers to draw on, including Crosland and Jenkins, who both entered the cabinet in 1965, and Tony Benn, who joined in 1966.

Harold Wilson would win four of the five general elections he contested as leader yet would be Prime Minister for just eight years, from 1964 to 1970, and between 1974 and 1976. Despite Wilson's Congregationalist roots and 1962 Conference rhetoric stating Labour was 'a moral crusade or it is nothing', the 1964 victory remains a highpoint of technological utopianism within the party and of the utilitarian economics many in its leadership had long favoured. For the first few years with the new Ministry of Technology and a revived Department of Economic Affairs (DEA), Wilson, the academic economist and admirer of Soviet planning, maintained a highly interventionist approach to labour productivity, investment and growth. A significant shift towards a more centralized corporatist economy took place. Yet Wilson was then forced to change direction and embrace spending controls, austerity and a November 1967 devaluation. One of the great tensions visible throughout Labour's entire history reappeared under Wilson, between the leadership's desire to expand the welfare of the people and their oversight of economic austerity. The tension emerged in Labour's first two minority administrations where the lack of policy development exposed the party's frailties with disastrous consequences. The same tensions would reappear in the late 1970s and after the financial collapse of 2007/8 as Labour's economic models proved incapable of securing growth and the party resorted to austerity.

With the government embracing a strategy of state planning and the modernization of industry, September 1965 saw the launch of the National Plan to stimulate economic growth. Yet on coming to office, the government was informed of an inherited £800 million trade deficit, much worse than anticipated. A further crisis occurred in July 1965 and the government agreed to give a new National Board for Prices and Incomes statutory powers to control wages. The situation deteriorated further in 1966 with money flowing out of the country and a difficult seaman's strike in May. In July the government announced spending cuts and a six-month wage and price freeze. Despite efforts to shore up the value of sterling, in November 1967 Wilson was finally forced into a devaluation of the pound from $2.80 to $2.40 alongside further austerity. By the summer of 1966, the National Plan had been abandoned along with its ambitious growth plans and the government had embraced Treasury orthodoxy, with the DEA finally being closed down in 1969.[1] For much of the remaining parliament the government followed strict public spending controls which, when coupled with the effects of devaluation, had by 1969 restored a balance of payments surplus, although this unexpectedly turned into a small deficit revealed just two days before the 1970 election.

Wilson renationalized the steel industry in 1967 in the favoured model of the public corporation but with no attempt to stimulate industrial democracy. Five new development areas were introduced in 1966 to successfully boost regional development. Between 1965 and 1970, two million new homes were built with nearly half council-owned. In education Wilson hoped the new Open University pioneered by Michael Young would demonstrate Labour's commitment to economic and social modernization by enabling the use of radio and television to aid the technological revolution. After years of planning and with the determination of Bevan's widow Jennie Lee and full support of Wilson, the 'University of the Air' finally received a royal charter in April 1969. Wilson also started the move away from academic selection at the age of 11, via Tony Crosland's Circular 10/65 of 12 July 1965, issued to local education authorities to plan for a conversion to a system of comprehensives, and greatly expanded the number of universities and polytechnics. Elsewhere, the 1969 Representation of the People Act reduced the voting age from 21 to 18. Wilson also eased means testing for non-contributory welfare benefits, linked pensions to earnings, and extended industrial-injury benefits. Despite resigning from Attlee's cabinet over the issue in 1951, as Prime Minister Wilson was forced to reintroduce prescription charges in 1968.

Wilson's *White Heat* agenda attracted Peter Willmott and Michael Young back to the Labour Party research department for the 1964 election. Both thought Labour's approach to modernization provided an opportunity to develop a policy agenda and strategy anchored within the social sciences; one that could help Labour build an agenda beyond questions of economics and statistics. In 1965, the Social Science Research Council was created, following the publication that year of the report of the Heyworth Committee on Social Sciences into the influence of academic research on government activity, established in 1963 by Rab Butler. Crosland offered the chair of the new committee to Young who quickly assembled a team of allies including the sociologist T.H. Marshall and social policy expert Richard Titmuss to coordinate the work and help build a progressive liberal democracy. Young stayed as chair for three years, establishing a new Social Survey Unit, an Industrial Relations Unit at Oxford to help the work of industrial pluralists like Clegg and Flanders and the Race Relations Unit at Bristol.

The 1964–70 Labour government is probably best remembered for the liberal social reforms of Roy Jenkins as Home Secretary from 1965 to 1967. The Race Relations Act 1965 created a new criminal offence of incitement to racial hatred, together with a Race Relations Board – the first piece of legislation addressing discrimination on the grounds of race. A second Race Relations Act followed in November 1968, outlawing discrimination in housing, employment and access to public services, prompting Enoch Powell on 20 April 1968 to react by quoting Virgil's epic Latin poem *The Aeneid*, predicting the equivalent of 'the River Tiber foaming with much blood'. Wilson responded weeks later in Birmingham on 5 May 1968 saying 'I am not prepared to stand aside and see this country engulfed by the racial conflict which calculated orators or ignorant prejudice can create.' Later the Race Relations Act 1976, though completed after Wilson had left office, extended protection to indirect discrimination, in response to the Sex Discrimination Act of 1975, which had covered indirect discrimination, and received Royal Assent around the time Barbara Castle's 1970 Equal Pay Act finally came into effect. In 1967 Welsh Labour MP

Leo Abse created the Sexual Offences Act, which partially legalized male homosexuality.[2] That same year David Steel's Abortion Act legalized terminations up to 24 weeks. Although introduced by means of private members legislation, by allowing sufficient parliamentary time, the government had tacitly supported the progress of both pieces of legislation.

Theatre censorship was abolished in 1968. The Divorce Law Reform Act of 1969, following another Abse campaign, introduced 'no fault' divorce. The Matrimonial Proceedings and Property Act 1970 allowed courts to order financial support for children from either spouse when marriages broke down, and also sought to correct the bias whereby both parties kept their earnings and inheritances post-divorce. In 1965, capital punishment was finally abolished, except for a small number of offences, most notably high treason, and in 1967 corporal punishment, still then applied in prisons, was ended, although it remained in schools. Cumulatively this represented a significant package enhancing liberal democracy.

In foreign affairs most notable was what the government didn't do. It did not send troops to Vietnam. Austere economic conditions forced the government to withdraw east of Suez. The Wilson government also established the Ministry for Overseas Development but ran into problems over decolonization. Having insisted on majority rule in Rhodesia, in November 1965 Ian Smith declared unilateral independence. Over Europe Wilson's political skills ensured short-term party unity. Britain applied for entry in 1967 with the knowledge that the French would oppose, which they duly did, thereby shunting the issue into the political mid distance.

War in Vietnam and the difficulties of decolonization saw a significant resurgence of the left alongside demands for greater sex and racial equality and ethnic pluralism across the UK. The New Left played an influential role in the wider social movements developing throughout the 1960s and 1970s. The *May Day Manifesto* was first published in 1967, before being revised the following year. Three figures from the first New Left – Stuart Hall, Raymond Williams and Edward Thompson – oversaw the project and edited the text, which sought to address the 'new international capitalism and a new kind of imperialism' and act as a counter-statement to the Labour government's failures. The seventy signatories, including Iris Murdoch and Ralph Miliband, were scathing about Labour and Wilson; an analysis that was to frame much subsequent left commentary of the Wilson era.

As we saw in the previous chapter, the New Left went through different phases and, although generally concerned to rehabilitate socialist humanism, was never a unified tradition. Moreover, the utilitarian, economistic Leninist left was also experiencing a resurgence after the pre-war defeats of popular front politics. The ecology of radical left politics also included a variety of Trotskyist and liberationist groupings. This complex picture reflecting splits, factions and assorted readings of Marxism would contain their own tensions and in different ways shape Labour politics over the decades to come.[3]

More generally, the centralization of the Wilson era looked at odds with the growing clamour for devolution and support for Welsh and Scottish independence. In response, Wilson established the Welsh Office. By-election successes for nationalist parties in 1966 and 1967 led to a constitutional commission under Lord Crowther and a Welsh Language Act in 1967. In 1970 both nationalist parties polled over 10 per cent. Across the Irish Sea, the clamour for civil rights amongst Northern Irish Catholics led to Protestant violence, forcing Callaghan to send in troops as peacemakers in August 1969. Yet they ended up staying until 2007 in what became the British Army's longest ever deployment. The 1970 Equal Pay Act was in part a response to the expanding women's movement in the 1960s. Despite the liberal advances secured under Wilson's equality legislation, the Commonwealth Immigrants Act was enacted in 1968 limiting the migration of Kenyan Asians with British passports into Britain.

In Place of Strife

The Wilson government's modernization agenda would also come to challenge long-held traditions of trade union autonomy and voluntarism, triggering years of industrial and political strife.

From being characterized as the 'workshop of the world' in the late nineteenth century, Britain gradually declined as an industrial power. Productivity growth had begun to lag that of the United States before the Second World War. Comparative decline within Europe began in the 1950s, becoming entrenched by the 1960s.

For many, the country's economic problems originated in its unique system of labour relations. Exceptional protections were available to unions as they remained immune from prosecution. Worker organizations were granted the freedom to strike and organize by being protected from civil damages following the 1906 Trade Disputes Act. This upheld the tradition of *voluntarism*, where the law was kept out of regulating employment relations. In part the Labour Party was created to retain this separation between labour relations and the law following the Taff Vale judgment.

By the 1950s, strains were beginning to show as low unemployment and labour shortages triggered strikes and inflation. Conservative politicians started to target comparative systems of labour regulation in their search for answers to questions of global competitiveness.[4] The narrative of the 'British disease' emerged and the tag of 'the sick man of Europe'. Voluntarism, it was argued, had created a fragmented industrial relations system which inhibited growth. Un-coordinated free collective bargaining was leading to wage drift, inefficient, restricted work practices and unofficial action.

The incoming Wilson government felt it necessary to confront the question of industrial relations reform. Initially, it drew on the diagnosis of a group of industrial relations academics including leading revisionists Hugh Clegg and Allan Flanders who advocated a model of British corporatism.[5] Their aim was to establish a tripartite union/employer/state architecture to integrate the organized working class into a national project to boost competitiveness and anchor post-war social democracy; an early version of stakeholder capitalism. In April 1965, the government established The Royal Commission on Trade Unions and Employers' Associations, with Lord Donovan as chair. The final report in 1968 upheld the voluntarist traditions of UK labour law. Instead of overhauling the system of labour legislation, the preferred solution was to be the reform and extension of collective bargaining. Donovan proposed reconciling competing systems of labour regulation and innovative factory agreements to boost productivity and formalize labour relations.[6] The report proposed an Industrial Relations Act to register collective agreements, extend collective bargaining and remove barriers to union recognition. The Commission resisted attempts to place legal restraints on unions, in particular over unofficial strike action, prompting a note of reservation by one of its members, Andrew Shonfield.

Yet strike levels and trade union influence were becoming more controversial political issues and Labour began to shift its position away from voluntarism and tighten the regulation of labour. From 1966, both inflation and unemployment began to creep upwards. Ray Gunter had pressed for action against unofficial disputes when at the Ministry of Labour. The department was renamed the Department of Employment and Productivity under Barbara Castle and she too sought new legal remedies. Controversial legalistic attempts to confront shop steward power emerged with the 1969 White Paper *In Place of Strife* and later reappeared in Conservative Prime Minister Ted Heath's 1971 Industrial Relations Act.

In Place of Strife proposed new government powers to settle unofficial disputes and enforce penalties for non-compliance, a 28-day conciliation pause and new ballot regulations. In early 1969, Castle met with strong opposition within the PLP whilst the TUC refused to discuss unofficial action. Within a few months it became apparent Castle and Wilson did not have cabinet support, with opposition being led by Callaghan, and with the TUC and NEC opposed, the White Paper was withdrawn. On 19 June Hugh Scanlon and Jack Jones offered a face-saving 'binding and solemn' agreement that the TUC would attempt to resolve unofficial disputes. Despite being abandoned, the White Paper weakened both the government and Wilson personally, reflected in diminishing approval ratings. In April 1970, a tepid Bill was unveiled, but the government was defeated before it even received a Commons second reading. Labour suffered a net loss of 76 seats and a swing of 4.7 per cent produced a Conservative majority of 31. Edward Heath was heading to Downing Street.

Who Governs Britain?

The 1970s would be an even more turbulent decade for Labour than the 1960s, although the party would quickly return to office after the loss to Heath in contrast to the long periods of opposition that followed the defeats of 1931 and 1951. Having defeated Wilson, Heath's Conservatives immediately faced problems of their own. They alienated the Ulster Unionists and Unionists in their own party after signing the Sunningdale Agreement. Heath's 1971 Industrial Relations Act included legally enforceable collective agreements, a National Industrial Relations Court, cooling-off periods and pre-strike ballots. The industrial reaction, including a one-day General Strike in support of the release of the Pentonville 5, alongside the miners' strikes of 1972 and 1974 and adoption of the three day week, an oil crisis and economic downturn culminated in a 'who governs Britain?' election of 1974.

In the short term the industrial upheaval and Heath's statutory pay policy helped re-establish relations between Labour and the unions after the difficulties of the late 1960s, culminating in the Social Contract agreed in 1973. Labourism had been rebuilt after the disaster of *In Place of Strife*. Despite this early reconciliation, the decade would see Labour's internal tensions re-emerge in ways that years later would eventually split the party and lead to the formation of the SDP. The left of the party advanced during the early 1970s, partly through the influence of the wider New Left, partly in response to the global capitalist crisis that brought with it a quadrupling of the cost of oil in 1973, stagflation and escalating industrial militancy and partly in response to the shortcomings of the Wilson government. In 1973, the Campaign for Labour Party Democracy (CLPD) was set up to push for greater MP accountability and wider constitutional reform in the party. At that year's Blackpool Conference, the party endorsed *Labour's Programme* pledging a major extension of public ownership and central planning and a 'fundamental and irreversible shift in the balance of power and wealth in favour of working people and their families'. It also opposed EEC entry until either a referendum or election.

The growth conditions favouring the cause of gradualism and Crosland's form of revisionism had evaporated. In its place many revisionists turned their energies towards the cause of Europe. Following pressure from Tony Benn, Wilson accepted the case for a referendum in March 1972, securing Shadow Cabinet support but at the cost of front-bench resignations including that of Jenkins, who also stood down as deputy leader. The Treaty of Accession was passed by parliament and the UK joined an enlarged EEC on 1 January 1973. Labour and the PLP remained opposed, although 69 MPs led by Jenkins had rebelled against the whip and voted in support in October 1971 with a further 20 abstentions.[7]

Return to Power

Labour returned to power after the February 1974 election, forming a minority government on 4 March after an election in which both main parties received less than 40 per cent of the popular vote, given a significant boost in support for both the Liberals and nationalists. After some quick wins which included repealing the industrial relations legislation and resolving the coal dispute, a second election was called for 10 October 1974 where Labour scraped a majority of four, gaining just 18 seats and taking its total to 319.

Having opposed the Tories over EEC entry in 1973, once back in Downing Street Wilson switched to backing membership, but the renegotiated terms were defeated at a special Party Conference on 26 April 1975, a position supported by approaching half of the PLP. Wilson allowed a free vote on the referendum. On 5 June 1975 the country agreed to continue Britain's membership by two to one.

On 16 March 1976, Wilson surprisingly announced his decision to stand down and was replaced by Callaghan a month later, who overcame five other candidates from various party traditions: Callaghan and Healy from the utilitarian and union right wing, Crosland and Jenkins from various shades of the revisionist right,[8] Foot from the Bevanite left and Benn, who was emerging as a tribune for both the New Left and old Socialist League Left. In the final run-off Callaghan defeated Foot, who then defeated Shirley Williams for Deputy. The Callaghan government was in a precarious political situation and faced extraordinary economic challenges with spiralling inflation in the midst of a global recession, rising unemployment and mounting industrial unrest.

On the industrial relations front there was no repeat of *In Place of Strife*. Labour re-embraced the voluntarist tradition and sought to enact the Donovan programme through five basic statutes: the Trade Union and Labour Relations Act (TULRA) 1974 and its 1976 amendment together with the 1975 Employment Protection Act and Sex Discrimination Act, followed a year later with the Race Relations Act. This substantial wide-ranging programme inherited from the Donovan Report offered employment protection against unfair dismissal, discrimination on the basis of sex, race, marital status and pregnancy, a union-recognition procedure, a series of other collective rights, such as time off for union representatives, and created new tripartite machinery including the Advisory, Conciliation and Arbitration Service (ACAS). Alongside this package, the Health and Safety at Work Act 1974 introduced a more effective workplace inspection regime, establishing the Health and Safety Executive.

Yet the approach failed to achieve the class reconciliation and industrial peace advanced by the industrial pluralists. As noted earlier, the years of opposition had brought a rapprochement with the unions after the debacle of the 1969 White Paper. The Social Contract sought new understandings regarding growth, employment and inflation, although little of it lasted much beyond the first year. Voluntary wage restraint would be part of a package including repeal of the Industrial Relations Act, rent controls and food subsidies. In July 1974, Heath's wage restraints were withdrawn. Yet inflation peaked at 26.9 per cent in August 1975 and this, together with rising unemployment, ensured the voluntary wage component of the Contract was short-lived. A £6 wage ceiling was imposed in the spring of 1975 which extended to zero above £8,500. Further wage restraints followed the next year of 5 per cent and £4 a week and inflation did start to fall, dropping to 7.4 per cent by 1978, a major achievement but one that came with significant costs. Callaghan had been widely expected to call a general election that autumn with opinion polls suggesting a narrow Labour lead. He decided to delay and extend the wage restraint policy for another year in anticipation of favourable economic conditions. The government's attempt to impose a 5 per cent limit on pay rises triggered widespread strikes during the winter of 1978–79, led by Ford workers settling for 17 per cent, and included lorry drivers, railway workers, local government and hospital workers. Terrible images of bodies not buried and mounting piles of rubbish dominated the news, not helped by the famous headline in *The Sun* tabloid newspaper 'Crisis, What Crisis?' following Callaghan's return from a sunny Guadeloupe summit in January which misreported what Labour's leader had actually said.

The radicalism of 1973 and *Labour's Programme* quickly dissolved in office, despite the efforts of Benn as Industry Secretary before he was moved to energy. A proposed wealth tax never materialized, and in 1977 the number of higher rate tax payers was reduced by a quarter. An initial fiscal expansion quickly shifted in favour of expenditure cuts and wage controls. An April 1975 austerity budget cut public spending for 1977–8 by £900 million. Labour was tacitly accepting the introduction of monetarism. In his first Conference speech, Callaghan explicitly rejected Keynes, saying:

we used to think you could spend your way out of a recession and increase employment by cutting taxes and boosting government spending. I tell you in all candour that that option no longer exists.

In the autumn of 1976, the government was forced to request a £3 billion IMF loan, with the December deal accepting billions of public spending cuts. Despite resistance from both the left and revisionists, Healey prevailed in cabinet without any resignations, although it later emerged that the Treasury assumptions that necessitated the loan application were flawed. The government subsequently sold assets and announced cuts of £2 billion spread over the next two years, although it only drew on half of the loan and was able to pay it back in full by 1979. Yet the budgets of April and October 1977 also included a 'Rooker–Wise' amendment that indexed income tax allowances to cost-of-living rises and in April 1978 included tax cuts and increases in child benefit. Overall, between 1974 and 1977, real disposable incomes fell by 7 per

James Callaghan
Source: Christian Lambiotte, European Communities, 1975.

cent, yet by 1978/9 the living standards of most household types had almost been restored to the levels Labour inherited on taking office.

In terms of the wider record of the government, in 1975 Labour set up the National Enterprise Board (NEB) to channel public investment across the economy and offer state support to ailing industries. British Leyland was part nationalized in 1975 along with the British National Oil Company the next year, followed by British Aerospace in 1977 as well as what remained of the shipbuilding industry. The Development Land Tax of 1976 introduced an 80 per cent tax on development gain after the first £160,000. Pensions increased by 20 per cent in real terms between 1974 and 1979, and the government helped preserve disposable incomes by rent controls and food and transport subsidies, as well as indexing a number of benefits to movements in prices or earnings depending on which was highest. In addition, the government initiated new benefits for the disabled and infirm. Housing Action Areas were introduced and public sector completions rose steadily before falling back below 1974 levels by 1979. Between 1974 and 1979, nearly 1,000 new comprehensive schools were established, and by Labour's final year in office over 80 per cent of children attended such schools. Significant investments were also made in nursery, primary and special schools budgets.

The Supplementary Benefits Act 1976 introduced new levels of financial support for those on little or no income. For families with children, the system of child cash and tax allowances was replaced in 1977 by a universal Child Benefit for all families with at least one child. For those at work, a supplementary pension scheme was introduced to provide members of the workforce with an additional income in retirement. Maternity leave was introduced in 1975. Domestic violence legislation enabled both married and cohabiting women to apply for non-molestation or exclusion orders and injunctions from magistrates' courts to stop domestic abuse. Homeless legislation required local authorities to permanently house women made homeless as a result of domestic violence.

This was all done whilst the Wilson and Callaghan governments lacked a workable majority in the Commons. The October 1974 majority of just four seats dissolved away through by-election defeats, leaving Labour as a minority government, including the loss of the Walsall North seat in October 1976 following the faked death and disappearance of John Stonehouse.

In March 1977, the Lib/Lab pact was brokered, but this ended by August 1978, followed by later deals with the SNP and Plaid, who held 14 seats between them. In return, the nationalist parties demanded devolution. In July 1978, the devolution legislation cleared parliament, although it was amended to include a threshold of the total population in support. March 1979 referendums saw the outright rejection of the Welsh plan and a narrow Scottish majority in favour, but below the required threshold of 40 per cent, thereby invalidating the result. Consequently, the SNP withdrew support and the government fell after the Conservatives put down a vote of no confidence, which passed by one vote on 28 March 1979. At the 3 May election, Labour was defeated by Margaret Thatcher, who was the beneficiary of both the ailing Liberals and a surge in turnout. Labour received its lowest vote share since 1931 and returned just 269 MPs.

Through the late 1970s it was not just the left and unions challenging post-war consensus; elements of the political right also broke ranks. By 1979, the corporatist state was being systematically undermined with the wide-ranging intellectual challenge we now describe as 'Thatcherism' reacting to widespread industrial militancy, the breakdown of pay policy and recurring stagflation. Thatcher's embrace of economic liberalism signalled a reorientation away from the concerns of post-war bipartisan corporatism and cross-party support for the Attlee welfare state.

A traumatic Labour government had been ended, one squeezed between a resurgent New Right, the unions and New Left. The party would be out of power until 1997. Once again, a failure to engineer the anticipated growth ensured the party relegated both its programme and ambitions in the embrace of austerity. Both Keynesianism and the Social Contract could not be sustained once in office and relations with the unions again crumbled. With hindsight, Healey's request of an IMF loan was unnecessary, the product of Treasury miscalculation. Such a mistake and the wider failures of the period helped usher in a New Right committed to dismantling the architecture of corporatism and deregulating the economy, whilst the advance of the left would by 1981 split the party. Yet having navigated the European and IMF challenges, the perils of stagflation and some extraordinary global events, by the end of

1978, the Callaghan government looked to be in relatively good shape despite the manoeuvrings on the left, disgruntled unions and cornered revisionists.

The basic political reality for Labour was a straightforward yet recurring one. The leadership view of the route to socialism continued to overwhelmingly involve a labourist politics of redistribution and this focus on distributional justice required capitalist growth. Whilst the period also saw highly significant interventions from the liberal revisionist left, from within social policy and a growing New Left, orthodox thinking remained focused on questions of resource distribution, which stagflation derailed. Once Keynesianism had been rejected and protectionism withdrawn as an option through EEC membership, it was difficult to see a party strategy beyond managed austerity. Utilitarianism could not deliver without growth to redistribute. When nationalizations did occur, little was done to alter the governance of industry due to a failure to embrace questions of power and democracy in the workplace beyond traditional voluntarism. A conception of justice based on resource distribution continued to hold back Labour just as politics and economics were about to be revolutionized under Margaret Thatcher around questions of self-interest in response to the failings of the 1960s and 1970s.

9

Wilderness
(1979–1987)

Having been rejected by the electorate in 1979, Labour sank into factional conflict and would remain in the political wilderness as Margaret Thatcher reordered the British economy and society with profound consequences for the future of the party.

The election of Michael Foot as leader on 4 November 1980 was swiftly followed by the departure of four recent cabinet ministers to form the SDP. A year later, Denis Healey narrowly defeated Tony Benn in a bitterly fought deputy leadership campaign after the introduction of an electoral college to widen the franchise beyond the PLP. Whilst the early 1980s saw significant advances for the left, it would fail to secure any enduring control over the party. After some of the most difficult years in its history, Labour was heavily defeated in 1983, winning only 27.6 per cent of the vote, its lowest share since 1918, and receiving just half a million more votes than the SDP-Liberal Alliance. Labour was in the political wilderness. Its economic approach had failed, it had split and descended into factional conflict. It lacked the intellectual resources to rebuild and the death question loomed large.

Foot was replaced by Neil Kinnock with Roy Hattersley as his deputy. The miners' strike ensured a difficult start for the new leadership team, yet by 1985 their reform strategy showed signs of success, notably in the battle against Trotskyite entryism. With Kinnock gradually asserting his authority, Labour improved its performance in 1987, gaining a modest 20 seats yet being firmly re-established as the second political party in Britain as the Alliance once again failed to make a breakthrough in terms of seat numbers. By 1987, Labour was tentatively embracing new thinking and revising its approach to socialist change and a model of progressive justice in response to both its failures in office and the ascent of the Thatcherite right.

Thatcherism

On 14 November 1977, John Hoskyns, later to become Head of Policy for Margaret Thatcher in Downing Street, circulated a landmark report entitled *Stepping Stones*.[1] The document sought to reorder domestic politics through a reassessment of labour regulation drawn from textbook liberal economic theory; the conclusion of months of strategic discussion at the heart of an emerging, new radical right. The ambition was clear: 'national recovery will be of a different order from that facing any other post-war government. Recovery requires a sea-change in Britain's political economy'. The task was to instil 'a sense of shame and disgust with the corrupting effects of socialism and union power'. It worked alongside detailed planning whilst in opposition to confront and break the unions, revealed by the *Ridley Report* – a Conservative think-tank paper produced in 1977, which appeared to include a detailed blueprint on how to provoke and defeat the NUM.

Stepping Stones was a companion piece to an earlier document framing the politics of Thatcherism. In April 1975, two months after Thatcher won the leadership, Keith Joseph presented *Notes Toward the Definition of Policy* to the Shadow Cabinet.[2] These two key texts in the advance of the New Right were built on a self-critical assessment of Conservative involvement in post-war corporatism and a return to the liberal economics that revolutionized the discipline in the 1870s adapted with the insights of the likes of F.A. Hayek, Ludwig von Mises and the scholars of the Mont Pelerin Society. This intellectual redirection crystallized at the 1979 general election, where concerns about union power helped sweep Thatcher into power and prefigured a sea change in the management of the economy and British politics with dramatic consequences for Labour.[3]

Alongside the economic dogma of monetarism and the ideas of economists like Milton Friedman, three critical shifts in economic policy quickly followed. First, the government set about weakening or abolishing the tripartite institutions to assist and in some cases bail out ailing sectors and companies, improve the skills base, and check the problem of low pay. Industrial Training Boards and Wages Councils were axed. The institutional architecture of post-war corporatism – the NEB, Manpower Services Commission (MSC) and National Economic

Development Council (NEDC) – was dismantled altogether or significantly curtailed. Second, it embarked on an unfolding privatization programme. Modest at first, the sale of state-owned assets gathered pace during the 1980s, often at knock-down prices and gilded with the rhetoric of advancing 'people's capitalism'. The nationalized industries, the utilities (gas, water, electricity, telecommunications), the ports and shipbuilding industry, and many local authority services were transferred to the private sector.

Third, the government built a rolling legislative labour law programme. It removed statutory support for trade union recognition, undermined the closed shop and narrowed significantly the statutory immunities protecting unions' right to strike and organize. Legitimate industrial action was narrowed, detailed pre-strike ballot procedures introduced and important restrictions were imposed on secondary and sympathetic action. Trade unions could be sued and be liable to pay damages. The union itself could be restrained by the granting of an injunction, with the threat of contempt proceedings and possible sequestration. The political language used to describe economic affairs changed dramatically. From being labelled the 'sick man of Europe', one suffering from the British 'disease', the discourse shifted to embrace Thatcher's trauma therapy, one that quickly secured an economic 'miracle'.[4] This shock doctrine helped dismantle the sectors and institutions underpinning Labour's history.

Britain's employment structure changed significantly in the 1980s. Post-war demographic shifts, particularly the 1960s 'baby boom', helped to swell the available workforce by around 1.7 million. This expansion coincided with the erosion of employment opportunities in manufacturing, the rapid growth of private sector service employment, increased female participation rates and a threefold rise in unemployment in the first half of the decade. Full-time employment fell by half a million, while the number of 'non-standard' employees rose by about two million. In 1988, 'non-standard' employment accounted for more than a third of the total labour force and most of these were either self-employed or part-time workers. Women comprised three-quarters of the part-time workforce.

Manufacturing output and productive capacity fell sharply in the first half of the 1980s, as record bankruptcies scarred the industrial base while costing two million jobs. Output declined by a staggering 20 per cent between 1979 and 1981 and did not surpass its 1974 level until 1989. The service sector, in contrast, expanded rapidly. Two million additional jobs were created between 1979 and 1987 while output increased by 29 per cent. Seven in every ten employees henceforth worked in services.

In assessing the growth of service sector employment, three points stand out: most expansion took place in the private sector; many of the new jobs were part time and poorly paid; and the majority were filled by women. By contrast, of the two million workers who lost their jobs in manufacturing, the majority had worked full time, were trade union members and had their pay and conditions determined through collective agreements. De-industrialization, mass unemployment and the overhaul of labour legislation dramatically affected the position and power of the unions. The proportion of employees in unions crashed from 56 to 31 per cent. Britain became more unequal as post-war trends in income inequality literally reversed. In the battle between capital and labour, labour lost.

In short, the British economy shifted dramatically from the one underpinning the traditional base of the party to one inverting the Darwinian certainties of much Labour history. In the words of historian Eric Hobsbawm, the 'Forward March of Labour' might well have been halted, just as the party appeared to be ensnared in a factional doom loop.[5]

The Darkness

On 3 May 1979, the Tories emerged with 339 seats and 43.9 per cent of the popular vote, compared to Labour's 269 and 36.9 per cent. The following years would be Labour's worst since the early 1930s as its class and union constituencies fractured, the SDP broke away and internal divisions disfigured the party. The party had split before but never on this scale. After the 1979 defeat, the right of the party was split between those who anticipated a swift return to office and others actively contemplating a dramatic change of direction and the formation of a new party. Yet the battles were not really about policy or the nature of socialism, but about power within the party machine. From the left since the early 1970s, CLPD had spearheaded the campaign for internal constitutional reform to control policy and the accountability of MPs. After the defeat they felt emboldened, not just from the grassroots but because the unions shifted leftwards. Three sites of factional contest emerged: over NEC control of the manifesto, mandatory reselection of MPs and widening the franchise to elect the leader. At the 1979 Conference two of these were agreed – on reselection by 4,008,000 to 3,039,000 and for the NEC to be given final control of the manifesto by 3,936,000 to 3,008,000, although the second change was reversed the following year. Proposals for the party as a whole to elect the leadership were defeated by 4,009,000 to 3,033,000. The precise makeup of an electoral college for electing the leadership was finally decided at a special conference in January 1981. The closeness of all three votes suggested momentum was with the left but that the political direction of the party remained unresolved.[6]

Within Labour's drama, two unlikely figures moved centre stage, Michael Foot and Tony Benn. In several respects they swapped political lanes in their respective journeys from the factional terrain of the early 1950s. Both had family ties to Edwardian liberalism: Michael was the son of Isaac, a lifelong Liberal and MP from 1922 to 1924 and 1929 to 1935; Tony the son of William, Liberal MP from 1906, who in 1928 converted to Labour and served in MacDonald's second cabinet. Foot, the quintessential political romantic and biographer of his mentor Bevan, the 1960s rebel elected leader in part as a reaction to the orthodoxies of the Wilson and Callaghan years; Benn, the revisionist star of the 1950s whose response to the compromises of the 1970s propelled him to the leadership of what would become a more doctrinaire left. The harsh utilitarian edge to much of 1980s 'hard' left was not dissimilar to the political character of the right wing 'St Ermin's' group of the same period discussed later, a faction shorn of much of its liberal revisionism following defections to the SDP. Foot as leader sat at the intersection of these competing yet not dissimilar factions.

Compared to both factions Foot's socialism sourced from a different place, one less preoccupied with planning and state administration, anchored within English radical literary traditions that shared Ruskin and Morris's rejection of economic utility as the source of value. Benn offered a colder transactional socialism compared to Foot's political touchstones within early nineteenth-century literature. Benn's early references were dissenting Christian socialist, inherited from his mother's congregationalist activism, yet on entering parliament transitioned from early 1950s

Michael Foot
Source: Marcel Antonisse, Fotocollectie Anefo, Dutch National Archives.

revisionism through Fabianism towards the authoritarian left. By the early 1980s, his socialism resembled that of Foot's when active in the 1930s Socialist League. For Foot, the party was a democratic plurality of identities, the classic Labour alliance, a broad church of voices dating back to Hardie. For Benn, it was a tool for the grassroots membership, a mass movement broad enough to include dissenters of all persuasions.

In his biography of Foot Ken Morgan captures these political cross currents and where each had ended up by the early 1980s. He writes:

> Foot's socialism is evolutionary, and grows out of a sense of historic identity.
> It is an outgrowth of the radical liberalism in which he had been brought up.
> It is fundamentally based on his own idiosyncratic sense of history. Benn's by
> contrast, is not really historical at all, despite some observations about the
> Levellers and the Chartists. It is curiously abstract, focusing on structures
> and mechanics, and unrelated to the political antecedents. Foot's socialism

is literary, cultural and humane, drawing heavily on traditions of protest and demands for democratic change from the time of the French revolution. When he addressed mass marches on the meaning of socialism, Hazlitt and Byron were at his shoulder, he conveyed a sense of warmth and solidarity. Benn's socialism is neither literary nor cultural. His bleak analysis seems on paper peculiarly mechanical, even bloodless, curiously lacking in humanity for so personally charming and cultured a man ... Foot sees British socialism as the custodian of a culture. Benn sees it as a weapon to be mobilized for social transformation.[7]

Morgan locates both characters within wider intellectual traditions operating behind the backs of Labour's 1980s drama. Neither are significant socialist theorists, both very English, children of Edwardian progressivism, yet patrician, standing outside of the political mainstream. Foot, the romantic parliamentarian and Aristotelian, like Bevan distinguishing between democratic and undemocratic socialism. Benn, the populist more focused on designated ends, seeing the party as 'the priesthood of all believers' and generous to entryism. Their paths crossed after 1970. Benn, the Gaitskellite insider of the 1950s and 1960s, shifted dramatically left whilst Foot, the critic, writer and rebel, the 'natural heir of Hardie and Lansbury', came inside.[8]

But this wasn't the only reading of events and the nature of the Foot/Benn divide. Neither were socialist theoreticians; both men's politics tended towards the statist and economistic and were conditioned by the shifting politics of the Wilson and Callaghan governments and wider intellectual movements across the left. In the late 1960s, it was Foot who was seen as a tribune of the left. He had helped in the creation of CND but in reality was a prisoner to the Bevanism and Morrisonian nationalization the New Left rejected. By the 1970s, any Labour left politics based on the traditional model of state control, Keynesian expansion and welfare transfers looked increasingly anachronistic given the failings of the National Plan and *In Place of Strife*, the effects of devaluation and austerity and the realities of stagflation, capitalist crisis and militant trade unionism. Foot came inside politically because his radical alternatives offered diminishing returns and by the late 1970s, in government as Secretary of State for Employment and later as deputy leader, he was committed to making labourism work. It was Benn in the 1970s who would pioneer industrial democracy, reject traditional corporatism and embrace the guild insights of the Institute for Workers Control (IWC) and economists such as Geoff Hodgson.[9] It was Benn who, having renounced his own title, would challenge the unwritten constitution and make the case for modern democratic and constitutional renewal and embrace Charter 88. Benn was not a Marxist, but someone who would move away from Fabianism and revisionism in search of new ideas as the post-war boom ended and the growth premium that gradualism required diminished. Without the literary references of Foot, he could indeed appear cold and calculating but he had evolved into quite a traditional figure in Labour's history, a very English radical Christian socialist concerned with liberty and human fraternity rather than utility and labourism.[10] This is not to say that Benn rejected the doctrinaire utilitarian politics of elements of what would become known as the 'hard' left, rather it is to suggest the man himself at different stages of his political life embraced familiar traditions within the history of Labour.

At the time it was widely accepted Healey and not Foot would be the next leader. Days after the October 1980 Conference, but before the scheduled January special conference, Callaghan announced his resignation, having stayed on to help Healey yet only long enough to ensure the election of his successor would remain restricted to members of the PLP. Yet Foot, with Kinnock as campaign manager, narrowly beat Healey 139 to 129. The formula for an electoral college for future leadership elections was finally agreed at a Wembley conference on 24 January 1981 made up by 40 per cent trade union votes, 30 per cent party members and 30 per cent for MPs, thereby taking significant power away from the PLP, the option favoured by the left.

For many on the right this vote in the aftermath of the election of Foot was the final straw. The next day a 'Gang of Four' former Labour cabinet ministers – Shirley Williams, Bill Rodgers, David Owen and, having just returned from Brussels, Roy Jenkins – announced a new Council for Social Democracy, their aims set out in the 'Limehouse Declaration'. The formal split from Labour occurred on 26 March 1981 when the SDP was launched, initially attracting 12 Labour MPs, rising to 27 of the 1979 intake. In September 1982, the Liberal-SDP Alliance formed. Although the departing group reflected different shades of opinion across the Labour right, the liberal left tradition within Labour revisionism shaped much of the thinking of the SDP. Questions of liberty and democratic renewal were central concerns, so too human rights and electoral reform, and an appeal to international procedural justice, especially European. The split reflected both the declining influence of Crosland's economic framework and the often uncomfortable relationship between Labour and liberalism throughout the twentieth century. Social liberalism had been an early significant force within the Edwardian party and later during the 1960s, yet at other times it operated more as an external influence. By the early 1980s, apart from a couple of notable exceptions, much of the liberal revisionist wing within Labour looked to have departed; an exit not just of MPs but also of significant figures such as Michael Young, Polly Toynbee and David Marquand.

The new party performed well both in the polls and at by-elections. In July 1981 at a by-election in Warrington, the Labour majority collapsed from over 10,000 to just 1,750. At Crosby in November, Williams won a seat from the Tories and Jenkins followed suit in Glasgow Hillhead the following March.

The defections reset the Labour right, the majority of whose MPs still remained loyal to the party. The highly effective Manifesto Group, created in 1974 to counterbalance the left and support moderate PLP members, was compromised by the breakaway after many members left, including its founder Dickson Mabon MP. The group was replaced in February 1981 by the Labour Solidarity Campaign led by Roy Hattersley.

Following the 1981 special conference and decision on mandatory reselection empowering the grassroots left, a group of senior union leaders[11] from the traditional right wing of labourism moved to organize the NEC and General Council fightback and regain control. Meeting secretly every month, they took their name from the location of their initial meeting, the St Ermin's Hotel. MPs such as Denis Howell, John Golding, Denis Healey and Giles Radice were regular attendees.

Then in April 1981 Tony Benn announced his challenge to become deputy leader and replace Healey. It was a decision made against the advice of some of his closest supporters and one that carried political consequences. The disagreement ultimately divided the left between a Tribune Group of MPs and the newly formed more Bennite Socialist Campaign Group, a division between a 'soft' and 'hard' left. After a tough and at times ugly campaign, Benn failed by 50.43 per cent to 49.57 per cent, in part due to the abstentions in the final ballot of a number of 'soft' left MPs, including Kinnock, fearful of further internal carnage and defections. Benn won by a large margin in the constituencies but lost heavily amongst both the unions and PLP. With hindsight, it was arguably the decisive moment in the factional struggles of the early 1980s and the ascendancy of the left. From 1980 on, moderate forces gained places on the NEC, and an emerging alliance developed between the right and soft left on Labour's ruling body, one of the most consequential developments of the Foot era.

After the 1982 Conference, Tony Benn and Eric Heffer were rejected as chairs of the critical Home Policy and Organisation Committees, which would prove to be critical sites for the political consolidation of Kinnock's Labour after the 1983 election. In a sign of things to come, the leadership also made its first tentative moves against the entryism of the Trotskyist group Militant Tendency, who had successfully gained control of a number of CLPs and Liverpool City Council, and would at the 1983 election return two MPs in Dave Nellist and Terry Fields. In 1981, the NEC set up an inquiry into the organization which led Conference in 1982 to agree a register of approved groups. Militant was proscribed by the NEC in December 1982 and members of its editorial board were later expelled.

This all occurred as the Thatcher government struggled economically. Its first two years saw a doubling of unemployment alongside negative growth and rising inflation, whilst a deflationary 1980 budget brought substantial welfare cuts. Yet the Falklands conflict following the 2 April 1982 Argentine troop invasion saw her popularity rise sharply. Labour offered support against a fascist aggressor, yet the 1982 Conference once again supported unilateral disarmament and at best Labour appeared uncomfortable with the patriotic fervour unleashed by the conflict. More generally, privatizations, tax cuts and an idea advocated by Labour in 1970, for the right of residents to buy their council houses, proved attractive. With the anti-Conservative vote divided and after some initial difficulties her economic position improving, Margaret Thatcher looked unbeatable and felt confident enough to call an early election for June 1983.[12]

Labour's 1983 manifesto *The New Hope for Britain*, dubbed by right-wing Labour MP Gerald Kaufman 'the longest suicide note in history', pledged abolition of the House of Lords, a defence policy both multilateral and unilateral, the repeal of the Conservative union legislation, withdrawal from the EEC and return to the public sector of the industries privatized after 1979. Many cynically hoped that a landslide defeat would discredit both Foot and the left. Yet it also contained pledges around industrial democracy and constitutional reform that suggested new thinking regarding traditional forms of state control and new liberal equalities legislation.[13] Labour faced relentless press attacks over both the manifesto content and style of campaign in contrast to the professional Conservative approach, one which played on fears of a repeat of the Winter of Discontent.

Labour was on the wrong end of a landslide, winning only 27.6 per cent of the vote, and just 209 MPs, its worst seat performance since 1935. It lost three million votes compared to 1979 and won only half a million more than the SDP-Liberal Alliance whose vote distribution and the effect of the electoral system meant they came away with just 23 MPs. Thatcher's majority rose to 144 despite the fact that the Conservative vote share fell by 1.5 per cent.

Consolidation

Michael Foot resigned and on 2 October 1983 the new electoral college elected Neil Kinnock as leader and Hattersley deputy. The leadership moved quickly to secure organizational change. With the aid of new public finances, so-called 'short money', the office of the leader was significantly strengthened with the employment of figures such as Dick Clements, Charles Clarke and Patricia Hewitt. A new Campaign Strategy Committee was established under the control of the leader, whose position was strengthened when the traditional right gained effective control of the NEC in 1983. In 1984 new joint Shadow Cabinet and NEC policy committees were set up to overcome factional rivalries and competing sites of power between the parliamentary leadership and NEC. At the 1984 Conference, Kinnock proposed One Member One Vote (OMOV) over candidate selections and mandatory reselections to challenge the role of activist-controlled constituency General Committees (GCs). Although narrowly defeated by 3,592,000 votes to 3,041,00, the direction of travel was established and in the coming years OMOV would become a political touchstone for party 'modernizers'. Yet in the short term the reform agenda stalled in the face of the 1984/85 miners' strike and challenges posed by local government rate capping.

The strike originated in March 1984 after the Coal Board announced cuts both in production and jobs in Scotland and Yorkshire. As the dispute widened, flying pickets migrated primarily out of South Yorkshire to the Scottish, Nottingham and Kent coalfields to convince working miners to join the fight. Heavily policed mass picketing at key locations, including outside Ollerton Colliery in Nottinghamshire where David Jones, a 24-year-old Wakefield miner, died on 15 March and at the so-called 'battle of Orgreave' at the Rotherham coking plant on 18 June 1984, became some of the most contentious moments in British industrial relations history. The Conservative union legislation played its role when the South Wales Mineworkers, having been fined £50,000 for contempt, were sequestrated, and the NUM, having been fined, also had its assets seized. On 3 March 1985, the strike eventually ended without any agreement following a special delegate conference. The violent images, with echoes of Labour's difficulties over the 1926 General Strike, made it an extraordinarily challenging period for Kinnock, whose family were South Wales miners. Politically much of the PLP, the grassroots and union activists were actively supportive of the miners. Since the 1909 shift in their allegiance to support Labour over the Liberals, the miners had played a pivotal, although often difficult role throughout the party's history. Kinnock's approach focused on the lack of a ballot for the action and culminated in an attack on Scargill's leadership of the dispute at the 1985 Party Conference. Twenty-five years later, he would accuse Arthur Scargill of 'suicidal vanity', whose leadership was a 'gift' to the Thatcher government.[14]

However difficult for Kinnock and the party, in the longer term the defeat of the miners demonstrated that for a party of labour, grounded within male trade unionism and a manual working class within certain rapidly declining sectors, to ever win again things had to change. Its defeat by a government determined to correct the humiliation of 1974 helped realign political forces within Labour and support the argument that 'New Times' meant the party had to change or die.

In the short term, Kinnock made more progress demonstrating political change over Trotskyite entryism than the miners' strike.[15] In 1985, in an act of confrontation with the government over budget

Neil Kinnock
Source: Rob Bogaerts, Fotocollectie Anefo, Dutch National Archives.

setting, Liverpool City Council issued redundancy notices to its 31,000 workers, offering Kinnock an opening to attack how 'a rigid dogma' produced 'grotesque chaos' in his Conference speech that year, in part aided by Eric Heffer walking out. The NEC then set up an inquiry into the situation in Liverpool from which, in 1986, the district party was suspended. The NEC battles over Militant helped consolidate the breach between the hard and soft left, reflected in the changing political contributions of key figures such as Margaret Beckett, Michael Meacher, David Blunkett and especially ex-Bennite Tom Sawyer in his position as Chair of the Home Policy Committee. It also led in 1986 to the introduction of the National Constitutional Committee with final say over discipline, limiting the rights to appeal to Conference and strengthening the hand of the leader.

1985 also saw Kinnock's preferred candidate Larry Whitty take over from Jim Mortimer as General Secretary, moving swiftly to rationalize the operation at Head Office. In October a new Director of Communications was hired, Peter Mandelson, to professionalize media strategy, who in association with Philip Gould and Deborah Mattinson introduced a new Shadow Communications Agency (SCA).

Beyond Militant there were other challenges for the leadership in its relations with Labour local government and groups derided by opponents as the 'loonly left'. The term misrepresents political constituencies which included civic leaderships emerging form the New Left and wider liberation movements together with more orthodox Trotskyite and Leninist elements. In the early 1980s, much of the left regarded local authorities as part of an extra-parliamentary movement challenging the ruling Westminster party and defending areas of greatest need and those taking the full brunt of expenditure cuts. Councils were meanwhile having their powers and assets stripped back with the 'right to buy' and opt-outs from Education Authorities. In 1985, a total of fifteen councils, including Blunkett-led Sheffield, Lambeth under Ted Knight and the Greater London Council (GLC) under Ken Livingstone and chair of Finance John McDonnell, joined in a rate-capping rebellion and refused to set a rate for 1985/6. Yet the fight against the government veered into a series of internal battles within Labour groups over the setting of legal budgets, most of which were eventually resolved although others were disqualified from office and surcharged. In March 1987, after a difficult Greenwich by-election loss, a leaked letter from Patricia Hewitt stated the 'loony left' tag was taking its toll on the party.

On the policy front Kinnock began to emerge as a revisionist. He tacitly moved to challenge Clause IV, stating that renationalization of the post-1979 privatizations would not be a priority, although accepting the case for the 'social ownership' of Telecom and British Gas. In terms of industrial relations reform, Thatcher's balloting procedures were accepted. On defence the party remained unilateralist, including the removal of American bases from the UK. More generally Kinnock agreed in 1985 that a fresh reassertion of Labour's basic principles was required, an idea promoted by Blunkett and his friend and tutor Bernard Crick, to contest the philosophical successes of Thatcherism. The NEC set up a group to reconsider the 'Aims and Values' of the party, although Kinnock rejected several initial drafts and the project for the time being stalled.

The 1987 election was called for 11 June. After what many regarded as a good professional campaign, one which included 'Kinnock the Movie' directed by Hugh Hudson, Labour secured just 229 seats, up 20, and 30.8 per cent of the vote. The government majority was cut from 144 to 101, granting Margaret Thatcher her second landslide. However, Labour had succeeded in defeating the Alliance and retaining second place, a result which would see the Alliance begin to unravel, eventually leading to the creation of the Liberal Democrats. Despite this relative success, Labour appeared bereft and remained in the political wilderness. It lacked a coherent economic agenda, many of the leading liberal revisionists had departed to the SDP and years of coarse factional struggle had diluted Labour's moral purpose. Labour's three traditions of justice had withered and the death question was ever present.

Revival
(1987–1997)

Following the defeat Kinnock moved to gain systematic control over party organization and policy. The NEC successfully resumed disciplinary actions against Militant and launched a wholesale Policy Review. In November 1990, Thatcher resigned and was succeeded by John Major. Despite confident Labour expectations, the 1992 election saw the Conservatives returned once more, albeit with a much-reduced majority of 21. Kinnock immediately resigned as leader and was succeeded by John Smith. Within months, the so-called 'Black Wednesday' of September 1992 damaged the Conservative government's reputation for economic competence and Labour looked set for victory. Tragically, Smith died from a heart attack in May 1994, an event that would see the emergence of New Labour.

Despite another ten years in opposition, the period would see a significant intellectual revival within Labour. On the economic front a 'supply-side socialism' would revise Labour's approach to growth and redistribution. The period would once more see a reorientation towards questions of liberty and justice expressed in renewed commitments to legislate to enhance equality, together with the pursuit of constitutional and political reform and the expansion of human rights. Finally, under the leadership of both John Smith and Tony Blair, Labour consciously sought to re-embrace the history of ethical socialism. Labour's three traditions of justice would all be re-engineered in ways that would ultimately foreshadow the party's longest period in government.

Policy Review

The disappointing 1987 defeat intensified the momentum behind change. Kinnock embarked on a major overhaul of the policy process. In September 1987 the Conference agreed a two-year Policy Review to be made up of seven joint NEC and Shadow Cabinet Review Groups with an interim document presented to the 1988 Conference and final conclusions the following year. To set the scene a report by the SCA entitled *Labour and Britain in the 1990s* was presented to the NEC on 20 November 1987 which forced Labour to confront the death question by setting out the social and attitudinal challenges facing a party which, they argued, was too readily associated with the past, the poor, high taxes, weak defence and industrial militancy.

The review is generally seen as a simple exercise in political repositioning driven by the SCA; a two-year fix to ditch unpopular policies and unburden the party of polling negatives, a shift to the right on the instructions of a cadre of increasingly influential, shadowy communications people. Yet it can also be seen as an attempt to rebuild Labour's economic framework, given both the inherent limitations of Crosland's revisionism and the positions of the early 1980s in relation to spending and public ownership, and at the same time more fully embrace a more liberal approach to questions of justice. Morrisonian nationalization was rejected in favour of social ownership and regulation. So too were commitments to Keynesian spending and full employment, replaced by an emphasis on training, investment and research; an economic reorientation branded 'supply-side socialism' in autumn 1988.

Resolving the widespread perception of Labour as a party of high taxation was in part helped by the Conservative Chancellor Nigel Lawson. In his fifth budget of March 1988, Lawson abolished the 60 per cent upper rate meaning no one would pay more than 40 per cent and reduced the basic rate from 27 to 25 per cent. In contrast, John Smith suggested a five-band approach between 20 and 50 per cent. Throughout March and April 1989, Gordon Brown went through all the group reports to strip away any uncosted spending pledges and consolidate this emerging framework.

On industrial relations the People at Work Policy Review Group, initially led by Michael Meacher, at first stumbled over secondary and sympathetic industrial action and the definition of a trade dispute, and proposed reforms that went further than the TUC had suggested in its own submission. In October 1989, Meacher was replaced by Tony Blair. Blair's clarification, when challenged by Employment Secretary Michael Howard over Labour's support for both the closed shop and the Social Charter,[1] the latter containing the right not to be a union member, essentially ended the party's support for compulsory union membership. Later the final report of the review group shifted policy away from traditional immunities in a significant challenge to labourism.[2]

On defence policy, the final review ditched unilateralism, despite a 1,244,000 Conference majority backing it in 1988. Following a New Year 1989 trip to Moscow, and after tense negotiations with NEC soft-left members and an impassioned address by Kinnock himself, a multilateralist position within NATO was finally adopted by 17 votes to 8 at the two-day NEC meeting at Transport House to agree the final group reports. With both the National Union of Public Employees (NUPE) and the Union of Shop, Distributive and Allied Workers (USDAW) swinging in behind the defence review, the 1988 unilateralist majority was overturned a year later.

Yet the Policy Review was not simply about discarding unpopular policies. Arguably it was the first serious attempt since the 1950s to revive a liberal revisionist project within Labour. For the left, the traumas of the Labour governments of the 1960s and 1970s had exposed the shortcomings of any return to Bevanism. But revisionist social democracy was also in retreat as the growth that Crosland had assumed to be a permanent feature of post-war Britain to power social change and distributive justice proved elusive.[3] After the defeat in 1987, Kinnock returned to the stalled 'Aims and Values' project to help ideologically anchor the Policy Review, handing the project to Hattersley.

Before the election Hattersley had published *Choose Freedom*,[4] which began: 'The true objective of socialism is the creation of a genuinely free society in which the protection and extension of individual liberty is the primary duty of the state.' The book echoed many of the themes of Crosland's *The Future of Socialism* but updated the approach to include the insights of John Rawls in *A Theory of Justice*.[5] Kinnock's deputy sought to re-establish the ideological case for socialism with recourse to questions of liberty and freedom, and this Rawlsian liberalism informed his drafting of Labour's new statement of purpose. Echoing the start of *Choose Freedom*, the final *A Statement of Democratic Socialist Aims and Values* began: 'To be truly free a man or woman must possess the ability to make the choices that freedom provides … The more equal distribution of wealth increases the sum of freedom'. In both documents, equality remained the means and liberty the ends of socialism.

The title of the party's 1986 'Freedom and Fairness' campaign had first signalled Labour's liberal intellectual reorientation. Yet the 'Aims and Values' journey continued to be difficult. It was subject to criticism, not just from the left but from within the Shadow Cabinet right, specifically from John Smith for an overreliance on the market. This reflected long-term divisions within revisionism. Smith's socialism descended from Tawney and the post-war ethical revisionist wing whereas Hattersley's was routed through Crosland and more recently Rawls. The early draft was subject to countless amendments, including additions that reflected the more communitarian concerns of Blunkett and concluded with the NEC agreeing to insert Clause IV into the final publication. In the end the final text was accepted by the 1988 Party Conference after a lacklustre debate and by then Kinnock had clearly lost interest. The project had diminished and proved intellectually inconclusive, especially over Labour's approach to the market. Yet the ideological reference points of the 'Aims and Values' process acted as a 'staging post' in delivering the overall Policy Review.[6] It retains an albeit unrecognized significance in the overall liberal reorientation of Labour throughout the period, including what later would emerge as New Labour.

The final Policy Review Report, whilst certainly incomplete, laid the footings for an emerging revisionist political reimagination within Labour; one established under Kinnock but which would be further developed over the next two decades. Whilst it rejected orthodox left-wing political positions regarding taxation and expenditure, nationalization and Clause IV, immunities and unilateralism, the final documents also offered a series of new positive openings for the party. John Smith emerged as a staunch advocate of a national minimum wage of £2.80 an hour,[7] a radical departure given the history of British labour law. This reorientation was supported by a wider package of employment law proposals offering protections for all workers and highlighted the need for innovative family-friendly legislation including child care, flexible working and new rights for women workers. The review also called for a new Ministry of Women.[8] Support for the Social Chapter, following the visit of Jacques Delors to the 1988 TUC Conference, signalled an embrace of a European social model and forms of judicial oversight at odds with much of the Eurosceptic and the voluntarist traditions that had defined 90 years of labourism. This was complemented by a new focus on the environment as well as on constitutional rights, reform of the Lords and regional representation pushed by Hattersley, and consumer rights advocated by Blunkett, echoing earlier concerns of Michael Young. A week before the 1992 election Kinnock engaged with Charter 88's 'Democracy Day', a significant challenge to Labour's traditional utilitarian concerns, and later Kinnock, after leaving office, even flirted with electoral reform having set up the Plant Commission to consider the issue. The Policy Review offered a signal of what was to come under Smith and also Blair in terms of the rewriting of Clause IV in 1994/5 and further policy modernization.

Overall, the Policy Review was a partial, incomplete and overcautious beginning. Despite being often overlooked, it intimated the possibility of a deeper revisionist reformation by establishing a new liberal basecamp within Labour, but one more aligned to the market economy than 1950s revisionism. It did not just ditch policies but tentatively embraced new thinking around individual rights, liberty and democratic renewal, equality and discrimination, Europe and the environment. One that at least acknowledged the changing social and economic conditions of Britain in the late 1980s, signalled in the wider debates around 'New Times' within *Marxism Today* and initiatives such as *Charter 88*, which vigorously challenged Labour traditionalism in advocating a bill of rights, written constitution, proportional representation, a democratic, non-hereditary second chamber, and wider redistribution of power between local, regional and national government.[9] Whilst we can make the case that the review was a foretaste of Labour in government after 1997, we also have to accept that with the compromises and amendments and overall failure of the 'Aims and Values' project, the Policy Review lacked an overarching intellectual framework. Citizenship was initially considered to frame the overall project before being rejected in favour of modernization and change,[10] once more signalling the review's role as a tributary towards a New Labour project built around themes of economic and social modernization. As we discuss in the next chapter, New Labour, rather than a breach with what went before, was a political project erected on the foundations of the Kinnock years.

The response from within the Campaign Group[11] to the Policy Review was a leadership challenge to Kinnock from Benn, the first against a sitting leader since Wilson's challenge to Gaitskell in 1960 and Tony

Greenwood's failed attempt a year later, and Hattersley from Heffer. As it had in 1981 with the breach between the Tribune and Campaign groups, the decision split the left. Four resigned from the Campaign Group over the challenge: Margaret Beckett, Clare Short, Joan Ruddock and Jo Richardson. With the backing of the 'soft left' Labour Coordinating Committee (LCC), John Prescott then entered the deputy contest. The result announced on 2 October 1988 was an overwhelming victory for Kinnock, 88.64 per cent against 11.73 per cent. In the constituency section Benn had scored less than 20 per cent, and received the backing of just 38 MPs. For deputy Hattersley received 67 per cent of the vote Prescott 24 per cent and Heffer 9.5 per cent.

The decision to challenge Kinnock had consolidated his position, this after a difficult summer with the Shadow Cabinet resignation of Denzil Davies over defence policy and rumours of growing support for Smith as an alternative leader. It also helped consolidate the significant role of the 'soft left' linked with the Tribune Group and the LCC in the constituencies, a group founded from the left in 1978 but in the 1980s acting as an early modernizing force.[12] From 1987 to 1992, the alliance between the Kinnock leadership of the right and soft left ensured control of the party.

On the organizational front, following the 1987 election, the NEC resumed disciplinary action against members of Militant, leading to further expulsions including the two MPs who supported the group. In 1987, OMOV was introduced for the membership section in selections alongside a vote for the unions with a ceiling of 40 per cent. Later it was agreed that the full reselection of MPs would only proceed after a full trigger ballot in favour. The NEC also tightened control over by-election candidates after defeats in Greenwich in 1987 and Glasgow Govan in 1988. Membership was also centralized after the 1989 Conference accepted central membership recruitment from regional and head offices. A national membership system was launched in January 1991 pulling power further to Head Office. An indication of the shifting internal political dynamics was the 1989 Conference announcement that Livingstone had been voted off the NEC. That same year Brown and Blair came top and fourth respectively in the Shadow Cabinet elections.

The Policy Review would also trigger wider organizational change in terms of policy development. In the second phase of the review, a series of listless 'Labour listens' events convinced many of the case for a wider institutional overhaul. The Institute for Public Policy Research (IPPR) was created in 1989 as a new policy incubator for progressive thought. The first moves away from the annual disorder of resolutions and overnight compositing, and towards a two-year 'rolling programme' based around a new National Policy Forum, were addressed in the document *Democracy and Policy Making for the 1990s* at the 1990 and 1991 Conferences; key changes that would foreshadow future reforms under both Smith and Blair.

As the Policy Review reached its conclusions, Labour's fortunes began to revive. By the spring of 1989 the two former Alliance partners were fighting each other at the Richmond and Pontypridd by-elections. At the May 1989 European elections, Labour secured 45 seats and the Conservatives 31. Throughout 1989 the Conservatives were increasingly split over Europe and economic policy. By the last day of the 1989 Conference, Labour had a 10-point poll lead in the *Evening Standard*, a comfortable lead they would retain for a year, and within a month Lawson had resigned. By November 1990 Thatcher had also gone and been replaced by John Major, after a series of events triggered by the resignation of her deputy Geoffrey Howe. The fall in government support was blamed largely on the poll tax and an economy sliding into recession.

With both Thatcher and the 'Community Charge' gone, Labour's campaign of 'It's Time for a Change' lacked its earlier political punch. Kinnock was now the longest-serving leader of any of the major political parties. Labour's 14-point lead in the November 1990 'Poll of Polls' was replaced a month later by an 8 per cent Conservative lead and throughout much of 1991 they continued to top the polls.

The 1992 election was widely forecast to produce a hung parliament or narrow Labour majority, yet the Conservatives were again returned to power, albeit with a much-reduced majority of 21. Labour was victorious in 271 seats and secured 34.4 per cent of the vote. It amounted to a net Labour gain of 42 seats, although in percentage terms it was less than the party achieved in 1979.

The Quiet Radical

Labour's fourth defeat in a row brought with it similar responses to those of the revisionists in 1959, this time from so-called 'modernizers', figures such as Blair, Mandelson and Brown. The death question reappeared. Any future victory would require an 8 per cent swing and there was widespread doubt Labour could ever win again, certainly not without dramatic change. There remained deep unease about the party's future prospects given the failure to unseat a 13-year incumbent in the midst of recession and high unemployment. Many blamed John Smith's 'Shadow Budget' for giving the Tories an opening to attack Labour's 'tax bombshell'.[13] Others looked to blame the controversy over the 'Jennifer's ear' health campaign and triumphalist 'Sheffield Rally' held eight days before the election. Throughout Kinnock had been vilified by *The Sun* with headlines such as 'Nightmare on Kinnock Street' and the election day front-page 'If Kinnock wins today will the last person to leave Britain please turn out the lights'. He resigned on the steps of the Walworth Road Head Office in the early hours immediately after the defeat, blaming the right-wing media for Labour's failure.

In July 1992 at London's Royal Horticultural Hall, John Smith defeated Bryan Gould to become Labour leader, having secured 97.7 per cent support amongst the constituencies, 96.2 per cent of the union vote and 77.3 per cent in the PLP. The 20 per cent PLP nomination threshold ruled out a candidate from the hard left. Gould had stood on a Keynesian platform, sceptical of European exchange rate mechanism (ERM) membership and fixed exchange rates. Margaret Beckett beat Gould and Prescott for the deputy post.[14]

Aged just 53, Smith had piloted Labour's devolution plans through parliament during the last Labour government, and on replacing Edmund Dell as Secretary of State for Trade became the youngest member of the Callaghan cabinet. His election brought forward the most self-confidently religious Labour leader since Lansbury. Smith's socialism was of an ethical kind familiar within much of Labour's prehistory, the type that would later enjoy a fashionable renaissance under Tony Blair. Consequently, Smith's election in 1992 saw a revival in the profile and influence of the Christian Socialist Movement (CSM). Launched in 1960, CSM brought together the Socialist Christian League and the Society of Socialist Clergy and Ministers under the leadership of Donald Soper. It affiliated to Labour in 1998 and renamed as Christians on the Left in 2013. Throughout, it sought it uphold the early tradition of ethical socialism and questions of human virtue in Labour's debates about purpose and justice.

John Smith
Source: Allstar Picture Library Ltd, Alamy.

In his March 1993 CSM Tawney Memorial Lecture entitled 'Reclaiming the Ground', Smith anchored his socialist convictions within his faith, attacking Thatcher's destructive individualism in ways that would have been welcomed by Edwardian social liberals and the disciples of T.H. Green. He remained very much at ease in linking his moral and liberal instincts back to the early Tawney whilst simultaneously using these ethical touchstones to help recast revisionism, making the case for 'positive liberty – the freedom to achieve that is gained through education, health care, housing, and employment. An infrastructure of freedom that would require collective provision of basic needs through an enabling State. It is this richer conception of freedom for the individual in society that is the moral basis of democratic socialism.'[15] It was a speech that revived memories of Attlee's thinking around welfare reform, economic and social rights and a post-war British New Deal.

In less than two years John Smith would be dead, but in that short time he quietly defied the caricature of the conservative lawyer pinned on him by some modernizers, one suggesting a safety-first traditionalist and advocate of 'one more heave' disinterested in party modernization. Smith was far from the inert leader. He embraced incremental reform whilst healing a party drained of confidence after successive defeats, but not by simply defining himself against his party, a tactic overused by less personally secure leaders. Smith managed to unite the party, proved to be an agile policy innovator and oversaw significant organizational renewal.

After the defeat of 1992 and having surveyed the success of Bill Clinton's 'New Democrats', in November 1992 the modernizers sought dramatic change, including Jack Straw, who once more pushed for a rewriting of Clause IV. Tensions with the modernizing flank heightened after Smith resisted the clamour to immediately push for OMOV at the 1992 Conference, a wise move given a defensive nervousness amongst the affiliated organizations at the time given a widespread anti-union sentiment in the party. Smith chose instead to initiate a more systematic and far-reaching review of the constitutional relationship between the party and unions whilst securing agreement that the block vote at the 1993 Conference be reduced from 90 to 70 per cent.

As the wheels turned on the organizational front, Smith used his parliamentary skills to help bury what was left of the Conservative reputation for economic competence following the so-called Black Wednesday of 16 September 1992 and Britain's exit from the ERM. A year earlier he had created room to manoeuvre by subtly shifting Labour policy towards greater flexibility over currency alignment. With an economy stalled and a government split over Europe and tax hikes and awash with accusations of sleaze, Labour's astute parliamentary manoeuvres continued into 1993 over the Maastricht Treaty ratification process and the Social Charter opt-out. It culminated on 22 July in a government defeat followed by a vote of confidence the next day; the government appeared broken.

Smith also proved to be an innovative leader regarding policy. In December 1992 on the 50th anniversary of the Beveridge Report, he established a Commission on Social Justice, based at the IPPR under Gordon Borrie, the former Director General of the Office of Fair Trading, and David Miliband as secretary, which eventually reported after his death on 24 October 1994. Commissioners included academics

Bernard Williams, David Marquand, Tony Atkinson and Ruth Lister and future Liberal MP Steve Webb. In part the commission was a vehicle for Smith to bury the legacy of his own 1992 Shadow Budget.[16] Yet it also sought to build a 'new Beveridge' through 13 issues papers covering tax and benefits, employment and training, housing and early years provision and education.[17]

The Commission helped systematize the evolution of the new liberal revisionism detectable in the earlier Policy Review. In an echo of FDR's four freedoms, it sought to rethink social justice through the prism of four human rights: the right of citizens to meet basic needs, the right to life opportunities, the equal worth of all citizens and the right to be free from unjust inequalities. Although Blair spoke at the launch of the final report and the 'enabling' welfare state embraced by New Labour aligned with the commission's recommendations, after Smith's death the new leadership balked at the egalitarian tenor of the report.

Most significant of all in terms of rethinking Labour's purpose was Smith's reorientation of the party towards electoral and constitutional reform. His Charter 88 speech on 1 March 1993 was arguably the most comprehensive embrace of democratic renewal by any Labour leader in history. According to the head of Charter 88 Anthony Barnett, 'Smith intended it to be a turning point and it was. It transformed Labour from a constitutionally conservative party into a radical, reformist one'.[18] In it, Smith embraced the incorporation of the European Convention on Human Rights into British law, an independent statistics service to end government deception, a Freedom of Information Act and decisive actions over corporate governance to remove cover-ups. He committed to making legal aid available to all and advanced the case for a modern European constitution – a 'shift away from an overpowering state to a citizen's democracy where people have rights and powers'.

In terms of economic rights to sit alongside this package of civil and political entitlements, at the 1993 TUC Conference Smith pledged a substantial package of labour law reforms and day one employment rights for all workers. The same speech also saw a subtle reorientation away from the orthodoxies of Labour's 'supply siders' by favouring a return to full employment as an act of public policy and the use of all levers of government macroeconomic policy to achieve this goal. In doing so Smith tacitly challenged long-held assumptions dating back to

MacDonald that capitalist growth would secure socialist change, instead reorientating economic policy to secure the desired social outcomes. This was a consistent theme since his days as Shadow Chancellor where he had privately embraced the case for a revised neo-corporatism, a 'National Economic Assessment', a modern social partnership or economic stakeholding favoured by the post-war industrial pluralists, within Labour's Economic Policy Sub-Committee set up to coordinate economic thinking after the Policy Review had been completed.[19] Smith consistently sought to challenge orthodox economism within Labour and recast economic strategy around questions of ethics and morals consistent with his personal commitment to the foundations of ethical socialism. According to his former Head of Policy David Ward,[20] Smith also planned to push for new financial regulations in the wake of 'Black Wednesday' and although Smith would not have sought to scrap Clause IV, he had planned a revised 'Aims and Values' consultation at the 1994 Conference to embed this emerging model as a statement of Labour's purpose.

At the 1993 Conference Smith successfully introduced OMOV. The Trade Union Review Group set up after 1992 first met on 20 July 1992. Smith had initially pursued a package that included a revised 50/50 split between members and the PLP and European PLP (EPLP) in the vote for the leadership, OMOV for candidate selection and reductions in the union vote at Conference linked to increases amongst the individual membership.[21] In the end after a difficult summer where OMOV appeared to be in deep trouble, Smith secured a substantial package of reforms. It created a revised third/third/third electoral college for leadership elections based around OMOV and the individual votes of Labour-supporting levy payers. The reforms included the long-desired OMOV for candidate selections and the abolition of the Conference block vote to be replaced by individual delegate voting, arguably the most significant change at Conference since the creation of the party.[22]

John Smith also oversaw the introduction of the National Policy Forum (NPF), first suggested by Larry Whitty in 1990. In 1992, the 81-strong body with 41 women was agreed to oversee the start of a rolling policy programme, its first meeting taking place on 7–8 May 1993. On 30 November 1993 a Joint Policy Committee was created to oversee and clear all policy documents and report to the NEC. Under

Smith's leadership, all-women shortlists were introduced in half of vacant Labour-held seats and marginal targets, which would have a significant effect in boosting female representation in the PLP.

By the end of 1992, Labour had a comfortable lead in the polls. The lead remained strong throughout 1993 despite the end of recession, a pick-up in growth and fall in unemployment. Labour's healthy position had been consolidated by the Tories abandoning privatization of the Royal Mail and remaining on the back foot over plans to introduce VAT on domestic fuel and lighting.

John Smith died suddenly aged just 55 on 12 May 1994,[23] with Labour 20 per cent ahead in the polls and just seven days after the Tories lost over 500 seats in the local elections. His deputy Beckett stood in as acting leader and oversaw the successful European election campaign, which resulted in the party winning 60 of the 87 seats. For many, Brown remained the heir apparent, yet in 1993 Blair topped his ally in the Shadow Cabinet elections. As Shadow Home Secretary, Blair's popularity rose inversely to Brown's as Shadow Chancellor given the latter's role in enforcing spending restraint, always a difficult role within the Shadow Cabinet, and his positioning over ERM withdrawal, which for many meant Labour was unable to fully exploit the government's difficulties. A secret 31 May 'Granita' deal saw Brown withdraw from the race; the terms of the deal would be widely disputed and disfigure the subsequent Labour government.

With 57 per cent of the vote, Tony Blair, aged just 41, was elected as Smith's successor on 21 July 1994, following a three-way contest with John Prescott and Margaret Beckett. Prescott defeated Beckett to become deputy leader. The result was emphatic with Blair winning in all three sections of the electoral college, securing 61 per cent of MPs and MEPs, 68 per cent amongst the individual membership and 52 per cent of the affiliated members.

1994–1997

On being elected leader, Blair was only too aware of the limited powers at his disposal. The only institution that he could change to demonstrate his ambition to modernize the nation was the party itself. With four initiatives – over Clause IV of the party constitution, a plebiscite on the draft manifesto, the removal of the block vote and over Labour's policy making and executive structures – he sought to overhaul the party to symbolize the change he would bring to the country if elected Prime Minister.

The rebranding of the party as New Labour dates from a Conference slogan first used in 1994 which later reappeared in the title of the 1996 draft manifesto *New Labour, New Life for Britain*. It signalled modernization and a break with the past.

At the same 1994 Conference, his first as leader, Blair held back the last three pages of his speech both for theatrical effect, and to ensure total secrecy over his plans to modify Clause IV of the party constitution. Without addressing the specific clause, Blair declared that 'parties that do not change die, and this party is a living movement not a historical monument ... It requires a modern constitution that says what we are in terms the public cannot misunderstand.'

Yet his plan to challenge statism, place a line under party history and remove associations with 'Old' Labour got off to a bumpy start. Later the same week the Conference passed Composite 57, reaffirming support for the old Clause IV by 50.9 per cent to 49.1 per cent, signalling that change was no foregone conclusion. A 'New Clause IV Campaign', notionally based in South London but run from the Walworth Road headquarters, was established to support the leadership agenda. Its aim was to convince CLPs to ballot their membership on the revised wording to circumvent activist control of the process and undermine local mandates to preserve the status quo. Blair embarked on a nationwide tour making the case for change. The NEC agreed to encourage CLPs to ballot their membership; in the end a total of 441 CLPs agreed to follow their advice.

After much consultation and revision, the draft of the new Clause IV went to the NEC on 13 March 1995. In the final negotiations Blair had to reluctantly accept a number of changes including a key amendment reasserting collective action: 'by the strength of our common endeavour we achieve more than we achieve alone', moved to counterbalance an initial wording which for many was too enthusiastic in its embrace of a 'dynamic market economy'.[24] With backing from the soft left, the NEC agreed the new draft by 21 votes to 3 with 5 abstentions. Barbara Castle emerged as the most high-profile opponent of change, although this was not surprising given that she had been active in the Socialist League, was a leading Bevanite and had opposed Gaitskell's earlier attempt to revise Clause IV.[25] At the Special Conference on 29 April 1995 the change was backed by 65.23 per cent to 34.77 per cent. Thirty-six years after Gaitskell's failure, the new constitution was supported by 54.6 per cent of the union vote, despite opposition from both the TGWU and UNISON, and 90 per cent of the membership, in a Conference split 70:30 between the affiliates and members. Blair had successfully challenged Labour's tradition of statism.

Blair's next target was the tradition of labourism. The following April Blair pressed for another individual ballot of the membership, this time over the draft manifesto, although this second reform failed to repeat the spectacular success of the Clause IV process. Years earlier Blair had proposed the move in the Trade Union Review Group set up by John Smith where it was overwhelmingly rejected. On becoming leader, he returned to the issue in order to circumvent the role of both the activists and unions and build a direct relationship between himself and the mass membership. Aware that this could delegitimize their role in the policy process, the unions moved quickly to ensure their inclusion in it. The initiative then lost any real political salience, apart from revealing the desire of the leadership to maximize its control over policy.[26] After the draft was agreed by the 1996 Conference, it was ratified in the ballot by 95 per cent of the membership on a 61 per cent turnout and by 92.2 per cent of the union membership after a 24.2 per cent poll.

The third element of the strategy concerned a reduction in the unions' voice at the Conference. The Trade Union Review Group anticipated a phased reduction of the union vote down to a 50/50 split with the membership, to be phased in once the membership exceeded 300,000. By the end of 1994, it had reached 305,189 and by 1996 over 400,000. Following negotiations between Blair and the unions, it was agreed there would be an immediate move to a 50/50 split at the 1996 Conference, and individual delegate voting in the union section rather than the wielding of any single block vote, symbolically ending the practice. Despite Blair wanting to go further, the agreement stuck.

The final part of the strategy was arguably the most significant. It involved a series of moves designed to avoid the battles of the late 1970s with competing sites of power between the cabinet and NEC, and the spectacle of MPs, including cabinet members, challenging their own government within the institutions of the party. In January 1996, the NEC agreed four task forces under a 'Party into Power' project to revise the working relationships between the party and a future Labour government. The four groups covered the work of the NEC, links between the party and government, policy making and the operation of annual Conference.[27] The proposals included a revised Joint Policy Committee chaired by the Prime Minister to oversee a two-year 'rolling programme', an expanded 175-strong National Policy Forum, the overhaul of the Conference composite system, replaced by a system of contemporary resolutions and NPF papers, the removal of the NEC women's section, replaced by quotas, and a reduced NEC membership section of six seats with MPs prohibited from standing. On 30 July, the NEC backed the package by 19 votes to 1 and it was then agreed by the post-election 1997 Conference, overhauling the historic arrangements of the Conference, the regions and the party policy-making infrastructure.[28]

The party appeared to be going from strength to strength in the pre-election period. Between 1994 and 1997 membership increased by around 40 per cent (Appendix A), partly in response to the outpouring of grief following the death of John Smith and the extraordinary energy generated by the Blair leadership. In 1995 Labour unveiled a slick new Campaign Centre at Milbank Tower on the Thames close to Westminster, where staff were placed on an election footing and redesignated into twelve election task forces. In contrast to the growing professionalism of Labour's operation, the Conservative implosion continued with ongoing sleaze allegations, including 'cash for questions' in parliament, forcing Major to set up the Nolan Committee on Standards in Public Life. The charges of financial wrongdoing hung over the 1997 campaign after the independent journalist Martin Bell successfully challenged the sitting Conservative MP in Tatton, Neil Hamilton, over taking cash from Mohammed Al Fayed in return for parliamentary favours.

The government also appeared hopelessly divided over policy and direction, especially over the festering issue of Europe. Events cracked open in June 1995 when John Major sought to face down his critics and resigned the party leadership, challenging his critics to 'put up or shut up'. John Redwood took up the invitation and was soundly defeated, although his 89 votes revealed the size of the faction mobilized against the Prime Minister. Later in November the Referendum Party was launched by Sir James Goldsmith, escalating tensions across the right. The sense of imminent change and the momentum behind Blair was displayed through massive poll leads for Labour and securing the support of Rupert Murdoch's *The Sun* and *News of the World*.

Whilst Blair and New Labour maintained many of the policy priorities of the Kinnock and Smith eras, the public-facing strategy, especially over questions of economics, sought to offer reassurance and caution. Labour's pre-election policy agenda reinforced the supply-side economic reorientation on display since 1988 with a public acceptance of significant elements of the Thatcherite agenda. In a detailed insight into the thinking of the leadership in their book *The Blair Revolution*,[29] Peter Mandelson and Roger Liddle set out on page 1 that New Labour's strategy 'is to move forward from where Margaret Thatcher left off' and embrace an agenda they labelled 'One Nation Socialism', a phrase that would reappear years later under Ed Miliband. It advocated the by now familiar embrace of free markets alongside social justice and public and private sector partnerships. With an election approaching, Gordon Brown made clear he would not raise the basic or higher tax bands and VAT rates and would maintain the Conservative spending plans for the first two years of office, placing distance between New Labour and the 1992 Shadow Budget. Any spending commitments would be paid for by a one-off windfall tax on the privatized utilities, a popular measure given widespread disquiet about the actions of 'fat cat' bosses in those sectors. The famous election pledge card symbolized an agenda that offered limited commitments but plenty of economic reassurance.[30] The process culminated in the 1997 manifesto, *New Labour: Because Britain Deserves Better*, unveiled on 3 April 1997, literally signed by Blair; his personal contract with the British people. The one slight deviation to the overall direction of travel occurred in 1995 following the publication of Will Hutton's remarkably successful book *The State We're In*. In response, in early 1996, Blair looked to tentatively embrace a model of economic stakeholding but it was soon dropped. We return to this in the next chapter.

Given his predicament, John Major delayed calling the 1997 election until as late as possible, eventually announcing the inevitable on 17 March. Polling day on 1 May 1997 saw Labour gain 418 seats, up 147 compared to 1992, the Tories 165, down 171, and the Lib Dems 46, up 28. On a 71.3 per cent turnout Labour secured 43.2 per cent of the vote, the Tories 30.7 per cent, and the Lib Dems 16.8 per cent. The Labour majority was greater than Attlee's landslide of 1945, the number of Conservative MPs was the lowest recorded since 1906 and the Lib Dems' performance was comparatively the best third party outcome since 59 Liberals were returned in 1929. As dawn broke over the South Bank, Blair told a rapturous crowd that 'we ran for office as New Labour, and we shall govern as New Labour'.

In reality, New Labour was the fortunate depository of a decade-long process of party revisionism that had re-engineered a new supply-side economic framework and, as a consequence of the Kinnock and Smith years, embraced a radical agenda to enshrine into law the next phases of Labour's decades-long commitment to expand equalities legislation and introduce new innovative constitutional reforms. Moreover, Blair and Smith had both sought to rehabilitate Labour's spiritual and ethical traditions. The stage was set to see how these traditions might combine in government and reveal the true nature of the New Labour project.

Landslides
(1997–2010)

Tony Blair would become Labour's longest serving Prime Minister, the only one to achieve three consecutive victories and the first to win an election since Wilson in 1974.

The creation of New Labour in 1994 was in part a response to the successful 1992 presidential campaign of Bill Clinton who presented himself as a New Democrat. It can also be seen as a response to the emergence of the New Right and its embrace of neo-classical economics. The Thatcher revolution demonstrated the political potency of newness and ideological reformation, yet also offered an opening for Labour as it failed to recognize the 'socially embedded nature of our being' and our mutual independence; space which Blair would successfully occupy by excavating party history.[1]

This push of the new and pull of the old ensured that New Labour always contained a paradoxical quality. Many, and not just on the left, regularly suggest New Labour was antithetical to the party's history and traditions. Much of the New Labour rhetoric supports such an interpretation, given the way it regularly counterposed its liberal modernity with a stale, conservative party history.[2] Yet Blair regularly justified its creation by seeking to embed the project within Labour history and by reclaiming neglected socialist traditions.[3] Modernization therefore implied a retrieval rather than simple rejection of Labour's historical purpose. Specifically, it consciously sought to embrace early ethical and liberal socialist traditions to supplant later statist ones. By separating political means from ends, the role of nationalization was thereby replaced with an emphasis on social justice and personal liberty.

New Labour's antecedents were not just within nineteenth-century socialism and Edwardian New Liberalism, however. They also included post-war revisionism, with its emphasis on consumer choice and human freedom, and the modernization of the Kinnock and Smith eras discussed in the previous chapter. Despite Blair's emphasis on a political rupture and a break with the past, the idea of modernization was hardly new. Years earlier, when Shadow Home Secretary, Blair had himself set out 'why modernization matters'.[4] He argued economic and social upheaval meant Labour had to re-establish the virtues of community and personal responsibility. Whilst modernization would become the hallmark of the New Labour era, in reality it had been used to shape the Policy Review and direction of the leadership since the 1987 defeat. In turn the intellectual foundations erected by Kinnock, Hattersley and Smith, to reconcile the modern party with its liberal heritage, were major concerns within various strands of post-war revisionism.

Other signature New Labour themes were drawn from party history. Blair's embrace of a 'Third Way' between socialism and capitalism had echoes of the 'middle way' advanced by the Commission on Social Justice under John Smith.[5] Going further back, the 'Third Way' was used by Allan Flanders and those around *Socialist Commentary* in the late 1940s.[6]

So, what did set the agenda of Blair and New Labour apart from what went before? Arguably until 1994 Labour had yet to find a 'governing formula'[7] of social and economic reform that retained voter trust and could answer the *death question* – the sense that its forward march was over; that its key class constituencies were on the wrong side of history. As we discussed in the previous chapter, after 1987, reform was uneven and precarious, its leaders appeared hesitant and at times unconvincing; reform tended to present as a series of discrete moves lacking any confident overarching worldview. Blair provided the political intensity and clarity required for disparate elements to cohere. But more than that, for the first time since Attlee, Labour under Blair successfully welded together key elements drawn from the liberal, ethical and utilitarian heritage shaping the party's history. At its best New Labour was an extraordinarily rich, elegant composite of the three philosophical traditions regarding questions of justice.

Yet two key questions related to history and justice emerged from the New Labour composition. The historical question is part of left mythology and centres around whether New Labour was drawn from Labour's past or antithetical to the party's history. Was New Labour a reclamation project or built on political rupture and a rejection of party history? How this was answered would inform factional rivalries for years to come. The justice question centres around which of the three traditions distilled into New Labour would come to dominate as the government evolved. The answer to this helps account for the limitations and missed opportunities of the New Labour era and how the project truncated and diminished over time.

Tony Blair
Source: Pavel Golovkin, European Union, 2010.

Arguably Blair's unique contribution, the ingredient that pulled together the various tributaries shaping Labour's reformation, was in weaving them into a story of national and spiritual renewal, thereby creating New Labour's emotional potency.[8] Yet Blair's brilliant oratory and unique theatrical gifts would come with a downside. The rhetorical heights he reached when evangelizing a 'New Britain' would feed into disappointment, anger and rejection when the promised renewal failed to materialize, especially given the loss of trust and moral purpose following the invasion of Iraq. Blair's governments would be judged against their own proclamations of national reformation rather than more mundane criteria of incremental change and service delivery, where the record of the government was substantial.

The New Labour Triptych

Through the blending of competing approaches to justice, New Labour erected a brilliant three-part political composition. A merger of traditions helps account for its range and power but also subsequent decline and diminishment. Through an astute reading of Labour history, Blair rehabilitated early ethical concerns along with the spirit of New Liberalism to anticipate the renewal of a nation. This was underpinned by years of economic growth, the type denied to any of his predecessors, to help deliver the utilitarian priorities of many of his colleagues. This positive sum environment was aided by the dire state of New Labour's political opponents. Yet over time the project lost moral clarity, liberal direction and the growth that helped engineer it, the same forces that had brought energy, vitality and the capacity for material change.

The central panel of the triptych was Blair's embrace of ethics and morality, unfashionable terrain for much of the left. The modern liberal social contract theory of John Rawls, the type that had such a profound effect on Crosland, Hattersley, and shades of progressive revisionism, had helped re-establish for the left the notion of liberty, yet it was not an approach uncritically embraced by all progressives. It recoiled from moral questions because of an insistence on liberal neutrality on what constitutes the good life. It was built around the idea of the unencumbered self, detached from families, localities and communities, and from shared traditions, interests and faiths. It remained too legalistic, remote and individualistic. In the 1980s, Rawls's approach was challenged by more 'communitarian' thinkers such as Michael Sandel, Alasdair MacIntye, Michael Waltzer and Charles Taylor, writers concerned with civic, national and spiritual renewal; with ethics, human flourishing and concern for what constitutes the good, rather than the simple provision of rights.[9] This philosophical turn suited Blair who, as both a student and MP, had been inspired by similar philosophical, spiritual and political concerns. Through an adherence to philosophers such as John Macmurray,[10] he had sought to build a political appreciation of the common good and personal and mutual flourishing. The consistent theme in Macmurray's work was the task of building community through an appreciation of our mutual dependency, in contrast to the neo-classical identification of solitary economic agents or indeed the abstractions of Blair's later cosmopolitanism. Macmurray's work retains similarities with the approach known as personalism. Moreover, he positively engaged with the 'early' Marx and humanist traditions that inspired the First New Left. These concerns were apparent in Blair's 6 July 1983 maiden speech to parliament where he argued that 'British democracy rests ultimately on the shared perception in the benefits of the common weal', a conscious reference to William Morris. A distinct ethical approach was ever present before becoming Prime Minister.

Blair's speeches often retained the moral cadence of the nineteenth-century religion of socialism. On accepting the party leadership he said his was a 'mission to lift the spirit of the nation ... a country where we say, we are part of a community of people – we do owe a duty to more than ourselves ... a country where there is no corner where we shield our eyes in shame ... the power of all for the good of each ... that is what socialism means to me'. His early speeches often resembled parables. In 1994 he argued for 'a new spirit in the nation based on working together, unity, solidarity, partnership. This is the patriotism of the future. Where you child in distress is my child, your parent ill and in pain is my parent, your friend unemployed or homeless is my friend; your neighbour my neighbour. This is the true patriotism of a nation'. In 1995, as leader, Blair echoed Tawney when suggesting 'socialists have to be both moralists and empiricists'. In the 1996 *Why I am a Christian*, Blair disowned utilitarianism and demanded a return to the ethical traditions within party history. Earlier in 1995, he was embracing the 'moral reformers' of Tawney and Morris, Cobbett and Owen.

Blair's embrace of sociologists such as Amitai Etzioni and Robert Putnam reflected a communitarian, or associational, turn within political philosophy and a reaction to Rawls's focus on liberal rights, but also long-standing personal concerns. Such thinking informed key elements of the New Labour agenda in government, including confronting poverty pay, strengthening communities, literacy and numeracy challenges, citizenship, crime and anti-social behaviour, welfare reform, public health and the roll-out of the Sure Start early years programme. It stretched as far as Blair's ethical foreign policy, culminating in his 'Chicago' speech, making the case for a 'doctrine of the international community' on 22 April 1999, a month into the Kosovo War, which detailed the circumstances that warrant the international community intervening in the affairs of other nations.[11]

This policy agenda was influenced not just by US sociologists, however. It also drew on neglected strains of post-war revisionist thinking discussed in chapter 6, including the work of John Bowlby, the pioneer of human attachment theory, pre-war colleague of Evan Durbin and an influential figure in the career of Michael Young. Bowlby's work at the Tavistock centred on the experiences of loss and suffering experienced by juveniles. In March 1996, many key New Labour personalities – Blair, Mo Mowlem and Tessa Jowell included – assembled at the institute for a conference entitled 'The Politics of Attachment'. The early Sure Start centres sought to ground public policy within some of Bowlby's basic insights regarding fraternity, association and civic renewal; ideas that resolve anxiety and the discharge of political rage in relation to childhood through patterns of care, family support, friendship and befriending within communities. The influence of post-war industrial pluralism and revisionists such as Allan Flanders and Hugh Clegg was also detectable in the early labour market policies of the New Labour era including the architecture of, and appointments to, the Low Pay Commission, the trade union recognition legislation and 'family friendly' employment rights.

A second panel of the New Labour triptych was supplied by a return to the New Liberalism of the Edwardian era. In 1995 Blair gave a speech to the Fabian Society to mark the fiftieth anniversary of the 1945 victory,[12] in which he embedded New Labour within the work of J.A. Hobson and L.T. Hobhouse, pioneers of 'liberal socialism', idealists making the case for positive freedom through collective action; advocates of an early 'third way' mutualism resting between classical or old liberalism and state socialism. Blair emphasized how the common good is nurtured by individuals having sufficient freedom to realize their full potentials whilst embedded in their community. Liberty was a necessity of any true society but not gained at the expense of others or the product of atomized exchange. It could be compromised by the coercive power of the state. As such, neo-classical economics was incomplete; it required a deeper understanding of the moral obligation of both the individual and state to cultivate true freedom. Blair argued that his agenda for rights and responsibilities tied in with the mutualism of the New Liberals. In contrast to nineteenth-century socialist ideas of the 'moral economy', both assumed capitalism to be sufficiently creative to deliver such social reforms and provide genuine freedoms; although once in office, the tensions between mutualism and capitalism were resolved by Blair in favour of the latter, for example over demutualization of parts of the banking system.

The purpose behind Blair's embrace was to reunite liberal and socialist traditions, a modern 'LibLabism' that had resulted in Labour's first MPs in 1906 and the common campaigns of 1910. In so doing he stood against the early social evolutionists in Labour such as MacDonald who considered socialism as the logical and superior descendent of liberalism. For Blair, the objective was a new Progressive Alliance to avoid a repeat of the Conservative domination of the twentieth century.[13] Despite the lofty intellectual ambitions to rebuild liberal socialism, Blair's motives at root were born of calculation, to build an anti-Conservative coalition to win and retain power. In 1983, the Alliance had secured 25.4 per cent of the vote with Labour on 27.6 per cent. The 1992 defeat meant many modernizers remained fearful Labour might never again secure an outright victory. Blair had begun to meet privately with Alliance leader Paddy Ashdown to explore the future reconstruction of the left. Once leader he privately stated to Ashdown that his 'preferred option' was to include LibDem representatives in his government.[14]

The landslide of 1997 removed the electoral imperative behind such changes; proposals that were never popular with figures such as John Prescott, Brown and Jack Straw. Yet Blair offered Ashdown membership of a Joint Cabinet Committee (JCC) to consider constitutional change, chaired by Blair himself with equal representation from the two parties. Moreover, in December 1997, Blair established the Jenkins Committee to recommend alternatives to the voting system, which in October 1998 proposed 'AV plus'. Yet the momentum behind reform ebbed away, and in January 1999 Ashdown stood down as LibDem leader and the JCC was eventually suspended in September 2001. By then the government had also introduced a proportional system for the 1999 European elections, and an element in the systems for the devolved administrations in Scotland, Wales and London.

The strong liberal left influences within New Labour were in part historical and part tactical but also reflected the growing influence of a vaguely defined European Social Model, especially since Jacques Delors visited the TUC in 1988. It was part of a wider embrace of more legalistic and international approaches to justice across the left, one that echoed the long-standing concerns of Roy Jenkins and other members of the 'Gang of Four'. It also spoke to some of the themes developed by sociologists central to developing the 'Third Way'.[15]

In February 1998, the sociologist Ulrich Beck published the 'Cosmopolitan Manifesto'.[16] He suggested the basis for a new 'world citizenship' and 'ethical globalization' with two key stages in this entrenched modernity: the first, the legacy of freedom captured through various civil rights struggles; the second, brought on by our modern dissolved attachments where 'community, group and identity structure have lost their ontological cement'. Old progressive values had been replaced by a radical individualism especially amongst the well-educated and the young, expressed through emerging global 'cosmopolitan parties'. These parties reflect three broad political movements within and between nation states: first, a modern appeal to transcendent human values that appear in every culture and religion – 'liberty, diversity, toleration!'; second, an emphasis on global political action over local or national interventions; and third, attempts to democratize transnational regimes and regulators.

These different and at times competing liberal influences were on display in the early phase of New Labour. The government sought to establish a constitutionally grounded modern national identity expressed in an embrace of a human rights agenda traced back to the end of the Second World War and a wider internationalism in policies such as the establishment of a dedicated department for international development. It erected a substantial package of constitutional reforms, human rights initiatives and anti-discrimination programmes culminating in the 2010 Equality Act, which pulled together the liberal enactments of successive Labour governments of over 50 years.

The third panel of the New Labour composition, its utilitarianism, was reliant on the 'long boom' of the 1990s and early 2000s. New Labour was the political beneficiary of a combination of global forces that included the post-Cold War entry of the former Eastern bloc into a burgeoning global market and Chinese market reforms, a global supply of cheap labour and the onset of financialization, credit liberalization and rising asset values. The positive-sum domestic environment fuelled by this global boom financed the distributional priorities of the Treasury under Gordon Brown.

Brown's political career can be divided into four phases. An initial radical phase where he embraced ethical ideas of the moral economy and a rejection of capitalism, very much aligned with the concerns of the early ILP and Labour pioneers. His writings from the time were infused with the spirit of Hardie, Wheatley and Maxton, of whom he wrote a biography based on his PhD research. In his introduction to the Red Paper on Scotland, entitled 'The Socialist Challenge', Brown's politics are democratic, radical, even revolutionary, and willing to confront the failures of successive Labour governments.[17] Later came a second phase on entering parliament, where his politics appear more Wilsonian with an embrace of technological modernization and advocacy of a more technocratic supply-side socialism, best represented in his 1989 book *Where There is Greed*.[18] As Shadow Chancellor, this period included an early dalliance with economic stakeholding. In 1995, in the wake of Will Hutton's surprise best seller *The State We're in*, Gordon Brown, along with Tony Wright, advocated a 'stakeholder economy' over 'footloose capitalism'.[19] It was later picked up by Tony Blair who, on 7 January 1996 in Singapore, advocated a stakeholder economy where 'no group or class is set apart'. In the six months between the Singapore speech and draft manifesto *New Labour, New Life for Britain*, the stakeholder model disappeared as it was deemed to be too corporatist and a throwback to the post-war social democracy voters had already rejected. It would prove to be a major turning point in the evolution of New Labour given the agenda's implications for constitutional and corporate governance and the regulation of the economy. It amounted to New Labour's economic path not travelled.

A major missed opportunity was the 1998 Company Law review and subsequent 2001 White Paper, which eventually led to the 2006 Companies Act, which stated directors should 'have regard to' other stakeholders, yet retained the underlying supremacy of shareholder interests. Reporting requirements on companies to make clear how they served non-shareholder interests had been dropped in 2005.

The rejection of stakeholding marked the beginning of the third phase of Brown's intellectual journey, with his wholesale embrace of the market and classical liberal economic ideas advanced since the Enlightenment.[20] The influence of Hardie, Wheately and Maxon was by the late 1990s replaced with those of Adam Smith, David Hume and Francis Hutcheson. Brown re-emerged as a powerful advocate of the city, the market, light-touch regulation; of globalization and trade liberalization. In part this can be accounted for by his engagement with American policy experts, notably economists such as Larry Summers. Many would argue that this intellectual turn amounts to a rejection of Labour's political economy. Yet Brown's strategy was a familiar one within party history; he was taking the inevitability of gradualism to its logical conclusion, with socialist change engineered from capitalist growth. The final, fourth phase was when Brown sought reinvention as Prime Minister and saw him transition from questions of economic utility towards a renewed focus on rights and liberty. In this final phase Brown emerged as the advocate of a new constitutional settlement, of devolution, and a new progressive agenda – the born-again republican.

Whilst Blair was making the ethical case for change, Brown was gravitating towards a Fabian statecraft of micro management plus central prescription, a benign focus on globalization and light-touch regulation, macroeconomic stability and fiscal prudence. Within the Treasury, and anticipated by Bill Clinton's New Democrat policies, there was a working assumption that declining real wages across the West would be one of the immediate effects of globalization and heightened international competition. Whilst the political and economic outlook remained mainstream utilitarian Labour, concerned to bolster working-class disposable incomes, the means to do so diverged. No longer was this to be pursued by the traditional methods of the post-war welfare state, but through new tax credits funded by a growth engineered through an alliance with finance capital. Policy focus was consciously directed towards remedial cash transfers to alleviate the declining living standards of the working class, especially its young families and older pensioners. This redistribution worked in tandem with a refinancing of public service safety nets, achieved through asserting an 'end to boom and bust' and henceforth sharing the proceeds of growth secured by a lightly regulated compact with the city. It can be seen as a long-standing Labour approach to growth and socialism but one adapted to the economic specifics of 1990s capitalism. The big question about New Labour's economics was whether such a model, built around private debt and an over-reliance on poorly regulated financial markets, was sustainable. Advocates argue it helped secure sixty quarters of economic growth and three massive majorities in 1997, 2001 and 2005. Yet as was often the case throughout Labour history, when the growth stopped the party would struggle to define an economic agenda beyond the embrace of austerity and latent party tensions would quickly resurface.

New Labour: From Boom to Bust

1997–2001: Radicalism

In the years following the 1997 election, the three strands of justice that have shaped Labour's history successfully came together. The New Labour triptych remained resolute and delivered a very successful first term in power. Blair became the century's youngest Prime Minister on taking office on 2 May 1997. He would hold the position until his resignation on 27 June 2007. His extraordinary presentational gifts were once again on display on 31 August 1997 following the death of Princess Diana. During his first term in office Blair, and as a consequence Labour, appeared to have achieved the position of the 'political arm of the people', a status that would have been warmly welcomed by Ramsay MacDonald.[21]

The incoming government was committed to a very limited number of specific policy positions, yet expectations were excessively high given the powerful rhetoric of national renewal that propelled New Labour to power. There were few surprises in Blair's first cabinet with Brown going to the Treasury, Robin Cook becoming Foreign Secretary, Blunkett overseeing education, Frank Dobson at health, Straw the new Home Secretary and Prescott in charge of a vast department covering environment, transport and the regions. Five women were given cabinet positions, drawn from the 101 female Labour MPs. From the outset the operation was highly centralized. Peter Mandelson was appointed Minister Without Portfolio to co-ordinate the various government departments. Alastair Campbell established a Strategic Communications

Unit, a central body whose role was to co-ordinate the party's media relations and ensure a unified press image. Jonathan Powell as Chief of Staff oversaw civil service relations.

The most significant reforms of the first term were constitutional, reflecting the liberal character of the government, although many at the time did not regard Blair as being particularly committed to the agenda, much of which he accepted as part of John Smith's legacy. On 11 September 1997 a clear majority of Scottish residents voted in favour of their own parliament, followed a week later by Welsh voters, albeit by a much narrower margin. Legislation forming the Scottish Parliament and Welsh Assembly quickly followed, with the first elections held in 1999. The Greater London Authority and the position of Mayor of London were established in 2000 and Regional Development Agencies were set up in the English regions.[22] An IRA ceasefire was unveiled in July 1997, after which Blair met Gerry Adams in October. In 1998, the Good Friday Agreement created a 108-member power-sharing Northern Ireland Assembly.

In 1998, after 700 years, the right of hereditary peers to sit in the House of Lords was largely abolished.[23] A Freedom of Information bill was introduced in May 1999, although the proposed legislation backtracked on earlier commitments.[24] The Human Rights Act was given the royal assent on 9 November 1998. Other reforms included the introduction of a Supreme Court and Electoral Commission. The age of consent was equalized at 16, the ban on homosexuals in the armed forces was lifted and Labour made its first unsuccessful attempt to repeal the notorious Section 28 ban on the promotion of homosexuality. These liberal reforms were reminiscent of the achievements of the Wilson government in the 1960s.

In terms of the economy, the government gave the Bank of England powers to set interest rates. Brown's first budget in July 1997 saw cuts in corporation tax and VAT on fuel and the introduction of the promised windfall tax on privatized utilities to finance the new welfare to work programme. Economic stability underscored the activities of the government whilst the creative use of the Private Finance Initiative and Public Private Partnerships built new infrastructure without excessive borrowing or taxation, allowing the government to maintain the Conservative spending plans. Throughout, Brown's 'Golden Rule', that over the cycle the government would borrow only to invest rather than fund current spending, helped reassure sceptics of his and Labour's fiscal 'prudence'.[25]

Other substantial interventions included the June 1997 signing of the European Social Chapter, a national minimum wage of £3.60 per hour for those over 21 and £3 for 18–21-year-olds, new union recognition procedures, and a New Deal for the young unemployed. The March 1998 budget introduced a Working Family Tax Credit. That same year Anti-Social Behaviours Orders (ASBOs) were first introduced. Public expenditure on education, health and social security rose rapidly, with substantial increases in pensions and child benefits.[26] On 18 March 1999, Blair unveiled an imaginative 20-year programme to end child poverty.

On foreign policy, the creation of the Department for International Development shifted global development policy away from the Foreign Office to an independent ministry with a cabinet-level minister. On Europe, in October 1997, Brown said the government favoured entry into monetary union but not in the first term and only after a referendum. In December 1998, the euro was launched without the participation of the UK. In 1999, Blair became a major advocate for a ground offensive in Kosovo following the failure of airstrikes to constrain Slobodan Milošević. It proved successful as did a limited intervention against rebel forces in Sierra Leone the following year. British forces were also involved in a four-day bombing campaign in Iraq led by the US in December 1998. Including later invasions in Afghanistan and Iraq, in total between 1997 and 2003, Blair ordered British troops into combat on five separate occasions.

Throughout Labour's first term the government appeared united and resilient. In contrast, their Conservative opponents struggled under their own young leader William Hague. The Labour leadership faced only limited internal difficulties. Cuts in Lone Parent Benefit saw a rebellion of 47 Labour MPs and 14 abstentions in December 1997. Apart from one defeat in 2000 over pensions, there was little conflict within the party's new policy making and Conference procedures. In general, the unions remained content, and a force for internal stability. There were ongoing tensions with certain leaders within the devolved institutions, noticeably Rhodri Morgan in Wales and Ken Livingstone in London, the latter elected as an independent before being later readmitted back into the party. In 1998, four 'Grassroots Alliance' candidates were elected onto the NEC CLP section. Significantly, given his modernizing and Rawlsian agenda, Roy Hattersley emerged as the most thoughtful of the government's critics, taking the government to task on grounds of both freedom and equality. The most challenging opposition came with the September 2000 fuel protests. The most difficult ethical challenges concerned suggestions of sleaze, specifically over a £1 million donation by the head of Formula One Bernie Ecclestone and ties to tobacco advertising and the December 1998 resignation of Mandelson over home load declarations. Mandelson would return in October 1999 but be gone once more in January 2001 over another donations row linked to passport applications by the wealthy Hinduja brothers. Later, in 2004, he was appointed an EU Commissioner.

With Labour looking unassailable it was no surprise that Blair decided to go early and seek to renew his mandate. Polling was set for 3 May 2001 but delayed until 7 June following an outbreak of foot and mouth disease. On polling day Labour took 412 seats, a fall of 6, the Tories 166, up 1, and the Lib Dems 52, up 6. Labour's share fell from 43.2 to 40.7 per cent on a noticeably low turnout of 59.4 per cent. The new majority now stood at 166 seats after a second stunning New Labour landslide.

2001–2005: Turbulence

Tony Blair became the first Labour Prime Minister to win a full second term. On 3 August 2003, he became the longest continuously serving Labour Prime Minister, surpassing Attlee. On 5 February 2005, he became the longest-serving Labour Prime Minister, surpassing Wilson. Blair swiftly embarked on significant changes in personnel. Cook was demoted to the Leader of the House and replaced by Straw. Chris Smith and Ann Taylor were dropped. Prescott lost his super department and was sent to the Cabinet Office. Blunkett replaced Straw at the Home Office whilst Tessa Jowell, Patricia Hewitt, Hilary Armstrong and Estelle Morris were all promoted to the cabinet.

The government focus was henceforth to be on public service delivery. This would become the key internal battleground throughout the second term. This was not a strict left/right debate, however, but between centralizers and those who favoured more devolution. It also reflected divisions between utilitarian and ethical traditions. The former, centralizing tendency argued that Labour should do whatever was necessary to ensure public satisfaction with public services including use of the private sector, the latter insisting on support for the public realm and ethical resistance to the role of the market in the interests of equality and citizenship rights. Yet three months into his second term, the September 11 attacks reshaped Blair's priorities with the onset of the 'war on terror' and the invasions of Afghanistan and Iraq; events that would redefine the Blair years and for many forever undermine his other extraordinary achievements.

Blair was proactive in helping build the international coalition to overthrow the Taliban and in November 2001 Kabul was taken by the invading forces. On the question of Iraq, he drew on the themes of his Chicago speech and his personal, deeply held belief in the moral case for liberal interventionism and just wars.[27] His early successes in Kosovo and Sierra Leone, both without the authority of the UN, and the triumph of the Good Friday Agreement undoubtedly brought a heightened self-confidence to his foreign policy interventions. Like Bevin in the post-war period, a fear of US isolationism and unilateral action in an uncertain post-Cold War era informed Blair's need for proximity and active dialogue with the US. He was also convinced of his gifts of communication and persuasion, and personal capacity to influence the Bush administration over the direction of US policy.

The government's case for war rested on Iraq's alleged possession of weapons of mass destruction (WMD) and violation of UN Resolutions. On 24 September 2002, the government published a dossier based on the intelligence agencies' assessments of Iraq's WMD, which reported recent intelligence that 'the Iraqi military are able to deploy chemical or biological weapons within 45 minutes of an order to do so'. A further briefing on Iraq's alleged WMDs was issued to journalists in February 2003. This document was discovered to have taken text without attribution from a PhD thesis widely available on the internet. It subsequently became known as the 'dodgy dossier'. On 15 February 2003, a million people demonstrated against the war. Robin Cook resigned on 17 March 2003, Clare Short eventually followed. A total of 139 Labour MPs voted against the war on 18 March.

A year after the 2002 dossier, the weapons expert Dr David Kelly was revealed as a source behind claims that Downing Street, and in particular Alastair Campbell, had intervened and 'sexed up' the document to make it more exciting. On 18 July, Kelly was found dead having taken his own life, after which Blair set up a judicial inquiry under Lord Hutton. His 28 January 2004 report cleared the government of any wrongdoing and of deliberately inserting false intelligence into the September dossier. A month later, Blair set up the Butler Review into the accuracy and presentation of the intelligence relating to Iraq's alleged WMD. In July 2004, Butler concluded the key intelligence used to justify the war had been unreliable and that Blair honestly stated what he believed to be true at the time, though implied the government's presentation of the intelligence had been exaggerated.

Blair's popularity collapsed. From once having received the highest recorded approval ratings of any Prime Minister, the onset of the Iraq War and the carnage that followed saw him record some of the lowest.[28]

On the home front, after the election the Prime Minister's Delivery Unit was set up to monitor and accelerate public service reform, specifically over education and skills, health, transport and the Home Office. In April 2002, in his sixth budget, Brown announced a 1 per cent increase in National Insurance to specifically finance a £6.1 billion increase in health spending following the publication of the Wanless Review of NHS finances. The reform agenda saw the introduction of the Foundation Hospital scheme, which allowed NHS hospitals financial autonomy, leading to escalating tensions with Brown, alongside widespread use of the private sector to reduce waiting times. Overall maximum waits for planned NHS operations tumbled from some 18 months to 18 weeks, and public satisfaction with the NHS almost doubled. Education brought the biggest test of Blair's domestic authority in January 2004 when the government scraped home by five votes over the second reading vote on controversial plans to introduce university top-up fees of £3,000 a year.

At the Home Office, immigration policy continued to be driven by both the needs of the economy and demand for labour and the liberal and cosmopolitan approach of many of the party's key figures. Under New Labour net migration quadrupled, averaging 200,000 a year. The primary purpose rule was relaxed as were work permit qualifications. In

2004, 'transitional controls' over new European accession state migration were rejected, with the government estimating relatively small amounts of net migration per year of between 5,000 and 13,000. In the event the actual figures estimated by the Office for National Statistics were up to ten times higher between 2004 and 2012. Whilst the government banked the macroeconomic utility of migration in terms of constraining inflationary pressures and enhancing labour market flexibility, the political salience of the issue rose sharply.

Throughout the spring and summer of 2001, riots broke out in parts of Bradford, Oldham and Burnley. The 11 September attacks soon followed and the climate of fear and cultural suspicion intensified, inflamed by an emboldened British National Party under Nick Griffin. The political and media climate changed and became less tolerant. In response, the language deployed within the Home Office in dealing with asylum and immigration issues shifted. The political significance of the issues ratcheted up, becoming key concerns for many Labour voters in areas disproportionately taking the numerical strain, yet often lying outside the key political battlegrounds of middle England. These tensions would infect Labour politics for the next two decades.

2003 was a very difficult year for Blair given the events in Iraq plus personal and health-related issues. He would also disappoint many of his closest supporters over Europe. In June 2003, Brown announced that of his five tests regarding entry into the euro, only one had been met, effectively parking the issue indefinitely. In April 2004, Blair announced that a referendum would be held on the ratification of the EU Constitution. After the French and Dutch rejected the constitution, the plans were suspended and the Parliamentary Bill to enact a referendum was suspended indefinitely. In September Labour lost the safe seat of Brent East and the following July the traditional seat of Leicester South, both to the LibDems campaigning strongly on opposition to Iraq and Labour's top-up fee proposals. Yet Michael Howard, the new Conservative leader who had replaced Hague's successor Iain Duncan Smith in late 2003, was unable to take advantage. By late summer 2004, Blair's fortunes looked to be slowly improving after the July publication of the Butler Review and party unity being maintained by a successful NPF meeting at Warwick University and with Labour still ahead in the polls. On 30 September 2004 after the Party Conference, Blair signalled the coming election would be his last. He announced he would serve a 'full third term' but would not contest a fourth election and give 'ample time' for his successor to establish him- or herself.

Despite escalating tensions between Blair and Brown throughout the second term and the co-opting of Alan Milburn to oversee election strategy, a truce was brokered to help secure a third victory with Brown pulled back into the core campaign strategy team. Blair's electoral 'masochism strategy' of not hiding from the difficulties of the previous four years proved electorally adroit. On 5 May 2005, Labour suffered a net loss of 57 seats, the Tories a gain of 32 and the Lib Dems 10.[29] Labour lost the popular vote in England and was therefore increasingly dependent on its Scottish seats, a sign of the trouble that lay ahead. Although with Labour on 355, the Tories 198 and Lib Dems on 62, Blair had delivered a third substantial majority of 65 seats. After eight years in power and the profound difficulties of the second term and lingering disquiet over the Iraq War, it amounted to an extraordinary result.

2005–2007: Trauma

Many in Labour considered the 2005 result a disappointment, however. Throughout his last years in office Blair would be faced with ongoing disquiet within the PLP and repeated questions over the timing of his resignation and a likely Brown succession. To add to his difficulties, on 6 December 2005 the Tories elected David Cameron, a dynamic 39-year-old communicator as their new leader, who would prove to be an increasingly able combatant. Just like in 2001, Blair recommitted to public services reform. Just like in 2001, unanticipated events quickly reshaped his immediate priorities. On Thursday 7 July 2005, four suicide bomb explosions struck London's public transport system during the morning rush hour. Fifty-six people were killed and 700 injured. Two weeks later, on 21 July 2005, a second series of bombings was reported leading to four controlled explosions. In the short term, Blair's handling of the crisis boosted his popularity. The legislation that followed proved to be highly controversial, however, and damaging to the government's liberal reputation. Six days after the attack Blair announced new anti-terror laws including against those 'glorifying' terrorism, which ran into trouble in both the Lords and Commons. In November 2005, the proposal to allow terrorist suspects to be held for questioning for up to 90 days was defeated by 31 votes, with 49 Labour MPs rebelling. It was Blair's first defeat on the floor of the House of Commons as Prime Minister.

Trouble mounted over education reforms, which restricted the involvement of Local Education Authorities in opening new schools, leading to a rebellion of 52 Labour MPs on 15 March 2006. Blair's difficulties mounted amid speculation over secret 'cash for honours' arrangements to boost party finances to offset a dramatic collapse in party membership throughout the second term (see Appendix A).[30] A covert system of financial loans was revealed, avoiding Labour's own regulation of political donations. With suggestions that the loans were unlikely to be repaid and allegations they were linked to places in the Lords, a police investigation followed. Blair was eventually interviewed by the police in December 2006 and a second time on 26 January 2007 after the arrest of one of his Downing Street officials.

During a stay in Barbados in August 2006, Blair faced mounting PLP pressure after refusing to endorse calls for a ceasefire in Lebanon. On his return to the UK, he showed little sign of stepping down any time soon despite growing calls for him to go. On 5 September a letter signed by 17 junior ministers and MPs demanded his resignation. Seven of the signatories then resigned from the government. On 7 September, Blair announced that the coming Party Conference would be his last as leader and the growing rebellion was called off. On 2 May 2007, on the tenth anniversary of the 1997 victory, Blair announced that he would be stepping down in a matter of weeks. On 10 May 2007, one week after defeat to the SNP in elections to the Scottish Parliament and major losses in the English local elections, Blair revealed that he would step down as Prime Minister on 27 June 2007.

2007–2010: Descent

Brown launched his leadership bid on 11 May 2007. From the left, both John McDonnell and Michael Meacher stated their intention to stand. As the only candidate that cleared the nomination threshold of 12.5 per cent of the PLP, Brown was elected leader. The result was formally declared on 24 June at a Special Conference in the Manchester

Conference Centre with Harriet Harman elected as his deputy. In his acceptance speech Brown sought reinvention and a breach with the New Labour years, stating a desire to build 'a new government with new priorities to meet the new challenges ahead'; he would build a new 'progressive consensus', implying the Blair era was over.[31] Blair resigned three days later and immediately stood down as an MP. For Brown, the man who helped deliver the growth that powered the Blair governments, the next three years would be painful. On ascending to the highest office, he was almost immediately forced to navigate a terrible economic and social reckoning as the 'long boom' went bust.

Before the fragility of the economy was fully revealed, the early months in office were good ones for Brown. He assembled a competent top team. Alistair Darling was sent to the Treasury, David Miliband to the Foreign Office and Jacqui Smith became Home Secretary. He pulled in outside experts without any necessary loyalty to the Labour Party

Gordon Brown
Source: HM Government, The National Archives.

to fulfil a desire to create 'a government of all the talents', including figures such as Digby Jones from the CBI. A series of early crises were managed effectively, including terrorist attacks in London and Glasgow and flooding outbreaks. By August the polls showed double-digit Labour leads, dubbed a 'Brown Bounce'. Plans for a quick general election were widely publicized, although never officially announced, with 1 November the preferred date.

The speculation was allowed to run throughout the 2007 Party Conference season. Labour's plans for tax reform were dramatically outtrumped at the Conservative Conference by a George Osborne pledge to raise inheritance tax thresholds to £1 million. Overnight, the polls looked to have significantly tightened in the key marginal seats. It all culminated on 7 October with Brown having to confirm he had scrapped any plans to go to the country. The 'election that never was' proved to be a watershed moment with echoes of Callaghan and Foot's 1978 decision to play long. The humiliation and backtracking would hang over the Brown government as the political tables turned and Labour's polling advantage vanished. Meanwhile a sub-prime mortgage crisis as a result of the collapse of the US housing market was preparing to detonate the economy.

2008 saw the first run on a domestic bank for 129 years. On 18 February 2008, Darling announced the nationalization of Northern Rock. Wall Street experienced its worst ever week. 'Black Friday', 10 October, saw a global bank run and credit freeze. Vulnerable banks such as HBOS and Royal Bank of Scotland faced collapse. Over that weekend Brown and Darling brokered a £37 billion bank bailout. Months later, prior to a successful 2009 G20 London Summit, Brown travelled widely to negotiate a $1 trillion stimulus to avert further disaster. Despite his extraordinary leadership role in pulling together the international response, the highpoint in his tenure at 10 Downing Street, the economy fell off a cliff. Recession fed surging unemployment, massive borrowing and subsequent austerity. The disaster was particularly uncomfortable for Brown, who, since 1997, had been responsible for the light-touch regulatory framework underpinning the crumbling debt regime.

The tragedy for Brown and Labour was that the economic crisis limited his capacity to establish the 'progressive consensus' he often talked of. Consequently, Labour failed to regroup around any semblance of a clear post-Blair agenda. Instead, Brown oversaw a bank bailout of staggering proportions, one that was supplemented with hundreds of billions of cheap credit through quantitative easing to boost the money supply, all the while continuing to privilege finance over other sectors of the economy and areas of social need; a familiar story within Labour history but one now played out on an epic scale.

Yet glimpses of the different agenda had been displayed. Brown looked to be embracing democracy and equality as key organizing principles for a post-Blair revival with talk of a written constitution and radical embrace of devolution, issues he has recently returned to when offering guidance to current Labour leader Keir Starmer. Specifically, the landmark Equality Act of 2010 signalled the radical potential of a Brown administration in terms of advancing liberal justice and bringing together Labour's five generations of equality legislation.

The academic lawyer Bob Hepple described five generations of equality legislation. The first generation, 1965 to 1968, introduced legislation on formal equality and non-discrimination with the Race Relations Act 1965. The second generation, from 1968 to 1970, covered the Race Relations Act 1968, which extended the initial legislation to cover employment, housing and provision of goods and services. The third generation, from 1970 to 1997, saw legislation extended to cover discrimination on grounds of sex with the Equal Pay Act 1970 and Sex Discrimination Act 1975. The concepts of indirect discrimination and positive action were introduced and the Equal Opportunities Commission was created for the purposes of enforcement. The Race Relations Act 1976, now covering indirect as well as direct discrimination, was enacted and the Commission on Racial Equality was created. Some 20 years later, in 1995, disability was protected by law with the Disability Discrimination Act. The fourth generation covered the New Labour years from 1997 and 2007, which saw a raft of regulations resulting from an EU directive extending protection against discrimination to age, disability, religion or belief and sexual orientation. The fifth generation, from 2000, involved a move towards transformative equality, with amendments to the Race Relations Act in 2000 imposing a so-called positive duty to promote race equality in the public sector. Similar public sector positive duties in respect of disability and gender were introduced in 2005 and 2007, respectively. This generation culminated in the single Equality Act 2010. These five generations of equalities legislation form the centrepiece of the contribution of the liberal conception of justice within Labour's history.[32]

The thinking behind the 2010 Equality Act is important. Signing the EU Social Chapter in 1997 led to the extension to Britain of the Framework Employment Directive and a series of equality regulations. It brought forward a raft of new equality legislation covering religion and belief, age and sexual orientation, including the removal of Clause 28 and equalization of the age of consent. As a consequence, various strands of equality legislation lacked an overall framework and appeared fragmented. Human rights and equality campaigners called for harmonization of legislation and enforcement institutions. The Equality Act brought that coherence, consolidating Labour's record dating back to the 1960s, and also managed to gain cross-party support and commitment to its introduction from the incoming Coalition government in May 2010, an example of the 'progressive consensus' Brown desired.[33]

Yet despite these suggestions of political renewal, things deteriorated electorally, exposed by the May 2008 local elections and disastrous by-election defeats in Crewe and Nantwich and Glasgow East. In the 2009 European elections, Labour was pushed back to third. Revelations in April 2009 of a bullying culture surrounding Brown involving the smearing of opponents' private lives hardly helped and rested uneasily with his talk of a 'moral compass'. Relations with some of his cabinet colleagues including Darling plunged. The MPs expenses scandal further hemmed in his government with the prosecution and jailing of a number of Labour MPs. Plots and positioning within the cabinet intensified, especially after a *Guardian* article by David Miliband on 30 July 2008, in which he appeared to set out his stall for the leadership.[34] A more substantial plot to unseat Brown appeared to be underway after James Purnell resigned as polling stations closed on local elections night 2009, quickly followed by the departures of Hazel Blears, John Hutton, Geoff Hoon and Caroline Flint, but came to nothing as Miliband dodged the immediate fight. In January 2010, calls by Hewitt and Hoon for a leadership election were rejected by all the likely candidates to challenge Brown from within the government.

Finally, on 6 April an election was announced for 6 May. The campaign was dominated by the fluctuating fortunes of the party leaders given the introduction of live TV debates. The personal low point for

Gordon Brown was being recorded describing a pensioner named Mrs Duffy as a 'bigoted woman' following an exchange about immigration on a Rochdale street.

It culminated in the first hung parliament for thirty-six years. Labour won 258 seats, 97 fewer than in 2005, receiving 29.7 per cent of the vote. The Tories 306 seats, up 108, taking 36.9 per cent of the poll, and the Lib Dems 57 seats, down 5 on 23.6 per cent. After five days of unsuccessful negotiations over a coalition agreement with the Lib Dems, Brown resigned on 11 May. Cameron became the Prime Minister and Clegg the Deputy Prime Minister in a cabinet containing 18 Conservatives and 5 Liberal Democrats. The New Labour era was over.

Diminishment

The 2010 election saw a 5.1 per cent swing from Labour to the Tories, the third largest since 1945. The party's seat loss was worse than at any other election apart from 1931, when MacDonald's National Government led to the defeat of 235 Labour MPs. In a sign of New Labour's contraction, by the end of 2009 party membership had fallen to the lowest ever recorded level.

Yet Labour had been in power for 13 years. Before Blair and New Labour, it had only ever won two working majorities. If we judge the government's record against what was possible, we can point to a number of notable achievements. These would include the introduction of the minimum wage and innovative early years provision and education reforms, a halving of child poverty and even more dramatic fall in pensioner poverty, the refinancing and rebuilding of public services and the collapse in NHS waiting times. There were also major reforms of the UK constitution including brokering the Good Friday Agreement. You could point to landmark rights for all citizens culminating in an Equality Act thereby consolidating over half a century of progressive legal enactments by successive Labour governments. Internationally you could identify the doubling of overseas aid, the ratification of the Kyoto Protocol and securing multilateral debt relief, all underpinned by the longest sustained period of economic growth in British history. It amounts to a solid record of achievements that united a variety of intellectual traditions within party history to change Britain for good.

Yet any honest assessment would also have to acknowledge that what began as a vibrant mix of political traditions and delivered three unprecedented majorities dramatically diminished over time. The liberal revisionist influences which dominated the first term in the end proved too hesitant and unwilling to provide the constitutional and democratic overhaul the British state desperately required. Blair's desire for Labour to return to its ancestral roots within New Liberalism by the end drew more influence from a restricted, individualized classical liberalism than from the Edwardian era. By the time of the 2005 Party Conference, Blair, the self-declared heir to Hobhouse, Hobson and T.H. Green, announced that 'the character of this changing world is indifferent to tradition. Unforgiving of frailty. No respecter of past reputations. It has no custom and practice'. Years before he would have rejected this as dehumanizing; now he embraced it and celebrated those 'swift to adapt'. What worked for him now was 'a liberal economy, prepared constantly to change to remain competitive'. He emphatically stated: 'In the era of rapid globalization, there is no mystery about what works – an open, liberal economy, prepared constantly to change to remain competitive.'

After leaving office Blair sought to both obscure and withdraw from his early political character and ethical concerns to help erect a modern liberal, cosmopolitan identity; a new Blair, whose liberalism was very different to that which once inspired him, the party he led and the country that supported him. The moral certainty and desire for spiritual renewal that from 1994 proved so attractive and which invested the party and government with ethical energy collided with the realities of US neo-con foreign policy and the Iraq War, after which Blair withdrew into the defence of an international liberal order. If a 5-to-4 Supreme Court decision in 2000, determining the presidency in favour of Bush rather than Al Gore, had gone the other way, then the disastrous consequences of supporting the President might have been averted, possibly limiting the post-9/11 conflict to just Afghanistan. Yet the diminishment of New Labour was not simply due to the fallout over Iraq.

At the Treasury the effects of the 'long boom' allowed Brown to hubristically claim to have delivered the economy from the 'boom-bust instability of the past'.[35] In his eleventh and final Budget he boasted 'the longest period of economic stability and sustained growth in our country's history'.[36] It was an extraordinary record that ensured Brown's utilitarian embrace of the market delivered significant advances in social justice overseen by a centralized Fabian statecraft. Interest rates were henceforth set by a Monetary Policy Committee of financial experts and neo-classical economists. The boom years would witness the triumph of economic orthodoxy reflected in Brown's embrace of Alan Greenspan, chairman of the US Federal Reserve. His decade in charge brought widespread advances in public services and significant improvements in child and pensioner poverty yet left a legacy of light regulation which triggered collapse, recession and austerity. Sixty quarters of growth brought with it an overconfident belief in the self-correcting capacity of modern capitalism to deliver sustained growth. It was reflected in an intellectual journey that by the end of his tenure at the Treasury saw Brown embrace liberal thinkers who claimed Adam Smith and the Scottish Enlightenment for the New Right.[37] The very system he had overseen would later derail his personal desire for radical political reinvention on becoming Prime Minister.

The ability to recycle a growth dividend into a distributional politics to alleviate poverty and refinance public services was derailed by the financial crisis, and many of the gains made were rewound by the austerity that followed. The strategy left unaltered, unmodernized, long-term productive weaknesses and failures of economic design in terms of ownership and power.

Overall, it is debatable what the key turning point was in the New Labour journey. Was it the consequence of Iraq or decided in 1996 – before even gaining power – with the rejection of economic stakeholding in favour of remedial cash transfers to the poor under the misplaced belief in unending growth? Either way it makes it difficult to conclude it was anything other than a missed opportunity. The missed opportunity had enduring consequences in the years that followed, played out in a long-term wage crash, flatlining productivity and the rise of populist authoritarian voices who scavenged on the resentments and concerns of people in industrial and post-industrial working-class communities, many of whom had invested heavily in the promise of a New Britain. New Labour failed to create the Britain its rhetoric promised and a unique growth dividend, huge majorities and weak Conservative opposition made possible. Over the next 14 years Labour would try several very different ways to try to make sense of it all.

Isolation
(2010–2024)

The legacy of the New Right continues to hang over Labour. The story of economic renewal under Thatcher, and Labour's struggle to repudiate its alleged achievements, remains an unfinished chapter in the party's history. In the early 1980s, the modernization of the Kinnock era sought to project a unifying, consensual variant of British socialism, in opposition to the divisive economics and politics of Thatcherism. Yet Labour's modernization would over time come to accept the legacy of the early 1980s. Under New Labour modernization meant upholding Thatcher's economic reforms, the embrace of the market and light financial regulation. Ultimately it led to economic collapse, recession and austerity in the aftermath of the 2007/8 banking crisis. The New Labour economic model proved to be unsustainable. Since the 2010 defeat, Labour has elected three very different leaders in Ed Miliband, Jeremy Corbyn and Keir Starmer. Each initially embarked on new strategic directions for the party and, in noticeably different ways, attempted to reconcile labour's three traditions of justice and move on from the politics of New Labour and the legacy of Thatcher. For all three it proved to be a difficult journey. Each leader was forced to change direction and revert back onto more familiar terrain within Labour history.

Escaping Thatcher

Nigel Lawson, Thatcher's Chancellor from 1983 to 1989, listed the Thatcherite ideals as 'free markets, financial discipline, firm control over public expenditure, tax cuts, nationalism, "Victorian values" (of the Samuel Smiles self-help variety), privatization and a dash of populism'.[1] Thatcherism is often compared to classical liberalism. Milton Friedman said that 'Margaret Thatcher is not in terms of belief a Tory. She is a nineteenth-century liberal'.[2] Thatcherism's embrace of economic liberalism signalled a reorientation away from the bipartisan concerns of post-war corporatism, and a renewed interest in deregulation, privatization and a minimal state, labour market flexibility, marginalizing trade unions and centralizing power from local authorities to central government.

Throughout the post-war period terms such as 'the sick man of Europe' and the 'British disease' have regularly been used by the right to lament the UK's post-war productivity performance, the effects of corporatism, systems of labour regulation and the actions of the Wilson and Callaghan governments.[3] The Thatcher revolution dismantled the corporatist state, embarked on wholesale privatizations and built a rolling legislative programme of labour reforms. Very quickly the economic language changed from 'sickness' and 'disease' to one of 'miracles'. As we previously noted, a decisive moment occurred in 1996 with Labour's rejection of an updated industrial pluralism in the form of economic stakeholding, in favour of more fulsome embrace of the market. Consequently, New Labour essentially conceded that years of underperformance and relative decline were arrested and reversed in the 1980s by Thatcher's economic policies. In his 2010 autobiography, Blair argued both that 'Britain needed the industrial and economic reforms of the Thatcher period' and that 'much of what she wanted to do in the 1980s was inevitable, a consequence not of ideology but of social and economic change'.[4]

The switch occurred at a time of surging growth and the benign economics of the long boom. Moreover, the switch went with the grain of an economic orthodoxy that praised Thatcher for conjuring an economic 'miracle' many thought would endure. The idea that her policies induced a productivity 'breakthrough' first gained traction with the economist John Muellbauer. He detected a significant upward lift in annual productivity growth from the third quarter of 1980 to form the empirical basis for the 'miracle' thesis. This became the new orthodoxy – across both the left and right. David Metcalf's work in the late 1980s explicitly stated that 'the pluralist course advocated by Donovan was tried and failed. By contrast, the methods pursued in the 1980s … seem to have done the trick'. The Donovan strategy of industrial pluralism, he insisted, was a 'conspicuous failure'.[5]

Fast forward to 2010. Labour lost the election and was replaced by a Coalition government formed in haste and committed to re-setting the public finances. Flagship Labour policies – Sure Start is a notable example – were starved of funding or ditched as austerity measures were enacted to shrink the state, with an ideological zeal reminiscent of the Thatcher years. Pursued with greater urgency following the Tories' 2015 electoral success, the cuts in public services merely amplified the hardship experienced by millions of households and workers on stagnant wages. Since 2008, there has been an unprecedented fall in UK productivity. This, when considered alongside poor wage growth and price rises, has produced a profound deterioration in living standards.

Today British output per hour and real wages are now no higher than they were prior to the global financial crisis of 2008/9. Between 2008 and 2020, average productivity growth was just 0.4 per cent. The UK ranks 31st out of 35 OECD countries in growth of output per hour from 2008 to 2017. Before Covid-19, our productivity growth was at its slowest since 2008. This wretched situation has led to 15 years of wage stagnation since the crash, a situation almost completely unprecedented.

Still the idea of a Thatcher 'miracle' persists. Yet close inspection of the evidence for that period is clear.[6] Thatcher was not a miracle worker. The deregulation of labour markets, the offensive against trade unions, and the privatization of utilities and other state assets did not resuscitate a 'sick' economy, still less induce a productivity 'miracle'. It shows that Thatcher initially benefitted from an arithmetical bounce in productivity measures while presiding over huge job losses and a decisive power shift in workplaces that incrementally, sometimes ruthlessly, degraded the conditions of work and workers. In that very specific sense, her legacy has endured. Thatcher's offensive against labour may have reduced the pressure on firms to undertake the investments in physical and human capital and research and development which support sustainable growth. Arguably the Thatcher years saw the consolidation of Britain's international standing as a base for low value-added operations. Despite not ageing well empirically, the enduring mythology of the Thatcher 'miracle' thesis has conditioned the politics of the left almost as much as the politics of the right.

The contest to succeed Gordon Brown was narrowly won by Ed Miliband. In response to the publication of Blair's memoirs on 1 September 2010, Miliband sought to draw a line under the past, disassociating himself from what went before: 'I think it is time to move on from Tony Blair and Gordon Brown and Peter Mandelson and to move on from the New Labour establishment ... I am the one at this election who can best turn the page. I think frankly most members of the public will want us to turn the page.'[7]

Miliband suggested New Labour had failed to sufficiently challenge the legacy of Margaret Thatcher. Both Blair and Brown had been unable to confront the worst excesses of global capitalism, failed to sufficiently regulate financial markets prior to the 2008 crash and presided over rising inequality. His focus would instead be on the contracting living standards of the 'squeezed middle' given the unregulated predatory character of modern capitalism that appeared to reward corporate abuse. Miliband initially sought to focus on questions of economic design and 'predistribution' to confront the long-term structural problems of the British economy in terms of productivity and living standards, in contrast to an orthodox Labour economic strategy built around class reconciliation and redistribution of the proceeds of growth familiar since 1924. Yet this strategy changed as Labour's polling position improved and Miliband tacked back towards safer and, for the ex-Treasury advisor, more familiar, utilitarian territory based around eye-catching fiscal transfers.

In 2015 Miliband was succeeded by the unlikely figure of Jeremy Corbyn, who offered a radical departure from the legacy of Thatcherism and the compromises of both the New Labour and Miliband eras, and the market orthodoxies of the other candidates competing for the leadership. In his first period as leader, Corbyn aligned the remaining survivors of the 1980s hard left with a new generation of activists radicalized after the financial crash and the student protests of the early 2010s. He successfully forged a populist socialist politics built around housing, student debt, anti-racism, anti-imperialism and ecological concerns, alongside support for unions and a wider precariat that in 2017 brought Labour close to securing one of the most astonishing election victories in British history. Yet two years later, his brittle political coalition had fractured over Brexit, charges of antisemitism and a corrosive internal party culture. Combined with rabid assaults from the media, Corbynism soon lost its ethical energy and vitality, withdrawing back into the more orthodox hard-left economistic politics of 35 years earlier as a 'Red Wall' crumbled and Labour succumbed to a Boris Johnson landslide.

After the brutal defeat of 2019, Keir Starmer promised the membership a different trajectory, one offering internal reconciliation, the benefits of

'Corbynism without Corbyn' and rejection of the economics of the New Right and New Labour. His successful campaign for the leadership was based on a conscious realignment of Labour's three traditions of justice and articulation of the 'moral case for socialism'. The radical human rights lawyer would preserve the policy potentials of the previous four years without the malign racist undertow and electoral negatives associated with the Corbyn leadership. Yet on achieving office, Starmer quickly retreated from the pledges that ensured his substantial victory. He subsequently embarked on a different path, in part a New Labour restoration project, but one that also subtly rejected parts of that inheritance in favour of a revamped supply-side socialism familiar in the Kinnock years. The degradation of the Conservatives under the Johnson and Liz Truss administrations ensured substantial poll leads for Labour from mid-2022; a turnaround unimaginable given the 20 per cent polling deficits of 2020. By early 2024, Labour looks to be on the cusp of victory, although the character of the modern party and its leader is vague and the policy prospectus has dramatically truncated.

Ed Miliband 2010–2015

Harriet Harman became the Leader of the Opposition and acting leader of the party following the resignation of Gordon Brown on 11 May 2010. Five candidates would contest the leadership: David and Ed Miliband, Ed Balls, Diane Abbott and Andy Burnham. Ed narrowly defeated David in the final run-off by 50.6 per cent to 49.4 per cent (see table 12.1).

On 25 September Labour elected its youngest leader, although the nature of his victory, defeating his elder brother with the votes of affiliated members, having lost amongst the MPs and the membership, would affect perceptions of his leadership.

Born on 24 December 1969 to New Left academic Ralph Miliband and activist Marion Kozak, both Jews originating from eastern Europe,[8] Ed and his brother David, four years his senior, were raised in a left-wing North London household. Both brothers joined the Labour Party as teenagers, both later attending Corpus Christi College, Oxford, to study Politics, Philosophy and Economics (PPE). After an internship in New York and working as a junior researcher on Channel 4's *A Week in*

Table 12.1 Labour leadership election, 2010

Candidate	Preferences round	Votes (%)				Result
		Total votes that round	MPs and MEPs	Party members	Unions & others	
Diane Abbott	1	7.4	0.9	2.4	4.1	ELIMINATED
Ed Balls	1	11.8	5.0	3.4	3.4	Go through
Andy Burnham	1	8.7	3.0	2.8	2.8	Go through
David Miliband	1	37.8	13.9	14.7	9.2	Go through
Ed Miliband	1	34.3	10.5	13.8	10.0	Go through
Ed Balls	2	13.3	5.2	4.2	3.8	Go through
Andy Burnham	2	10.4	3.0	3.3	4.1	ELIMINATED
David Miliband	2	38.9	14.0	15.1	9.8	Go through
Ed Miliband	2	37.5	11.1	11.1	15.2	Go through
Ed Balls	3	16.0	5.4	4.8	5.8	ELIMINATED
David Miliband	3	42.7	15.8	16.1	10.9	Go through
Ed Miliband	3	41.3	12.1	12.4	16.7	Go through
David Miliband	4	49.4	17.8	18.1	13.4	ELIMINATED
Ed Miliband	4	50.6	15.5	15.2	19.9	WINNER

Politics, he was offered a job as a researcher for Harman, the then Shadow Chief Secretary to the Treasury, and shortly after was recruited as an aide by the Shadow Chancellor Gordon Brown. He later became a Special Advisor in the Treasury, where he had a significant input over welfare to work, low pay and childcare policy.

First elected Labour MP for Doncaster North on 5 May 2005,[9] in government Miliband held posts in the Cabinet Office and as Chancellor of the Duchy of Lancaster before becoming Secretary of State for Energy and Climate Change on 3 October 2008; the same office he would shadow in opposition before being elected leader.

In his campaign for the leadership, Ed Miliband developed more space to challenge the legacy of New Labour's 13 years in office compared to his brother, who effectively became trapped as the 'Blairite' candidate.[10] Over the course of the campaign the younger brother offered a programme of economic and political reform critical of the New Labour era alongside an acknowledgement of strategic foreign policy errors given his opposition to the Iraq War, which unlike his elder sibling predated his election to parliament. Miliband's victory saw Labour record its first lead since the early days of Gordon Brown's leadership in a YouGov poll on 27 September 2010, partly due to disillusioned Liberal Democrat supporters defecting to Labour.

Miliband appointed Alan Johnson to Shadow Chancellor, although he would last just 3 months before being replaced by Balls, who switched across from Shadow Home Secretary. Yvette Cooper was appointed to the foreign affairs brief. Whilst Miliband retained strong support from the unions and amongst the activist base, he had much more difficulty within the PLP. Miliband inherited a Shadow Cabinet of which the majority had supported his brother. The early days were turbulent, with regular bouts of internal criticism, particularly over Miliband's harsh judgement of New Labour's record and his attempts to break with the immediate past, not least because all of the top team had played significant roles in the Labour government and many were determined to protect their own reputations and political legacy. Miliband's attempts at rethinking economic policy were particularly difficult given the powerful position of Balls as his Shadow Chancellor. His rather abstract intellectual concerns often attracted bouts of criticism and he was regularly attacked by a hostile and intrusive press especially over charges of disloyalty given the decision to run against his brother. It became essential for Miliband to establish his leadership by exerting greater control over his top team. On 5 July 2011, the PLP voted to abolish Shadow Cabinet elections, a decision subsequently ratified by the NEC and Party Conference.

In his first speech as leader, Miliband renounced the war in Iraq and sought to move beyond the Blair and Brown years with talk of a 'new generation' of leadership. Specifically, Miliband attempted to shift the party away from the wholesale embrace of markets through an emphasis on 'responsible capitalism', greater state intervention to alter the balance of the UK economy away from financial services and greater regulation of banks and energy companies. Miliband was attempting to reintroduce ethics into Labour's economic policy making and pivot away from the traditional utilitarian concerns of dominant Treasury-inspired thinking. It marked a subtle reorientation of Labour's approach with a desire to criticize 'predatory' economic behaviour and tackle vested interests and the closed circles that disfigured British society, best captured in the

Ed Miliband
Source: *Financial Times*, Flickr.

newspaper phone hacking scandal that erupted in July 2011. In contrast to New Labour and David Cameron, whose governments maintained close personal links with the Murdoch empire, Miliband captured the public mood of outrage when demonstrating a willingness to confront power elites and practically apply his critique of predatory corporate activity.

In his early period as leader Miliband embraced the idea of 'predistribution', the concern for active prevention of inequality through economic intervention to alter the architectural make-up of modern capitalism, rather than by remedial tax and benefits reforms administered by the central state, the traditional utilitarian Labour method. Miliband was attempting to update the post-war concerns of the industrial pluralists and reintroduce stakeholder themes rejected under New Labour. The emphasis on predistribution rather than redistribution implied a significant change of direction. It hinted at a more interventionist industrial policy and a desire to boost wages, for instance through the idea of a Living Wage – with distinct ILP associations – rather than through tax credits. Whilst Miliband struggled to define this new economic terrain and the meaning of 'responsible' capitalism and predistribution, his early attempts at reshaping Labour's ideological framework amounted to a significant intellectual intervention.

To support this change of direction Miliband appeared to embrace some of the ideas circulating around the communitarian 'Blue Labour' movement. Founded in 2009 by the academic Maurice Glasman, later created a life peer by Miliband, as a counter to New Labour through a reclamation of virtue ethics within the Labour tradition, the movement rose to prominence following a series of seminars held in 2010 and 2011 in London and University College Oxford. A resulting book of essays included contributions from Glasman, academics Marc Stears, Stuart White and Jonathan Rutherford, along with politicians such as David Miliband, James Purnell and David Lammy, together with a supportive foreword by Ed Miliband.[11] The overall approach was distinctly Aristotelian. Its focus was on community organizing, civic renewal, rebuilding working-class industrial and political representation – reminiscent of early guild and ethical socialist traditions – together with a renewed interest in Catholic Social Teaching. The movement sought to rehabilitate ethics and contest both the utilitarian and liberal Rawlsian influences shaping Labour's approach to justice.

These various themes cohered with the successful 2012 'One Nation' speech, Miliband's memorable and well-received Conference address, the high point to the Miliband leadership. Miliband envisioned 'a country for all, with everyone playing their part. A Britain we rebuild together', echoing progressive communitarian nation-building themes identifiable throughout Labour history. Miliband claimed his 'One Nation' approach descended from both Conservative Prime Minister Benjamin Disraeli's One Nation Conservatism, which sought to challenge the economic inequality splitting the country into two nations of rich and poor people, and Attlee's unifying approach to post-war reconstruction. The proponents of 'One Nation' Labour saw it as a possible successor to New Labour, although as previously noted, it was a phrase used by Mandelson and Liddle in 1996 in their analysis of the Blair Revolution, and was reminiscent of Kinnock's criticism of the divisive qualities of Thatcherism.

Miliband invoked a familiar Labour refrain of the national community, one that seeks to transcend the sectional concerns of labourism and class, that can be identified most closely with MacDonald. In his address Miliband commended New Labour for challenging Labour's traditional sectionalism and widening the party's appeal, yet argued that 'although New Labour often started with the right intentions, over time it did not do enough to change the balance of power in this country'. Miliband was also speaking to the sense of inclusive patriotic renewal on display at that summer's successful London Olympic Games whilst laying down dividing lines in defence of the union against a resurgent SNP.

Yet Miliband wouldn't follow through with the radical potentials of his first two years. By 2012 he was already becoming more cautious both to maintain party unity and to preserve a recent uplift in Labour's fortunes. Having outlined a relatively ambitious, radical agenda, Miliband tacked back to the centre with the first evidence of a potential election victory.

The 21 March 2012 'omnishambles' budget would be a decisive moment in the Miliband years, but not for the reasons many assumed at the time.[12] George Osborne's Budget cut the top tax rate, but also introduced a 20 per cent VAT on pasties and other hot foods sold by bakeries, triggering the so-called 'pastygate' crisis. Other rises also had to be rectified, including on static caravans and alterations to historic buildings. The budget proved to be a disaster and presented Miliband with a fresh opportunity to improve his standing. From that moment Labour often appeared to be ahead in the polls although Miliband's personal polling numbers were poor.

From late 2012 Miliband began to play safe, assuming that Labour's new-found poll lead would work alongside two significant movements amongst the electorate. First, the unpopularity of the Liberal Democrats following their capitulation within the coalition over a clear commitment to abolish student fees. Second, the growing threat to the Conservative party over Europe from Nigel Farage, UKIP and the populist right. Both movements appeared to work to Labour's advantage. Miliband looked to be the beneficiary of the two decisive electoral shifts in the parliament. It led to what became known as the 'small target' or '35 per cent strategy' to avoid risk and bank the electoral benefits of these shifts whilst preserving internal party unity.[13]

Miliband's early innovations in pursuit of policy and ideological renewal vanished, replaced with a programme of orthodox fiscal transfers to offset cost of living concerns. These included 2013 Conference pledges to freeze gas and electricity prices and 2014 plans to defend the NHS,[14] with strong echoes of Brown's Treasury model of distributive justice rather than Miliband's earlier attempts at progressive nation building. Whilst many of these retail policy offers were individually popular, they revealed a dramatic diminishment of the Miliband project, mocked at the time by David Axelrod, the US election guru hired by the party, as 'Vote Labour and win a microwave'. They also reinforced the Tory attack line that both he and Balls were 'deficit deniers', an argument strengthened when Miliband forgot the section of his 2014 Conference speech devoted to Labour's approach to fiscal responsibility, including a promise to 'eliminate the deficit as soon as possible'. Miliband's more conservative strategy was informed by a widespread belief in the inevitability of victory and at worst of a hung parliament with Miliband as Prime Minister. This position was confidently maintained right up to the release of the BBC Exit Poll on election day 2015, despite fluctuating polling numbers, underwhelming May 2014 local election results and after having finishing behind UKIP in European elections that year.

One other electoral shift would decisively upend Labour's strategy. The party's decline in the 2011 Scottish elections foreshadowed greater losses at the 2015 election. The 44.7 per cent vote in favour of independence at the September 2014 referendum implied a very strong SNP showing in any future general election conducted under first past the post. The referendum campaign saw the SNP use Scottish Labour's stance against independence as evidence of its 'anti-Scottish' sentiment and of being seen as 'in cahoots with the hated UK government'.[15] In the general election campaign Labour faced a classic squeeze between being seen as a unionist party amongst Scottish voters and by English voters as an electoral pushover for the SNP in the event of a hung parliament. The Conservatives almost accidentally had alighted on a potent strategy depicting a vote for Labour as a vote that would put Scotland's interests before those of England, releasing a campaign poster depicting Miliband in the pocket of a dominant Alex Salmond. It proved fatal, resulting in an overall majority for the Conservatives of 11 seats on 7 May 2015. The Conservatives won 330 seats and polled 36.8 per cent of the votes cast compared to a disappointing 30.4 per cent for Labour. The SNP won 56 of the 59 Scottish seats. The Liberal Democrats lost 49 of their 57 seats. Labour gained more than 20 seats in England and Wales, although it lost several of its own MPs including Ed Balls. It lost 40 of its 41 seats in Scotland, including the one belonging to its leader, Jim Murphy. The party lost a net total of 26 seats, falling to 232 MPs.

It was a dismal result for Labour and for Miliband personally. Having been elected from the liberal 'soft left', in the first couple of years he had sought to reorientate the party's approach to economic policy towards fundamental questions of ethics and virtue, the distribution of power and of economic design. Yet against his better judgement he quickly retreated back towards orthodox utilitarianism, but in ways that failed to politically resolve the deficit legacy of the Brown years. Leading and intellectually rebuilding the party after 13 years in power was never going to be easy. Yet Miliband struggled to reject Labour's historic statism and build a programme that aligned with a fracturing electorate and heightened demands for constitutional and electoral reform, not just in Scotland but across the north and in urban communities. In the end Miliband returned to Labour's safe space of distributional justice, preferring an underwhelming retail politics of cash transfers.

For some of his opponents, the most significant outcome of the Miliband years would only become apparent once he had left office. In general, Miliband rejected the New Labour trick of setting himself against his own party to attract media attention and establish his political *bona fides*. Throughout, he worked exceptionally hard to maintain party unity. Yet the misplaced impression could never be fully erased that the unions held disproportionate sway over the Labour leader given the way they helped him defeat his brother in 2010. In 2013, when Unite were accused of attempting to fix the selection of Labour's parliamentary candidate in Falkirk West, Miliband faced a renewed wave of criticism, including from Cameron, who used the Falkirk scandal at Prime Minister's Questions. In response, the Labour leader gave several interviews declaring that he would scrap the scheme that Unite had 'frankly abused' and stated that he 'was now determined to review Labour's relationship with the trade unions'. In the months that followed, Miliband, with the help of former General Secretary Ray Collins, achieved a widely praised, amicable deal with the unions. On 1 March 2014, a Special Conference at London's

ExCel Centre agreed rule changes that replaced the electoral college for future leadership elections with a full OMOV system including registered supporters, now able to join at substantially reduced rates. Henceforth union members would have to opt in rather than opt out of paying the political levy to the party. It was a remarkable initiative given that the move replicated the 1927 Trades Disputes Act. Unbeknown to many present, in just 18 months the changes agreed that day, appearing to challenge traditional labourism whilst also reversing the left's constitutional gains of the early 1980s, would help deliver the most dramatic internal victory for the left in Labour's history.

Jeremy Corbyn

The day after Labour's election defeat, Miliband resigned as party leader. Harriet Harman once more took interim charge. On 3 June Jeremy Corbyn confirmed in his local paper the *Islington Tribune* that he would stand for the leadership on a 'clear anti-austerity platform'. On Monday 15 June 2015, having received 36 nominations, one more than the required threshold, Corbyn entered the contest alongside three other candidates: Yvette Cooper, Andy Burnham and Liz Kendall. Despite having the lowest number of nominations, Corbyn emerged as the front-runner. On 12 September, Corbyn secured a landslide victory with 59.5 per cent of first preference votes in the first round of voting, with the runner-up Burnham obtaining just 19 per cent (see table 12.2).

Initially, Corbyn appeared to be the reluctant Campaign Group paper candidate, a similar role to that performed by Abbott in 2010. Yet a number of MPs outside of the hard left nominated Corbyn to help widen the debate given the similarities of the other candidates and in order to provide the membership with a wider range of political options.[16] Undoubtedly Corbyn benefitted from a significant number of registered supporters introduced under the Miliband reforms, but he also achieved a landslide amongst the individual members. This point is significant. Corbyn's election wasn't simply down to the Miliband rule changes. In Labour mythology, many now assume it was due to a unique chain of events starting late on 22 February 2012, when Labour MP Eric Joyce physically attacked fellow MPs in the Commons Strangers Bar. This led to a by-election in Falkirk, alleged abuses in the candidate

Table 12.2 Labour leadership election, 2015

Candidate	Party members		Registered supporters		Affiliated supporters		Total	
	Votes	%	Votes	%	Votes	%	Votes	%
Jeremy Corbyn	121,751	49.6	88,449	83.8	41,217	57.6	251,417	59.5
Andy Burnham	55,698	22.7	6,160	5.8	18,604	26.0	80,462	19.0
Yvette Cooper	54,470	22.2	8,415	8.0	9,043	12.6	71,928	17.0
Liz Kendall	13,601	5.5	2,574	2.4	2,682	3.8	18,857	4.5

selection process, Miliband's 2013 abolition of the electoral college and introduction of registered supporters, events that culminated in Corbyn's election in 2015. This overstates the role of Miliband's reforms in Corbyn's success, however, and neglects other reasons he was elected, and the fact he won a landslide of members as well as registered supporters. Corbyn would remain leader until 4 April 2020.

Corbyn, first elected as MP for Islington North on 9 June 1983, was born 26 May 1949 and enjoyed a relatively privileged upbringing in Shropshire. His father was an active member of the Labour Party. After moving to London in the 1970s, he worked as an organizer for the public services union NUPE and the AEEU engineering union. Between 1974 and 1983, he served as a Haringey councillor. He was a regular contributor to the hard-line *London Left Briefing* and on the executive of CLPD. He was active in the early 1980s push for constitutional rule changes to empower the membership and worked for Tony Benn's unsuccessful 1981 campaign for the deputy leadership. In parliament Corbyn was active and became the secretary of the Campaign Group. He consistently opposed war, including the Gulf War in 1991 and the Iraq conflict in 2003, and remained a long-standing supporter of CND. Between 1997 and 2010 Corbyn rebelled against the Labour whip on 428 occasions, more than any other MP.[17]

Corbyn's ascent was aided by several factors. He established early momentum through the endorsement of significant trade union figures including Len McCluskey, the General Secretary of Unite, and gained support from UNISON, the Communication Workers Union (CWU), the Transport Salaried Staffs' Association (TSSA) and the Associated Society of Locomotive Engineers and Firemen (ASLEF). The party's rules for electing the leadership had the unintended consequence of boosting Corbyn's candidacy by handing more weight to the votes of the party membership, historically to the left of the parliamentary party. Corbyn's inclusion in the contest brought an influx of new Labour members, many joining to vote for him. Notably, of the new Labour members who had voted for the Green Party in the 2015 general election, 92 per cent voted for Corbyn in the September leadership election.[18] Yet the most significant factor in Corbyn's success was his ability to chart a new direction for Labour's disenchanted support base. Corbyn was authentic and clear about what he opposed: capitalism, war, the deficit, New Labour, spending and welfare cuts, hostility to refugees and migrants and much more. His moral clarity appealed to disillusioned supporters who felt Labour had for too long compromised and betrayed the members. Throughout the summer, Corbyn's rallies and campaign events were packed with supporters, and full of energy and enthusiasm compared to events hosted by the other three in the contest. Despite Corbyn's associations with the orthodox economistic and statist traditions of the old hard left, for a younger generation he appeared virtuous and utopian in his rejection of New Labour's realpolitik.

Corbyn's candidacy offered the membership an unexpected choice, as the other candidates maintained a strict acceptance of austerity. The contrast was visible in July when along with 47 other Labour MPs he defied the whip in opposition to the Second Reading of the Welfare Reform and Work Bill. Corbyn offered moral clarity in his diagnosis of modern capitalism and through his long-standing commitment to peace and justice. He alone was the change candidate operating in a receptive climate, communicating to an expanding electorate in an untested electoral system.

The Corbyn Years: 2015–2017

After his victory, Corbyn appointed his long-term ally John McDonnell to be his Shadow Chancellor. In October 2015, he hired *The Guardian* journalist Seumas Milne as Labour's Executive Director for Strategy and Communications. Tensions soon emerged in his relations with the parliamentary party. Thirty-six MPs had nominated Corbyn for the leadership but a greatly reduced number had actually voted for him. In November

Jeremy Corbyn
Source: Jeremy Corbyn Portraits, Flickr.

2015, Corbyn opposed military involvement in the Syrian Civil War but allowed MPs a free vote. Sixty-six MPs voted for air strikes, eleven of whom were members of Labour's front bench, including Shadow Foreign Secretary Hilary Benn and Deputy Leader Tom Watson.

In the May 2016 local elections, Labour performed poorly. On Thursday 23 June the UK voted to leave the European Union by 51.89 per cent to 48.11 per cent. Corbyn was criticized for his indifference throughout the campaign, including by Alan Johnson, the head of Labour's yes campaign. Less than 48 hours later, Benn was sacked for coordinating resignations within the Shadow Cabinet to force Corbyn's departure. By Monday evening, 23 of the 31 members of the Shadow Cabinet had resigned. A no-confidence vote was tabled in the PLP by Margaret Hodge and Ann Coffey over criticism of the leader's 'lacklustre' performance during the referendum campaign amid widespread fear of an imminent election following Cameron's resignation. Despite lacking any constitutional legitimacy, on 28 June the motion was backed by 172 MPs with just 40 supporting the Labour leader. Yet the so-called 'chicken coup' failed. Corbyn refused to vacate his position, arguing that he derived his mandate from the membership and not the PLP. On 11 July 2016, Angela Eagle launched a leadership challenge, only to then withdraw 8 days later after the announcement of a rival challenge from Owen Smith. On 24 September, Corbyn was re-elected as leader by 61.8 per cent to 38.2 per cent. By the end of the contest Labour's membership had grown to more than 500,000.

Disputes over Europe continued. On 1 February 2017, 47 MPs broke a three-line whip over Labour's support for triggering Article 50 to initiate withdrawal from the European Union. With poll leads of over 20 per cent, on 18 April Theresa May announced a snap election for 8 June. The May 2017 local elections saw the Tories' best performance in a decade and Labour lose 382 council seats. The Conservatives looked to be heading for a landslide. Yet the election produced a hung parliament. Labour secured 40.0 per cent of the vote, its highest share since 2001, and made a net gain of 30 seats. Under Corbyn, Labour had achieved a 9.6 per cent increase in its vote share, the biggest increase in a single general election since 1945.

Unlike Corbyn, Theresa May proved to be a poor election campaigner. The Labour leader had defied his critics and established Labour as the anti-austerity party; one that stood, in a strap line shared with New Labour, 'For the Many, Not the Few'. Labour had crafted a radical, populist manifesto that pledged to end austerity, scrap tuition fees and introduce higher taxes on top earners, corporations and the city. Labour committed to boost public sector pay and repeal benefit cuts, deliver more affordable social housing and childcare. A Labour government would nationalize rail, water, energy and Royal Mail.

Whilst the document remained very much a traditional left utilitarian text with little to say about constitutional and electoral reform, citizenship and civic virtue, Corbyn and McDonnell brilliantly allied the remnants of the early 1980s hard left with a younger left politicized by the 2007/8 economic crisis who rejected both technocratic social democracy and neo-liberalism. Unbeknown to most of the PLP, the Labour leader had tapped into a radical intellectual renewal sometimes described as a 'New New Left'.[19] It was young, energetic and tech savvy. This new highly democratic movement maintained a rich, radical intellectual heritage within the European left and was inspired by the anti-globalization movements, and later the post-2008 Occupy actions and militant campus protests of the early 2010s. It embraced bold new ideas regarding economic design, industrial democracy, culture and the environment, and was well organized and networked including within Momentum, the organization that spun out of the Corbyn leadership election campaign, and amongst cadres of young activists in think tanks such as the New Economics Foundation, the revived IPPR, and Centre for Labour and Social Studies, and new platforms such as Novara Media.

Yet just two and a half years later, on 12 December 2019, the party would suffer its fourth successive election defeat and its worst result since 1935. The insurgent energy of 2017 would disappear and Labour would lose 60 seats, falling back to just 202 MPs polling only 32.1 per cent of the vote, down 7.9 per cent. After nearly a decade in power the Conservatives would secure a landslide, winning 365 seats, 48 more than in 2017, with a 43.6 per cent vote share. Given that the manifestos of 2017 and 2019 were very similar, what accounts for Labour's dramatic change in fortunes?

The Corbyn Years: 2017–2019

Despite the undoubted success of the 2017 election campaign, Corbyn's relations with the PLP continued to deteriorate. Hostile MPs remained ready to publicly criticize the leadership, and the leader's office tended to not engage with MPs they distrusted. In an early sign of how Brexit would come to dominate and further corrode the atmosphere, in late June 2017 Corbyn sacked three front-bench London MPs after they voted in favour of a Queen's Speech amendment calling for Britain to remain within the Customs Union and Single Market. In March 2018, Corbyn was heavily criticized by many of his own MPs furious at his reluctance to blame the Russian state for a nerve agent attack in Salisbury.

The leader's office at times appeared dysfunctional. After Labour's narrow 2017 defeat, staff reportedly viewed their campaign 'as a blueprint for future success', and missed an opportunity for more fundamental reorganization of both personnel and direction. Corbyn and his senior team 'presided over an organization widely seen as chaotic and dysfunctional, with inexperienced staff, high turnover and toxic office politics'.[20]

Corbyn and his team were damaged over a failure to take appropriate and decisive action against those accused of antisemitism. Concerns about the party's ability to deal with instances of antisemitism were raised soon after Jeremy Corbyn's election in 2015. Many new members were critics of Israel over Palestinian rights and settlement building in the occupied territories. The first major row emerged in 2016 when the Bradford West MP, Naz Shah, apologized for an antisemitic Facebook post. In an effort to defend Shah, the former London mayor, Ken Livingstone, claimed Adolf Hitler supported Zionism. Livingstone eventually quit the party after a lengthy disciplinary process.

The June 2016 Chakrabarti report into racism within Labour found that although antisemitism and racism were not endemic, there was an 'occasionally toxic atmosphere'. At the launch Corbyn remained silent as his supporter Marc Wadsworth verbally attacked a Jewish Labour MP, Ruth Smeeth, accusing her in a conspiratorial antisemitic trope of working 'hand in hand' with the *Daily Telegraph*. The controversy escalated in 2018 with media reports of bigotry on the social media pages of Corbyn supporters, and allegations that Corbyn's allies were blocking action taken against those accused of antisemitic statements. A new antisemitism row broke out in March 2018 after Corbyn conceded he was wrong to support a graffiti artist whose 'offensive' work was scrubbed off a wall in London's East End. In a Facebook post in 2012, Corbyn had offered his support to Los Angeles-based street artist Mear One, whose mural featured several known antisemitic tropes. In August, Corbyn drew further criticism after a video emerged of remarks he made at a conference in 2013 praising Manuel Hassassian, the Palestinian Ambassador to the UK. Corbyn also criticized the reception given to Hassassian's remarks by some members of the audience, whom he characterized as 'thankfully silent Zionists' who 'clearly have two problems. One is that they don't want to study history, and secondly, having lived in this country for a very long time, probably all their lives, they don't understand English irony, either.'

That same year three Labour Lords resigned over alleged antisemitism. In April 2019, the Jewish Labour Movement passed a motion of no confidence in Corbyn's leadership. In May 2019, Corbyn's long-term

CLPD ally and NEC member Peter Willsman was suspended after being recorded saying that the Israeli embassy was 'almost certainly' behind Labour's antisemitism row. That same month the Equality and Human Rights Commission (EHRC) launched a formal investigation into the Labour Party over allegations of antisemitism. Eight whistleblowers from Labour's staff spoke to the BBC for a *Panorama* programme broadcast in July 2019, with some saying they felt there was political meddling from Corbyn's office in the process for handling antisemitism complaints. In early November 2019, following a letter in *The Guardian* by public figures urging voters to reject Labour at the coming election, Corbyn spoke of suspending members for antisemitic activity and speeding up the complaints procedures. Whilst many of his supporters believed antisemitism had been 'weaponized' by his political opponents, few would dispute that the issue did him long-term damage.

In February 2019, seven Labour MPs resigned to form the Independent Group, later renamed Change UK, citing alleged antisemitism, dissatisfaction with Corbyn's leadership and the party's position on Brexit. Other MPs, including Frank Field and Louise Ellman, chose to sit as independents, citing antisemitism. Jeremy Corbyn's undisputed dominance of the party, including securing his preferred candidate Jennie Formby as Labour's general secretary, and control of the NEC and Party Conference, meant talk of a more significant split continued, often linked to the unlikely figure of Jonathan Powell, Tony Blair's former chief of staff. The media was regularly briefed about the likelihood of another more significant mass resignation of Labour MPs. It never materialized with anti-Corbyn sentiment in the PLP transferred into anti-Brexit groups including the People's Vote campaign.

Above all it was Brexit that drained the insurgent energy from Labour and its leader.[21] From 2016, the Brexit result left Labour facing an enduring strategic dilemma. Ninety-five per cent of Labour MPs supported Remain, but a majority of Labour MPs (61 per cent) represented constituencies that had a majority Leave vote. Yet a clear majority of Labour voters (68 per cent) supported Remain in 2016. After the 2017 election, the Labour Party was 64 seats short of an overall majority. To win power, it needed roughly to double the thirty net gains it made in 2017 and the majority of Labour's targets were Leave-voting seats. Any future victory was through Leave-voting territory yet Labour's existing base and PLP were firmly committed to Remain. Added to this was Corbyn's long-term Euroscepticism and the hostility of much of the PLP to their leader.

Cumulatively this strategic dilemma and the political hostility to the leader ensured that by the time of the 2019 election, Labour lacked any coherent position on the subject. In an election dominated by Brexit, Labour was open to criticism in Leave-voting heartlands of wishing to subvert the will of the people with its support for a second referendum. Following the 2016 decision to leave the European Union and prior to the 2017 election, Labour had shown political agility in ensuring Brexit did not dominate the campaign. In December 2016, the party set out the criteria to judge the government's negotiating strategy, and in March 2017, Keir Starmer issued six tests to assess any Brexit deal, including a requirement that any agreement delivers the 'exact same benefits' as the UK enjoys from being inside the Single Market and Customs Union, the same words that had been used by the Brexit Secretary David Davis two months earlier. The issue was thereby effectively neutralized.

After the 2017 election, Corbyn wished to embrace a progressive Leave agenda. Yet a Shadow Cabinet Brexit sub-committee failed to agree a strategy that could endure. It rejected suggestions of a deal with Theresa May and came to embrace the case for a second referendum after effective lobbying of the PLP and the unions by the People's Vote (PV) campaign following its launch on 15 April 2018. Labour's holding position was to reject Theresa May's Brexit, demand an election and make the case for a renegotiated Labour deal with a customs union, a 'jobs-first Brexit'. Yet by the time of the 2018 Conference, the position looked to be unsustainable. Scores of CLPs had by then submitted resolutions echoing the PV demand for a public vote with Remain on the ballot. An ambiguous composite resolution emerged that upheld the leadership line. Yet in his Conference speech, the Shadow Secretary for Exiting the European Union, Keir Starmer, accepted the case for a second referendum with an option for Remain. By late 2018, Labour had in effect become the party of Remain. The six tests that had been successfully deployed in the 2017 election to avoid Labour being defined by Brexit were now used to oppose any deal that emerged from Brussels and gradually align the party ever closer to the PV campaign. It would culminate a year later in a brutal election defeat defined by Brexit.

On 15 January 2019, May's deal was defeated by 432 votes to 202. The following month the Brexit sub-committee moved closer to publicly embracing a second referendum. A briefing was circulated to Labour MPs saying Labour would back a public vote between a credible Leave position and Remain. On 27 March following a second rejection of May's deal, MPs were given a series of eight indicative votes in which Labour MPs were whipped into supporting a second referendum, although all eight failed to gain majorities. In April 2019, a Labour negotiating team led by Starmer and McDonnell began discussions with Downing Street officials and ministers over a Brexit deal. The Conservative whips believed a negotiated deal with Labour could pass the Commons, although Labour's team advised Corbyn otherwise, also suggesting it would be disastrous for Labour to secure an agreement and play the role of May's saviour, thereby appealing to the party's innate tribalism. Eventually Corbyn withdrew his team from the talks, although some present thought a negotiated deal and a soft Brexit was achievable. The May 2019 European election saw the Brexit Party top the poll with 29 seats, followed by the LibDems on 16, Labour on 10 and the Tories on 4. The result incentivized advocates of the PV position, including Starmer, Diane Abbott and McDonnell and elements of the PLP fearful of a LibDem revival, who since before the 2017 election had aggressively pursued a second vote.

By July, Boris Johnson had taken power and with it came a more aggressive populist Brexit agenda, with the new Conservative leader usurping the iconoclastic, insurgent role that Corbyn had performed in 2017. Throughout the autumn, in a series of parliamentary manoeuvres, Labour was actively seeking to delay both an election and Brexit beyond the scheduled leave date of 31 October, in particular with the passing of the 'Benn Act', rechristened by Johnson as the 'Surrender Act'. In the end Labour settled on a policy of renegotiating Brexit once in office and putting the outcome to a second referendum alongside an option to remain. It proved to be an impossible position to communicate in an election defined by the issue, not least because Corbyn, in an echo of Wilson in 1975, would remain neutral and grant his MPs a free vote.

The demise of Corbyn and Corbynism played out through the Brexit process. The PV campaign helped achieve the very things it purported to be against: a hard Brexit, Conservative landslide and a more right-wing populist government. Many close to Corbyn believed that his enemies, having failed to unseat him through constitutional means in 2016, regrouped after 2017.[22] A twin-track strategy emerged of threatening mass resignations from the PLP whilst using Brexit and the PV campaign to weaken his leadership. Alongside the corrosive effects of charges of antisemitism, the cumulative effect was to shatter the intergenerational Corbyn alliance of 2017. Much of the old Bennite left, including the leader himself, retained their long-standing Euroscepticism in contrast to the younger elements attracted to Corbynism. Internal relations at the centre rapidly deteriorated, including between Corbyn and McDonnell.

The manifesto, *It's Time for Real Change*, was similar to the breakthrough document of two years earlier. Both had the feel of the 1973 party programme in their overall approach to nationalization. The 2019 version planned to introduce government bonds to nationalize the six most powerful energy companies along with the railways and the water industry, Royal Mail, the National Grid and broadband wing of British Telecom, the latter not included in the 2017 manifesto. It was estimated that the commitments would bring at least 5 per cent of the total UK assets currently held by private companies into public ownership, boost by over £200 billion the assets owned by the public sector and add over 310,000 to the size of the public sector workforce.[23]

Other fiscal transfers contained in the manifesto included the replacement of universal credit alongside increases in the national minimum wage and pensions. One gigantic expenditure not included in the manifesto but announced in the campaign was a £58 billion universal scheme to compensate more than three million women born in the 1950s who were given insufficient notice of changes to the state pension age, so called WASPI women. The manifesto also pledged a National Care Service to end and reverse privatization in the NHS, as well as a £400 billion 'national transformation fund' for infrastructure and green technologies. A new 'right to food' and 'worker ownership funds' suggested some innovative ideas around economic and social rights and industrial democracy but there was little regarding electoral and constitutional reform of the British state beyond vague support for a constitutional convention, Lords reform and votes at 16.

The election result was a disaster for Labour, the most decisive of four successive electoral defeats since 2005, suggesting a major realignment around class, education, age, geography and Brexit. Labour hung on to just 72 per cent of its 2017 voters, disproportionately losing Leave voters. Boris Johnson's victory came from winning over the lowest paid and least-educated amongst the electorate. Among those identified as social class DE, the Tories secured a 13-point lead compared with 3-point and 8-point Labour leads in 2017 and 2015. Fifty-eight per cent of those with education at GCSE level or below voted Conservative, 33 points ahead of Labour. Labour had a 16 per cent lead amongst graduates. YouGov data revealed 49 per cent of Labour–Conservative switchers cited Brexit as the reason for deserting the party.[24]

Charges of antisemitism had damaged Labour and undermined Corbyn's moral purpose. Labour's internal culture was sour and deeply unattractive to voters. Incoherence over Brexit, ongoing factional battles within the party and a disinterest in constitutional change had undermined the forces pushing for democratic renewal within Corbynism. The project had truncated and resembled an orthodox statist left restoration project; it had more of a Socialist League or Bevanite feel than the democratic insurgency and cultural agility of 2017. Following a 'Brexit realignment', Labour appeared to be losing its class base and regrouping around a new demographic of younger voters and graduates residing in cities and amongst social classes ABC1.[25] Like in other Western democracies, by 2019 Labour looked to have become part of a 'Brahmin left', highly educated, urban dwelling and cosmopolitan with a strong set of liberal values active from a position of relative economic strength within a 'new knowledge economy'.[26]

Within Labour, the post-election debate tended to be over-reliant on a Conservative diagnosis of the result and the emergence of the so-called 'Red Wall'. The 'Red Wall' was a term used to describe constituencies in the Midlands and Northern England which historically supported the Labour Party. In his original analysis, Conservative strategist James Kanagasooriam suggested that voters in those areas were actually demographically similar to more Tory areas yet for cultural reasons were less Conservative than you would have expected given their demographics. Brexit appeared to have helped realign these voters with the Conservative Party.

The 2019 result appeared to be part of a long-term trend. In 2014 Robert Ford and Matthew Goodwin documented the erosion by UKIP of the Labour-supporting working-class vote.[27] At the 2017 election, the

Conservatives lost seats overall, but did gain six Labour-held seats in the Midlands and North. In 2019, Labour suffered a net loss of 47 seats in England, losing approximately 20 per cent of its 2017 support in 'Red Wall' seats.

The effect of the 'Red Wall' phenomenon was to make many on the left wary of appearing socially liberal and counterposing communitarian concerns with liberalism in a general segmentation of the electorate. The tendency was to suggest that in order to rebuild social bonds and appeal to the working class, it was necessary to be illiberal over migration or equality; in effect that Labour's purpose henceforth was not to cohere different conceptions of justice but to *choose* between its virtue and liberal traditions. Such a diagnosis would have significant implications for Labour's direction under its next leader as, following the 2019 defeat, Corbyn announced he would stand down after the election of his successor.

Keir Starmer

Keir Starmer was first elected as an MP on 7 May 2015. Within five years he would be party leader. Soon after entering parliament Starmer joined Labour's front bench as a Shadow Minister for Immigration but resigned on 27 June 2016 as part of the 'chicken coup' against Corbyn. In October of the same year, he accepted the post of Shadow Secretary of State for Exiting the European Union – a position he would hold until the leadership election results were announced on 4 April 2020.

Born in Southwark, London, on 2 September 1962, Starmer, the second of four children, was raised in Oxted, Surrey, by his toolmaker father and mother, a nurse. Named after Labour's first leader, he joined the party at 16. After attending Reigate Grammar School, he headed north to study law at Leeds University. Having secured first class honours, he carried out postgraduate studies at St Edmund Hall, Oxford, graduating as a Bachelor of Civil Law in 1986. The same year Starmer joined *Socialist Alternatives*, a journal of the Pabloist International Revolutionary Marxist Tendency, a tiny anti-statist group that embraced ecology, feminism and democratic self-management. After the closure of *Socialist Alternatives* he became involved with the *Socialist Society*, a bridge between the Labour left and other socialist groups.[28]

By today's standards, Starmer had an unusual background, having never been a political advisor and someone who had enjoyed a successful career before entering politics. Starmer was called to the Bar in 1987 at Middle Temple. In 1990 he became one of the founders of Doughty Street Chambers, comprised of predominantly left-wing lawyers, as well as the secretary of the Haldane Society of Socialist Lawyers. He served as a legal officer for Liberty until 1990. He worked primarily on human rights, including defending death sentence cases in several African and Caribbean countries. He assisted on the notorious McLibel case on behalf of Greenpeace campaigners Helen Steel and David Morris in what became the longest trial in legal history. In 2002 he was appointed a QC. Starmer's involvement in Northern Ireland began through a Haldane Society study of alleged human rights violations under the Emergency Provisions in the early 1990s. He later became a human rights advisor to the Northern Ireland Policing Board, the body responsible for holding to account the Police Service of Northern Ireland in the early 2000s. Between 2002 and 2008 he was a member of the death penalty advisory panel of the Foreign Office. In July 2008 Starmer was appointed the new Director of Public Prosecutions (DPP) and head of the Crown Prosecution Service (CPS). He held the position until November 2013 when he returned to private legal practice and accepted an invitation from Ed Miliband to chair a Labour task force on victims' rights. In December 2014, Starmer was selected to succeed Frank Dobson as Labour's candidate for the safe seat of Holborn and St Pancras. He was elected in May 2015 with 52.9 per cent of the vote and a majority of 17,048.

In his early years in parliament Starmer focused on conventional, familiar criminal justice and human rights matters and remained unattached to any faction beyond the mainstream Tribune MPs group. He looked to be pursuing an orthodox liberal equalities agenda; a perception reinforced after being appointed to Labour's home affairs team. On his reappointment as Shadow Brexit Secretary following Corbyn's re-election, Starmer was emboldened in redefining Labour's Brexit position. He broke the party line in his 2018 Conference speech and became insistent on a second referendum and remaining part of the EU Customs Union, going on to play a key role in the failed April 2019 negotiations with the government. Starmer appeared to be a mainstream liberal lawyer turned politician. His pro-Europeanism reflected his North

Keir Starmer
Source: House of Commons.

London cosmopolitanism but also signalled a professional attachment to European procedural justice and legal oversight and the post-war architecture of international human rights. Starmer presented as an obvious leadership prospect from a mainstream liberal revisionist lane. However, when the vacancy arose, he shifted position.

Starmer: The Candidate

At first on entering the contest, Starmer's language reflected his liberal disposition. He preached the language of factional reconciliation and internal pluralism to rebuild an ugly internal culture and repair a defeated, demoralized party. For much of the membership it was a welcome antidote to years of internal upheaval and factional drive-by attacks. He deployed a language of generosity and emerged as an ethically robust, principled and reliable candidate; an honest choice in an era of post-truth authoritarian populism. His personal characteristics appeared to fit naturally with the concerns of the membership. However, a more cynical interpretation of this natural fit was that it had been manufactured through years of very detailed polling research of the membership privately conducted by YouGov for *Labour Together*, a policy platform run by his campaign chief Morgan McSweeney.

Starmer's political identity changed. His campaign cleverly reorientated his innate liberalism towards an explicit embrace of ethical socialism when advancing the case for modern justice. Starmer launched his campaign on 4 January 2020. On 15 January 2020, he wrote an article in *The Guardian* entitled: 'Labour can win again if we make the moral case for socialism.'[29] In it he argued:

> Labour lost the election. But the moral fight against inequality and injustice must continue … We can win again if we make the moral case for socialism, a moral socialism … There are three foundations to this: economic justice, social justice and climate justice … We should be arguing for a new economic model … Labour's values are my values: peace, justice, equality and dignity for all.

Starmer unveiled ten pledges to the membership that embraced all three of the competing justice traditions that define Labour's history. His campaign wasn't just about reconciling a party membership after years of factional struggle, but was now promising to reconcile all of Labour's political traditions and ideologies 'based on the moral case for socialism'.[30] Pledge one promised *Economic Justice*, two *Social Justice*, three *Climate Justice*, four promised to *Promote peace and human rights*, five *Common Ownership*, six to *Defend Migrant Rights*, seven to *Strengthen workers' rights and trade unions*, eight promised *Radical devolution of power, wealth and opportunity*, nine *Equality* and ten *Effective opposition to the Tories* and rebuild the party culture and internal pluralism.

Starmer would be the healer of the breach but not just between left and right. He was uniting the early ILP and the Fabians. On the one hand, Starmer was seeking to insert ethics back into Labour's economic debate with talk of a new economic model driving the moral case for socialism, with echoes not just of the early Miliband period and the approach of John Smith, but traced further back to Ruskin and Morris and Labour's early pioneers' advocacy of the idea of a moral economy.

On the other hand, his pledges restated the case for distributive justice, public ownership and the old Clause IV, more traditional statist utilitarian Labour traditions. He was also embracing labourism with his commitments to employment rights. Yet with his pledges Starmer was also simultaneously claiming inheritance to liberal revisionism and Labour's five generations of equalities legislation and the post-war legacy of human rights whilst re-establishing an ethical foreign policy. He had become Labour's everyman.

In January, he unveiled a video that brilliantly spliced together his work as a radical lawyer supporting striking miners, print workers and dockers, poll tax protestors, ecological campaigners and the McLibel activists. It detailed his legal judgment against an illegal Iraq War and his record marching against it. It culminated in an endorsement of his role at the CPS in standing up against the powerful by Doreen Lawrence, Labour peer and mother of the murdered teenager Stephen Lawrence. It had been crafted by Tom Kibasi, who as head of the IPPR had overseen its transformation into a radical think tank aligned with many of the more innovative elements around Corbynism. Starmer never looked back; his pledges and video sealed the election with the promise of 'Corbynism without Corbyn' – retaining a radical policy agenda without the unpopularity of the previous leader whilst removing the stain of antisemitism.

On 4 April, the victory that was never in doubt was formally announced. Starmer had won on the first ballot with 56.2 per cent of the 490,731 votes cast (table 12.3). In his acceptance speech, crafted by communitarian thinker Jonathan Rutherford, referring to antisemitism he promised to 'tear out this poison' and placed centre stage 'what really matters, our family, our friends, our relationships. The love we have for one another'. What Attlee and Blair had achieved in government,

Table 12.3 Labour leadership election, 2020

Candidate	Party members		Registered supporters		Affiliated supporters		Total	
	Votes	%	Votes	%	Votes	%	Votes	%
Keir Starmer	225,135	56.1	10,228	76.6	40,417	53.1	275,780	56.2
Rebecca Long-Bailey	117,598	29.3	650	5.0	16,970	22.3	135,218	27.6
Lisa Nandy	58,788	14.6	2,128	17.4	18,681	24.6	79,597	16.2

the alignment of Labour's justice traditions, Starmer had rhetorically promised to his internal electorate. There was room for every shade of member and every socialist variant. It was a straightforward ascent to power but on terms totally unsustainable. In the past Labour had aligned the three traditions of justice – and Labour's different internal constituencies – through creative leadership and building political alliances. Different factions within Labour emerged from these different traditions and so did previous Labour leaders. In contrast, Starmer was suggesting he personally represented all three, without any appreciation of how each emerged from very different philosophical belief systems in their preferences for how society should be organized. Starmer was using his late entry into politics to avoid definition. The drama of Labour's history, its conflicts and divisions, could in the short term be circumvented by ten campaign pledges and a four-minute video. The problem was an obvious one. In compositing Labour's traditions, he had failed to make an argument to his electorate and secure any distinct mandate. Such a tactical manoeuvre came with a strategic cost when he would seek to lead rather than tell members what they wanted to hear.

Starmer: The Leader

He appointed his first Shadow Cabinet the following day. The cast included Miliband as well as both of the candidates he had defeated. Anneliese Dodds became Shadow Chancellor, making her the first woman to serve in that position in either a ministerial or shadow ministerial position, although it was an appointment that revealed little in terms of Starmer's own approach to economics. Despite the constraints of lockdown, in the initial months the media welcomed Starmer's lawyerly, problem-solving method as a sign of Labour's new-found maturity and the party received a polling bounce.

Ascending to the leadership during pandemic and lockdown would have challenged any new leader. In his victory speech Starmer promised to 'engage constructively' in opposition. He faced an ongoing dilemma of both offering support in a national emergency while making legitimate criticism of the Johnson administration's handling of lockdown and the public health crisis, not least because Labour was the devolved government in Wales and pursuing similar policies. Despite supporting the government's overall approach, some viewed him as a 'nitpicking opportunist', unfairly condemning the government and spending 'too much time carping from the side-lines',[31] while others were of the view that he failed to adequately hold the government to account given the relatively high UK Covid death rates.[32]

By the summer Starmer was forced into some tough political decisions. On 25 June 2020, he sacked his former leadership rival Rebecca Long-Bailey, after a tweet appeared to endorse the views of actress Maxine Peake by linking to an interview she had given in *The Independent*. Starmer said that because the article 'contained anti-Semitic conspiracy theories', it should not have been shared by Long-Bailey.

By the autumn Corbyn was gone. In October 2020, the Equality and Human Rights Commission published its damning report on Labour's handling of antisemitism complaints under Corbyn, stating that its analysis pointed to 'a culture within the party which, at best, did not do enough to prevent antisemitism and, at worst, could be seen to accept it'.[33] Corbyn responded that the scale of antisemitism was 'dramatically overstated'. Shortly after, Starmer said those suggesting the issue was exaggerated 'should be nowhere near the Labour Party'. Corbyn was quickly suspended. Corbyn's allies suggested an agreement was struck between Starmer's office and Jon Trickett and Len McCluskey to remove his suspension but this broke down after resignation threats from his PLP enemies if he was readmitted to their ranks. In February 2023, Starmer confirmed that the former leader would not be allowed to run as a Labour candidate at the next election.

Four Pivots

As Starmer's leadership progressed, he quickly shed the everyman persona he had used to ascend to the top of the party. He deployed four key pivots, from his early commitment to internal pluralism, from his 10 campaign pledges, a pivot back to the supply-side socialism of the early 1990s and a shift away from Labour's tradition of liberalism.

The desire for internal reconciliation and the campaign pledge to restore the democratic culture of the party never materialized. Once in office, Starmer oversaw a brutal centralization of power on strictly factional lines and the removal of any signs of independent thought from prospective Labour candidates. During the 2020 leadership election, the organization promoting the interests of the party's traditional utilitarian right, *Labour First*, formed a joint venture with the more liberal Blairite group *Progress* called *Reclaiming Labour*, holding meetings around the country analysing why Labour lost. Following Starmer's victory, they jointly launched a new umbrella organization called *Labour to Win*, 'to bring about fundamental change in the party's culture and organization'. The new group, very closely aligned to key personnel in the leader's office and the party Head Office, then systematically routed the left and the centre in the constituency selection contests for new MPs. In October 2022, the same organization helped deselect Sam Tarry in his Ilford South seat. Scores of candidates from across the left and soft left were ruthlessly excluded from parliamentary shortlists. In June 2023, the elected Mayor of the North of Tyne area was kept out of the running to lead the new north-east region. Boundary changes saw sitting left-wing MPs defeated by the party machine. In June 2023, Neal Lawson received notice that he may face expulsion from the Labour Party – after 44 years of membership – because of a May 2021 retweet supporting closer relations between progressive parties. The move brought widespread condemnation as Lawson was the head of centre-left pressure group *Compass*, and a figure associated with internal reconciliation and liberal pluralist traditions within the party. On 4 September, in a reshuffle that substantially boosted the status of the Labour right, Starmer demoted Lisa Nandy, the Shadow Cabinet member most clearly identified with the party's soft left. Starmer's *first pivot* was away from internal pluralism.

His *second pivot* was over the campaign policy pledges he had made to the membership. Once elected, little was heard of the moral case for socialism. Both the distributional pledges of the campaign and key public ownership commitments were withdrawn, so too were key planks of his equalities agenda, especially regarding migrants. The commitment to implement tax rises for the top 5 per cent of earners was an early casualty. The abolition of tuition fees was abandoned in 2023. Starmer had initially supported common ownership of 'rail, mail, energy and water and an end to outsourcing in the NHS, local government, and criminal justice system'. He quickly rowed back on both energy and water, arguing they were no longer fiscally justifiable given economic constraints, although Labour remained committed to establishing a publicly owned energy company, GB Energy. The one commitment that remained intact concerned the railways, where Labour retained the option of public ownership as the contracts of the operating companies expired. Starmer also moved away from full voting rights for EU nationals, the promise to close immigration detention centres and the commitment to defend free movement after departing from the EU. On 30 May 2023, in the *Daily Express* he wrote, 'Britain's future is outside the EU. Not in the single market, not in the customs union, not with a return to freedom of movement. These arguments are in the past, where they belong.' In June 2023, a long-standing climate investment pledge worth £28 billion a year was diluted to the status of being phased in within Labour's first term, another commitment sacrificed because of the economic climate and the need to offer reassurance to the markets.

These changes met with a predicable reaction within the party. Much of the left was outraged, although such moves were inevitable given Starmer's strategy to get the top job. Having reunited Labour's various traditions, he was always going to have to make some difficult choices about political priorities and his direction of travel. The real problem he faced throughout 2021 and early 2022 was less about pivoting away from his early positions and more to do with the lack of any alternative destinations. Criticism quickly mounted, suggesting Starmer stood for little and lacked any clear vision for the Labour Party. One study found that 'the perceptions of the public suggest he is yet to produce a clear narrative of both the crisis, and his leadership'.[34] *The Guardian* would later suggest that 'Sir Keir wants to appear neither rash nor radical', arguing that 'without clear conviction as to its own purpose, his party lacks the dynamic that only conviction can provide'.[35] Shortly after being elected as Labour's everyman, Starmer appeared bereft of ideas.

The view emerged that Starmer was simply replacing his early 'Corbynism without Corbyn' strategy with a New Labour restoration project. The years of populist disruption in Labour were over. Fiscal restraint and austerity were now the order of the day. So too was attacking Conservative sleaze, embracing business and the market. Competent management was now in vogue. Gradualism was back in fashion at the expense of insurgency. The 'small target' strategy identifiable in the last years of Miliband swiftly reappeared. Veterans from the New Labour years welcomed Starmer shedding his campaign pledges over public ownership, tax and expenditure as signs of political maturity. The plan was to make the coming election a referendum on an unpopular government. The danger was similar to the outcome of the leadership election; securing victory without any mandate for change. From the left the strategy looked 'dispiritingly small and lacking in ambition, given the challenges of the age and a deep disillusionment felt in post-industrial, non-metropolitan England'.[36]

Yet Starmer's journey could be read in a very different way. Less a New Labour restoration than a traditional attempt to rebuild Labour's historical coalition anchored around a discernible labour interest and to re-engineer its relationship with the British working class. In this interpretation, whilst Starmer could still be criticized for his early positioning as Labour's everyman and in the failure to build a mandate for change, this should not disguise the subsequent scale of ambition of his leadership project. Starmer was consciously choosing to challenge political orthodoxy rather than revert to it. It was widely assumed that the 'Brexit realignment' of 2019 had consolidated new political binaries around Europe, age, education, geography and class and that these were here to stay. Yet rather than accept that the 'Brahmin left' was the new base of progressive politics, Starmer was now seeking to re-establish the traditional class base of Labour politics, win back the 'Red Wall' for Labour and claw back the long-term decline in working-class support. It was a bold strategy as many political commentators assumed that Starmer, as a cosmopolitan liberal lawyer who led the case for a second referendum, would be unable to re-engage the non-metropolitan communities that became disillusioned with the Labour Party after Brexit and Corbyn.[37]

To rewind the new political binaries Starmer deployed a *third pivot* away from his leadership campaign, one that embraced Labour's late 1980s and early 1990s 'supply-side socialism' alongside the industrial pluralism of post-war Labour revisionism. Such a supply-side approach focused on active state intervention to re-engineer growth through ambitious public investment, especially in regard to infrastructure and environmental projects, support for research and development, active regional policy, together with a renewed focus on questions of labour supply and human capital. It was very different to New Labour's general acceptance of Thatcher's economic reforms and the effects of the early 1980s supply-side deregulation. Rather than accept the terms of the Thatcher productivity 'miracle', Starmer's focus was to overcome her legacy of a comparatively weak productive performance achieved through muscular state intervention and partnership with business. The route to social justice and equality was to be less about remedial welfare in preference for rebuilding working-class jobs in pursuit of net zero. It looked to be a pivot away from orthodox distributional Labour politics towards an active industrial policy and embrace of a model of stakeholder capitalism informed by some of the earlier concerns of the ethical revisionist tradition and the 'Oxford School' central to the Wilson and Callaghan governments of the 1960s and 1970s discussed in previous chapters.

Starmer's return to post-war industrial pluralism was in part a response to the pandemic where human labour was politicized in ways thought unimaginable throughout the preceding decades. The market for labour stopped. The role of the state vis-à-vis labour was redefined. A Conservative government had to step in and regulate who works, where and under what conditions. Corporatism reappeared as the TUC re-emerged at the centre of economic life for the first time in over 40 years and helped to forge the most significant labour market intervention of living memory: a state furlough programme covering some 11 million workers.

At the 2021 Party Conference, Starmer's deputy Angela Rayner unveiled a Green Paper on Employment Rights. She said Labour's *New Deal for Working People* will be signed into law within the first 100 days of a Labour government. Labour would empower workers to act collectively through Fair Pay Agreements negotiated through sectoral collective bargaining. Labour's Green Paper included the creation of a single status of 'worker' for all but the genuinely self-employed.[38] The agenda would build on successive Labour governments' equalities legislation over rights to flexible working, extended statutory parental leave, bereavement leave and protections for pregnant women. Unions will be strengthened and a single enforcement body created to enforce workers' rights.

This active labour market and supply-side strategy predates the Blair leadership and suggests the Starmer agenda extends beyond a straightforward New Labour restoration exercise. The New Labour era assumed that the traditional class constituencies that underpinned Labour were in long-term decline and that the forms of labour market regulation advocated by Starmer would price people out of work in the global economy. Labour could only thrive by pivoting away from its dependency on working-class voters and their industrial representatives. Starmer was rejecting such assumptions and pivoting back to these traditional constituencies and re-establishing a more traditional role for his party. In this respect it implies a significant Wilsonian re-evaluation of Labour's purpose with the rehabilitation of an active state-led growth agenda and return to questions of economic stakeholding. New Labour it is not.

This political recalibration back to rebuilding relations with the working class involved a final, *fourth pivot*, possibly the most surprising shift of them all, away from the tradition of justice centred on questions of liberty and freedom. Having a background as a liberal human rights lawyer, as leader Starmer's party showed little interest in constitutional reform and the rights-based liberalism of Labour revisionism. The early concerns of the cosmopolitan liberal lawyer evaporated. In contrast to the first phase of the New Labour era and the earlier concerns of both Kinnock and especially John Smith, questions of constitutional and political reform were marginalized under Starmer's leadership, apart from one report received from Gordon Brown over devolution. The modern Labour Party has withdrawn from traditional progressive liberal concern for the structure of British state power and the architecture of the constitution. The modern party appears content to accept traditional utilitarian notions of state capture popular across much of the orthodox left. The defence of a threatened Human Rights Act was never considered a political priority. Starmer has failed to commit to repeal the Public Order Act's constraints on the right to protest nor oppose the 'Spycops Bill' protecting undercover activities. Ideas around a proposed constitutional convention disappeared. In part this approach was in response to Starmer being labelled an elite north London Remain lawyer by his media and political opponents. It might also reveal an alternative interpretation of Starmer's time as the DPP, rather than the radical story depicted in his campaign video when running to be leader.[39] The fourth pivot was deemed a political necessity in order for Labour to once again appeal to working-class 'Red Wall' voters. Yet it might also misread the voters that reside in this part of the electoral landscape.

As a corrective to this simplistic binary between the communitarian concerns of working-class voters and liberal conceptions of justice, in May 2021, YouGov released the results of a major survey of voters in the 'Red Wall'. It showed that 'Red Wall' constituencies 'contain a great diversity of opinions, and indeed widespread support for a range of what we might consider progressive policies and views'.[40] Moreover that 'where Red Wall voters do exhibit socially conservative attitudes, they are not significant stronger (or no more common) than the level of social conservativism which we see among the British public in general'. Starmer's strategy of splitting liberal and virtue justice traditions might misread the voters.

Starmer's fourth pivot might also be in response to shifts within liberalism itself and the rise of identity politics and fears of being trapped within endless culture wars. His repositioning appears intimately connected to a transformation in liberal politics away from nurturing citizenship and the common good towards relativism and a politics of the self. The character of the left has noticeably shifted away from a sacrificial contribution to the commons to one that sees politics as an authentic search for the self, aided by social media echo chambers. This assumes generalization is not possible given assorted personal experiences of privilege, inequality and exploitation. This shift suggests that liberal politics has turned inward to questions of personal identity in ways that threaten traditional conceptions of justice and the equality of rights and poses real challenges to leaders of progressive parties, vividly captured in debates about trans rights. The danger, however, is that Labour retreats from electoral and constitutional reform and misreads the degree of dissatisfaction with traditional British politics amongst the electorate. Cumulatively, Labour under Starmer appears intent on rejecting the liberal legacy of the Kinnock, Smith, Blair and Brown eras.

The cumulative effect of Starmer's four pivots is towards a more traditional statism within Labour and away from mainstream liberalism and the embrace of pluralism both in terms of policy and the internal culture of the modern party. Yet in terms of economic policy, it is a strategy that predates New Labour and, in its desire to re-establish Labour's historic coalition of class interests, is a radical departure form modern political orthodoxy. The wisdom of such a reorientation all depends on how successful it proves to be.

Upturn

Since becoming leader Starmer has seen his political fortunes fluctuate wildly. His initial positive approval ratings were high. Starmer's first real electoral test took place in May 2021 with the scheduled local elections – as well as those delayed in 2020 due to the pandemic. The Conservatives made significant gains and Labour lost 327 of its councillors and control of eight councils, and on the same day was defeated at a by-election in Hartlepool. In the immediate aftermath, a planned reshuffle was derailed following an outcry over leaks that Starmer planned to sack his deputy from her position as party chair and campaigns coordinator. Eventually Angela Rayner emerged with an enhanced role and Rachel Reeves was promoted to Shadow Chancellor, the latter move a sign of Starmer's turn towards the traditional Labour right. Starmer's precarious position slightly improved following a tight 323 vote victory at another by-election in Batley and Spen on 1 July.

What really altered Starmer's fortunes, suggesting he retained the key political ingredient necessary in politics, luck, was the so-called 'partygate' scandal that erupted in November 2021. Starmer effectively deployed his legal skills in the prosecution of Johnson throughout 2021 and 2022. On 30 November, *The Daily Mirror* first reported allegations of Downing Street staff parties that broke lockdown rules. Boris Johnson moved swiftly to deny any rule breaking but a week later a video emerged of his staff joking about such parties in a mock press conference. In January 2022, the police began investigating twelve gatherings, including some attended by the Prime Minister. Johnson, his wife and the Chancellor were all issued with fixed penalty notices. An independent inquiry by Sue Gray concluded there had been a 'failure of leadership'. The fall out included a defection to Labour of Conservative MP Christian Wakeford, the resignation of senior Downing Street aides and the referral of Johnson to the Parliamentary Privileges Committee over charges of misleading parliament. Public disquiet led to a fall in support for the Tories and a Labour revival, with the party taking control of five councils at the 2022 local elections. On 6 June, it was announced that Johnson would face a vote of no confidence. Johnson finally resigned following further by-election defeats in June at Wakefield and Tiverton and Honiton, a scandal over the Deputy Chief Whip Chris Pincher and the resignation of 31 MPs from government posts on 7 July.

On 6 September 2022, Liz Truss was appointed the new Prime Minister. On 23 September, a mini-budget proposed abolishing the top rate of tax and cuts to the basic rate, along with the cancellation of planned corporation tax and national insurance rises, all funded by large-scale borrowing. It amounted to an extreme right-wing supply-side strategy and a confident gamble, rejected by the markets, that tax cuts paid for themselves. Support for the Conservative Party collapsed as widespread financial instability and a fall in sterling led to the reversal of many of the measures, the sacking of the Chancellor and Truss's subsequent resignation on her forty-fifth day in office on 20 October.

Starmer's fortunes greatly improved through 2022. By year end the party was recording polling leads approaching 20 per cent. Strategically, Labour's position in Scotland changed overnight following the shock announcement on 15 February 2023 of Nicola Sturgeon's intention to resign as leader of the Scottish National Party, with twenty Scottish seats included in the top 130 Labour targets.[41]

The 2023 local election results suggested Starmer's strategy of pulling an estranged working-class base back to Labour was working. The Tories lost over 1,000 seats and Labour made over 500 gains. Crucially Labour did noticeably better in areas that voted Leave in the 2016 Brexit referendum, many of which Labour lost to the Tories in 2019. Labour achieved a seven-point swing in areas won by the Tories in 2019, compared to just under three points in areas won by Labour. Labour's best results were in areas of England with fewest university graduates where it netted a six-point swing. In places with more graduates, the swing was only three points.

Starmer appears to have alighted on a political strategy that separates him not just from the legacy of Corbyn but also from that of Thatcher and New Labour. The approach appears Wilsonian, although exclusively framed around growth without the liberal revisionism of the era. It marks a return to Labour gradualism and a politics of distributional justice powered by capitalist growth. Wilson's National Plan was abandoned. He delivered average annual growth rates of 2.2 per cent and his strategy was considered a failure, which culminated in wage restraint and strict spending controls. Starmer's strategy is extraordinarily ambitious. It is a restoration project but not to New Labour, as unfashionably it seeks to rebuild the class coalition and idea of a Labour alliance identifiable since the party's inception. Starmer has helped transform Labour's fortunes since the wretched defeat of 2019 and he appears to be on the cusp of victory. Yet there exists significant internal damage given his retreat from the strategy that helped secure the leadership.

Overall, since 2010 Labour has struggled to discover a unifying sense of purpose after the demise of New Labour and to effectively respond to austerity. In very different ways and with varying levels of success, Miliband, Corbyn and Starmer all attempted to realign the party's justice traditions. All three subsequently changed tack and resorted to a more limited reassertion of Labour's orthodox economism and statism, the familiar terrain of the party's traditional right- and left-wing factions.

Purpose

The challenge facing today's Labour Party is immense. Just a 3 per cent swing would cost the Conservatives their majority at the next election. Yet in 2019, Labour returned its lowest total of MPs since 1935. The party therefore requires something in the order of a 12 per cent swing to secure an overall majority. Labour has only achieved this type of swing twice in its history – in 1945 and 1997.[1] Attlee's extraordinary 1945 landslide was on a swing of 10.7 per cent and Blair's in 1997 was on a 10.2 per cent swing.[2] Labour has led in the opinion polls since January 2022, and by significant margins since 2022, following the catastrophic premiership of Liz Truss. In the three years prior to its 1997 election, Labour consistently recorded levels of support above 50 per cent in the polls, yet on election day itself received 44 per cent of the vote. In 1997, 56 of Labour's 418 MPs were from Scotland, one in seven of Labour's total. In 2019, there was just one Scottish MP elected in Labour's combined total of 202.[3]

It is precisely 100 years since Labour first came to power. There have been six periods of Labour government. The first two were minority administrations.[4] Labour's hold on power has often been precarious. Twice, between 1964 and 1966 and October 1974 and 1977, Labour held small single-figure majorities. Labour has won five major majorities – in 1945, 1966, 1997, 2001 and 2005. Yet having been defeated, it has often been out of office for long periods – 14 years after 1931,[5] 13 years after 1951, 18 after 1979 and approaching 14 years after the 2010 defeat. Excluding wartime coalitions, the party has been in power for a total of 33 years, 13 of which were under New Labour. Only six of the 23 party leaders have become Prime Minister.[6]

The record of past Labour governments is mixed. The primary achievement of the first minority administration between January and November 1924 was to demonstrate that the party was fit to govern. It made a significant intervention over housing policy, managed the effects of the 'Geddes Axe' and introduced some minor social security reforms. The 1929 election saw Labour emerge for the first time as the largest party, but with hindsight it was an unfortunate election to win. By the summer of 1931 the government was consumed by a political and financial crisis that ended disastrously, with the party collapsing from 287 MPs to just 52. Yet these epic events did not destroy the party. The resilience of Labour's class base ensured that by 1935 it had re-established a relatively healthy position amongst the electorate. The 1945–51 Labour government established the political settlement that defined much of the twentieth century with the creation of the welfare state and socialized medicine. Attlee's British New Deal was an extraordinary achievement given the conditions of post-war Britain.

The 11 years that Labour held office between 1964 and 1979 are more difficult to assess. The 1964–70 government embarked on what would become a half century of pioneering Labour equalities legislation culminating in the 2010 Equality Act. It also sought to build a modern growth agenda to resolve emerging challenges of comparative productive capacity that remain unresolved today. Yet it would be forced to retreat, concede defeat and buckle under international pressure and a failure to achieve domestic labour law reforms. The 1974–9 government is generally considered a failure. Yet given the challenges that confronted it, the administration achieved a great deal and skilfully survived a series of economic and industrial storms. By late 1978, it might well have been re-elected.

Controversy also surrounds the 1997–2010 government. The Good Friday Agreement remains an extraordinary achievement. The government's early record as a liberal reforming administration endures in terms of devolution, equalities and human rights reform. Its successes in health and education are often overlooked, although its housing policies were disappointing. Labour's record in recycling a growth dividend to rebuild public services and secure distributive justice was for a decade unparalleled. Yet much of it unravelled due to Labour's own culpability in helping create the conditions that led to a financial crisis, recession and austerity. The government also lost trust and moral purpose following the invasion of Iraq and became increasingly illiberal. Despite significant achievements, when set against Blair's 1997 Conference pledge to lead 'one of the great reforming governments in British history' and the benefits of a decade of growth, it is difficult not to conclude that it amounted to a missed opportunity.

Overall, on the 100th anniversary of the first Labour government, the party has much to celebrate, from a welfare state and free NHS to five decades of pioneering equalities legislation, the national minimum wage and the Good Friday Agreement. Labour has achieved many extraordinary things on behalf of the British people.

Vivid History

Labour's history includes some occasional, compelling victories. In 1945 it successfully defined the Tories as the party of the past; of mass unemployment and appeasement. Wilson offered the prospect of technological modernity and Blair a New Britain after the decline, drift and sleaze of the Major years.

More often it is a story of defeat. Even today, the disaster of 1931 still haunts the party after MacDonald, Thomas and Snowden entered the National Government. The rejection of a tired Attlee administration in 1951 still pains given the extraordinary achievements of that government. Thatcher's ascendancy in 1979 and Labour's threatened eclipse by the SDP scarred the party at large and a generation of its leaders. There was little in the way of intellectual and political reckoning following the New Labour years and the 2010 defeat, replaced with bouts of wretched factionalism and 14 years of isolation.

The Labour Party is complicated. It has always contained a vibrant mix of socialists and social democrats and a host of different traditions, factions and institutions. Keir Hardie's original idea of the Labour alliance has endured; in certain respects Keir Starmer is attempting to rebuild it today.

Labour has always been a home for socialists, even revolutionaries. Figures such as Jeremy Corbyn and Tony Benn are familiar ones within its history, despite recent assertions that, following his suspension, Corbyn is in some sense alien to Labour's traditions. Apart from between 2015 and 2019 the left has never been ascendant, although during the early 1930s, 1970s and 1980s it experienced years of relative strength. The three high points of the left came with the 1973 programme, the constitutional victories of the early 1980s and the 2017 manifesto. The right has generally been in control, yet despite the departures of the SDF and ILP, the left has been reluctant to break with the party. Despite what many regard as the failures of successive Labour governments, the electoral system ensures an ongoing socialist dilemma given the fortunes of the SDF, ILP and other communist and Trotskyist groups outside the Labour Party.

It is a story of bitter rivalries and factions. The events of 1931 led to ongoing tensions between the Socialist League and the new Fabians. In the 1950s it was between the Bevanites and revisionists, and throughout the late 1970s and early 1980s between the left and right, best captured in the 1981 Benn/Healey deputy leadership contest. In the 1990s, it took the form of 'modernizers' versus 'traditionalists' and then between 'New' and 'Old' Labour. Most recently we have had Jeremy Corbyn's ascent to power and his battles with the parliamentary party.

These stories are burnt into party mythology, although fights for internal supremacy often appear impenetrable to outsiders as they have regularly been fought over the minutiae of the party's constitution. Such battles have been over the union link, candidate selection and the method of electing the leader. They have included contests over the details of policy formation and ratification, the role of the NEC and annual Conference and over Clause IV of the original party constitution.

Despite the heroics and the mythology, any assessment of Labour's radical potentials has to acknowledge that it was created in part for defensive conservative reasons, to keep the law out of industrial relations and preserve the voluntarist tradition. Yet Labour has never been a narrow sectional party. In its relations with the unions, it has had recurring tensions including over responses to the 1926 General Strike, events surrounding the formation of the National Government in 1931, *In Place of Strife* in 1969, successive attempts at wage restraint, the Winter of Discontent in 1978/9 and throughout the 1984/5 miners' strike.

Inevitability and Contingency

Throughout the drama, two essential questions are ever present. First, the *origins question*. Was the rise of a party of labour inevitable given the antagonistic nature of capitalist relations of production, the social and economic demands of an expanding working class and the inherent limits of liberalism? Second, the *death question*. Is the decline of a party of labour inevitable given long-term changes in British class relations? This second question has informed waves of left- and right-wing Labour revisionism, rescued the party from tendencies towards sentimentality and nostalgia and ensured it has adapted in order to survive.

In the 100 years since the first Labour government, the party and the country have both changed beyond recognition. Yet Labour has proven to be both a remarkably resilient and politically agile institution in ways that belie deterministic assumptions of how and why it emerged and assertions of its imminent decline. In the 50 years following the first Labour government, despite assumptions about the inevitability of gradualism, Labour held office for just 15 years. In the next 50 years, when Labour's forward march was supposedly over, it held office for 18. Debates about the inevitability of Labour's rise and fall turn on questions of class and of class essentialism. Yet whilst Labour has historically drawn its strength from the working class, this has always been contingent on questions of geography, gender, race and age, and throughout its history the party has always aligned with elements of the progressive middle class.

Throughout the book we have emphasized questions of contingency. War is one such contingency. It is difficult to understand the first two minority governments and landslide of 1945 without the contingencies of two world wars. The first conflict shaped the contributions of leaders such as MacDonald and Attlee and fractured the Liberals. Wartime mobilization reset political thinking, not least in the ways it dramatically reconfigured the organizational reach and purpose of the state and shaped internal economic debate. As part of Churchill's wartime coalition, Labour's management of the domestic agenda helps us account for the 1945 victory. Labour benefitted from the extended range of state machinery mobilized in a cross-class pursuit of the war effort. Such a regime both legitimized and helped deliver a platform for state planning and ownership, welfare reform and redistribution; major elements of the post-war settlement.

From a very different perspective, the Second World War and a generation's exposure to fascism and authoritarianism brought with it renewed concern for questions of freedom and liberty and helped establish an international human rights architecture that shaped five decades of equalities legislation under successive Labour administrations. More recently the Falklands campaign reset the 1983 election and helped consolidate Thatcherism at the expense of Labour and its leader Michael Foot. The Iraq conflict derailed the Blair administration and still hangs over the party and the legacy of New Labour.

Labour's history has also been shaped by the contingencies of global economic events. The Wall Street Crash, post-war austerity and reconstruction, 1970s oil shocks and stagflation, the September 1992 sterling crisis termed 'Black Wednesday', the later crisis of 2007/8 and the politics of austerity all loom large throughout Labour history. Despite long-standing assumptions of social evolution through capitalist growth, in government Labour has regularly sacrificed its social programmes with the acceptance of austerity.

Personal contingencies also inform the story, including the early deaths of leaders such as Hugh Gaitskell at 56 and John Smith at 55.[7] So too do the contingencies affecting key decisions. After several ballots, Keir Hardie was elected as the first chairman of the PLP in February 1906 by just one vote over David Shackleton. Callaghan and Brown narrowly resisted early elections in 1978 and 2008. The invasion of Iraq might have been averted if Al Gore had not narrowly lost to George W. Bush in November 2000. A decade later David Miliband narrowly lost to his brother Ed. Labour' s history might have played out very differently if any of these marginal outcomes had gone the other way.

This is not to dispute that various intellectual influences have ensured that a sense of socialist inevitability has been a regular drumbeat throughout Labour history. These include, amongst others, a variety of religious influences, economistic assumptions of technological change, utopian ideas of social progress and the inevitability of gradualism. The story of socialist evolution was very much part of the 1945 story captured in *Let Us Face the Future*. Yet we have also seen how these same tendencies left Labour governments lacking in terms of intellectual resources, negligent in terms of policy, reactive and susceptible to outside events which they have been unable to influence. Assertions of inevitability have paradoxically often left the party at the mercy of events, especially at moments of crisis.

Purpose

Labour has no settled understanding of what it is for, its purpose, grounded in a single conception of justice. Arguably intellectual vagueness has helped keep the party together. Its various traditions, factions and organizations can cohabit and share common ground, such as a belief in parliamentary democracy, concerns for social reform and a commitment to trade union organization. They can cohere around certain policies and campaigns without an official shared ideology. Arguably this lack of creed is a strength rather a weakness; in order to survive, a modern political party requires a certain opaqueness regarding its purpose. Yet it can tilt into inertia and intellectual emptiness.

We have suggested an interpretation of Labour history which appreciates how competing theories of justice have sought influence within the party. This contrasts with the search for an essential Labour and socialist identity. There is no settled theory of socialism or understanding of Labour's purpose. We suggest Labour's successes and failures can be understood less in terms of its inevitable rise and fall but rather by its ability to unite and cohere three competing approaches to justice within an overall political organization and an agenda for government.

The book has identified three general philosophical approaches that underpin competing visions of how society should be organized. These are concerned with the expansion of human welfare, freedom and virtue. All form valuable and indispensable parts of the Labour tradition and the ways they have interrelated offers a method to understand *A Century of Labour*. The party has prospered when the three different traditions combine, notably under the Attlee government, during the brief leadership of John Smith and the first term of the Blair government. Yet this requires a self-confident culture of pluralism, internal generosity and creative leadership not often identifiable over the last 100 years.

Too often one approach has tended to dominate to the exclusion of others – the statist, labourist tradition of distributional justice. For both classical Marxism and Fabianism, socialism has a very specific meaning as a system of state ownership and economic planning to maximize the welfare of the people. From its creation as a party pursuing the interests of labour, there remained a dominant orthodox and instrumental interpretation of Labour's purpose – seen as the party of just rewards rather than grand theories. Yet hidden within this approach existed a grand theory – utilitarianism.

A focus on material welfare has often been at the expense of deeper moral or spiritual questions and concerns for human liberty and freedom, ideas which have existed throughout the history of the left. By contracting the concerns of Labour towards questions of utility, we have overturned the priorities of much radical thought developed over many centuries. Today, as a party, we suffer the collateral intellectual, cultural and political damage. We are losing the capacity to diagnose and resist that which politically concerns us most about contemporary capitalism. The paradox of the party's tendency towards utilitarianism is that Labour has often struggled to successfully manage the economy and engineer growth to contain austerity.

History demonstrates to us that Labour can successfully weave together different approaches to justice to successfully own a story of national renewal; one equipped with moral purpose that can rebuild civic virtue, enhance human rights and advance equality. Such an approach has in the past transformed the country and can do so again. Without this, Labour can often appear cold and transactional.

There are lessons here for the present Labour Party. It is vital that the current Labour leader seeks to rehabilitate a contemporary approach to justice that draws from and reconciles these varied approaches; the success of the next Labour government will depend on it. Yet at present the Labour Party appears intent on sacrificing its historical concern for questions of liberty and human freedom in pursuit of a stylized vision of the working class. History suggests that when Labour's justice traditions collide, the party fails to prosper. For Labour to succeed it requires its leadership to draw support and intellectual inspiration from all three traditions, yet left- and right-wing factionalism has often hindered such creative advances.

Without such reconciliation Labour often recoils into a default instrumentalism, reliant on capitalist growth to prosper. Such growth looks an unlikely immediate prospect. Stale technocratic social democracy will prove unable to resist the rise of authoritarian populism and challenge the forces that endanger the foundations of modern liberal democracy. Yet Labour is part of a rich radical tradition dating back to *Magna Carta*, the Peasants Revolt of 1381 and the Civil Wars. Its antecedents include those who embraced the religion of socialism and the pioneers who built the Labour alliance and later created the welfare state. Labour established five generations of equalities legislation and contributed to the international development of human rights. Labour has resources to draw on, traditions to excavate. Without such intellectual and political reconciliation, a party of labour could be destroyed by victory.

Appendices

Appendix: A

Table A.1 Labour Party Individual Membership

Year	Individual members*	Year	Individual members*	Year	Individual members*
1928	215,000	1960	790,000	1992	280,000
1929	228,000	1961	751,000	1993	279,530
1930	277,000	1962	767,000	1994	266,270
1931	297,000	1963	830,000	1995	305,189
1932	372,000	1964	830,000	1996	365,110
1933	366,000	1965	817,000	1997	400,465
1934	381,000	1966	776,000	1998	405,238
1935	419,000	1967	734,000	1999	387,776
1936	431,000	1968	701,000	2000	361,000
1937	447,000	1969	681,000	2001	311,000
1938	429,000	1970	680,000	2002	272,000
1939	409,000	1971	700,000	2003	248,294
1940	304,000	1972	703,000	2004	214,952
1941	227,000	1973	665,000	2005	201,374
1942	219,000	1974	692,000	2006	198,026
1943	236,000	1975	675,000	2007	182,370
1944	266,000	1976	659,000	2008	176,891
1945	487,000	1977	660,000	2009	166,247
1946	645,000	1978	676,000	2010	193,961
1947	608,000	1979	660,000	2011	193,300
1948	629,000	1980	348,000	2012	187,537
1949	730,000	1981	277,000	2013	189,531
1950	908,000	1982	274,000	2014	193,961
1951	876,000	1983	295,000	2015	388,103
1952	1,015,000	1984	323,000	2016	543,645
1953	1,005,000	1985	313,000	2017	564,443
1954	934,000	1986	297,000	2018	518,659
1955	843,000	1987	289,000	2019	532,046
1956	845,000	1988	266,000	2020	523,332
1957	913,000	1989	294,000	2021	432,213
1958	889,000	1990	311,000		
1959	848,000	1991	261,000		

* Officially there was no individual membership until 1918. No count of individual members was made until 1928.

Source: For the period before 1992, David Butler and Gareth Butler, *British Political Facts 1900–94* (London: Macmillan, 1994), pp. 146–7. For the period 1993 to 1999, Labour Party NEC reports. For the period 2000–21, Labour Party annual reports.

Appendix B

Table A.2 Governments Formed Following General Elections since 1900

Date	Party forming government	Prime Minister	Majority*
26/9–24/10/1900	Conservative	Lord Salisbury	
12/1–8/2/1906	Liberal	Henry Campbell-Bannerman	
15/1–10/2/1910	Liberal	H.H Asquith	
3–19/12/1910	Liberal	H.H. Asquith	
14/12/1918	Coalition (Con and Lib)**	David Lloyd George	283
15/11/1922	Conservative	Andrew Bonar Law	74
06/12/1923	Labour***	Ramsay MacDonald	None
29/10/1924	Conservative	Stanley Baldwin	210
30/05/1929	Labour	Ramsay MacDonald	None
27/10/1931	National†	Ramsay MacDonald	492
14/11/1935	National‡	Stanley Baldwin	242
05/07/1945	Labour	Clement Attlee	147
23/02/1950	Labour	Clement Attlee	6
25/10/1951	Conservative	Sir Winston Churchill	16
26/05/1955	Conservative	Sir Anthony Eden	59
08/10/1959	Conservative	Harold Macmillan	99
15/10/1964	Labour	Harold Wilson	5
31/03/1966	Labour	Harold Wilson	97
18/06/1970	Conservative	Edward Heath	31
28/02/1974	Labour	Harold Wilson	None
10/10/1974	Labour	Harold Wilson	4
03/05/1979	Conservative	Margaret Thatcher	44
09/06/1983	Conservative	Margaret Thatcher	144
11/06/1987	Conservative	Margaret Thatcher	101
09/04/1992	Conservative	John Major	21
01/05/1997	Labour	Tony Blair	178
07/06/2001	Labour	Tony Blair	166
05/05/2005	Labour	Tony Blair	65
06/05/2010	Coalition (Con and Lib Dem)§	David Cameron	77
07/05/2015	Conservative	David Cameron	11
08/06/2017	Conservative	Theresa May	None
24/07/2019	Conservative	Boris Johnson	None
12/12/2019	Conservative	Boris Johnson	81

* Government majority is calculated as the number of seats held by the governing parties minus the number of seats held by all other parties or independent Members. The Speaker is excluded when calculating the majority, but MPs who did not take their seats (e.g., Sinn Féin Members) are included.
** The Conservatives and Prime Minister David Lloyd George's wing of the Liberal Party contested the 1918 general election as a coalition. More than half of House of Commons seats were won by Conservative candidates, so that the subsequent coalition government was Conservative dominated. The majority of 283 is calculated including the 73 Sinn Fein Members who did not take their seats.
*** Labour formed a government after the 1923 election but the Conservatives had won the most seats (although not a majority).
† Prime Minister Ramsay MacDonald led a 'National Government' into the 1931 election, which consisted of the Conservative and Liberal parties along with a few National Labour Members like MacDonald. Conservatives won over three quarters of the seats, making the National Government Conservative dominated.
‡ The Conservatives contested the 1935 election again as part of a National Government. The Prime Minister before and after the election, Stanley Baldwin, was a Conservative. The National Government remained Conservative dominated as over half of House of Commons seats were won by Conservative candidates.
§ The Conservatives were the largest party following the 2010 election but did not have a majority. A coalition government was formed with the Liberal Democrats.
Source: Colin Rallings and Michael Thrasher, *British Electoral Facts 1832–2006*; Peter Joyce, *Politico's Guide to UK General Elections 1832–2001*; House of Commons Library, General Election 2017: results and analysis; House of Commons Library, General Election 2019: results and analysis.

Appendix C

Table A.3a General Election Results, 1918–2019: UK – Seats Won

Date	Con*	Lab**	LD***	PC/SNP	Other	Total
26/9–24/10/1900	402	2	183	..	83	670
12/1–8/2/1906	156	29	397	..	88	670
15/1–10/2/1910	272	40	274	..	84	670
3–19/12/1910	271	42	272	..	85	670
14/12/1918†	382	57	164	..	105	707
15/11/1922	344	142	115	..	14	615
06/12/1923	258	191	158	..	8	615
29/10/1924	412	151	40	..	12	615
30/05/1929	260	287	59	0	9	615
27/10/1931	522	52	36	0	5	615
14/11/1935	429	154	21	0	11	615
05/07/1945	210	393	12	0	25	640
23/02/1950	298	315	9	0	3	625
25/10/1951	321	295	6	0	3	625
26/05/1955	345	277	6	0	2	630
08/10/1959	365	258	6	0	1	630
15/10/1964	304	317	9	0	0	630
31/03/1966	253	364	12	0	1	630
18/06/1970	330	288	6	1	5	630
28/02/1974	297	301	14	9	14	635
10/10/1974	277	319	13	14	12	635
03/05/1979	339	269	11	4	12	635
09/06/1983	397	209	23	4	17	650
11/06/1987	376	229	22	6	17	650
09/04/1992	336	271	20	7	17	651
01/05/1997	165	418	46	10	20	659
07/06/2001	166	412	52	9	20	659
05/05/2005	198	355	62	9	22	646
06/05/2010	306	258	57	9	20	650
07/05/2015	330	232	8	59	21	650
08/06/2017	317	262	12	39	20	650
12/12/2019	365	202	11	52	20	650

* CONSERVATIVE COLUMN: Includes Conservative and Liberal Unionist for 1910; Coalition Conservative for 1918; National, National Liberal and National Labour candidates for 1931–5; National and National Liberal candidates for 1945; National Liberal & Conservative candidates 1945–70.

** LABOUR COLUMN: Includes Labour Repr. Cmte. for 1900 and 1906 election; Coalition Liberal Party for 1918; National Liberal for 1922; and Independent Liberal for 1931. Figures show Liberal/SDP Alliance vote for 1983–1987 and Liberal Democrat vote from 1992 onwards.

APPENDICES

Table A.3b General Election Results, 1918–2019: UK – Share of Vote (%)

Date	Con*	Lab**	LD***	PC/SNP	Other	Total
26/9–24/10/1900	50.2	1.3	45.1	..	3.4	100
12/1–8/2/1906	43.4	4.8	48.9	..	2.9	100
15/1–10/2/1910	46.8	7.0	43.5	..	2.7	100
3–19/12/1910	46.6	6.4	44.2	..	2.8	100
14/12/1918†	38.7	20.8	25.6	..	14.9	100
15/11/1922	38.5	29.7	28.8	..	3.0	100
06/12/1923	38.0	30.7	29.7	..	1.6	100
29/10/1924	46.8	33.3	17.8	..	2.1	100
30/05/1929	38.1	37.1	23.5	0.0	1.3	100
27/10/1931	60.7	30.9	7.0	0.1	1.3	100
14/11/1935	53.3	38.0	6.7	0.1	1.9	100
05/07/1945	39.6	48.0	9.0	0.2	3.2	100
23/02/1950	43.4	46.1	9.1	0.1	1.3	100
25/10/1951	48.0	48.8	2.6	0.1	0.6	100
26/05/1955	49.7	46.4	2.7	0.2	1.0	100
08/10/1959	49.4	43.8	5.9	0.4	0.6	100
15/10/1964	43.4	44.1	11.2	0.5	0.8	100
31/03/1966	41.9	48.0	8.5	0.7	0.9	100
18/06/1970	46.4	43.1	7.5	1.7	1.4	100
28/02/1974	37.9	37.2	19.3	2.6	3.1	100
10/10/1974	35.8	39.3	18.3	3.4	3.1	100
03/05/1979	43.9	36.9	13.8	2.0	3.3	100
09/06/1983	42.4	27.6	25.4	1.5	3.1	100
11/06/1987	42.3	30.8	22.6	1.7	2.6	100
09/04/1992	41.9	34.4	17.8	2.3	3.5	100
01/05/1997	30.7	43.2	16.8	2.5	6.8	100
07/06/2001	31.6	40.7	18.3	2.5	6.9	100
05/05/2005	32.4	35.2	22.0	2.2	8.2	100
06/05/2010	36.1	29.0	23.0	2.2	9.7	100
07/05/2015	36.8	30.4	7.9	5.3	19.5	100
08/06/2017	42.3	40.0	7.4	3.5	6.8	100
12/12/2019	43.6	32.1	11.5	4.4	8.4	100

*** The LD COLUMN includes the Liberal Party in the 1900, 1906 and 1910 elections.
† 1918 figures include all of Ireland. After the creation of the Irish Free State in 1922 Northern Ireland remained part of the United Kingdom.
Note: 1. For elections up to 1992, the Speaker of the House of Commons is listed under the party they represented before their appointment. From 1997 the Speaker is listed under 'Other'. University seats, numbering 15 in 1918 and 12 in the years to 1945.
Source: Colin Rallings and Michael Thrasher, *British Electoral Facts 1832–2006*. House of Commons Library, CBP7186; General Election 2015, CBP7979; General Election 2017: results and analysis, CBP8749. General Election 2019: results and analysis.

Notes

Preface

1 Newspaper Placard, 22 January 1924, quoted in J. Shepherd and K. Laybourn, *Britain's First Labour Government*, Palgrave Macmillan, 2013, p. 1.

Chapter 1: History

1 Revised in 1994, the original clause called for 'common ownership of the means of production, distribution, and exchange, and the best obtainable system of popular administration and control of each industry or service'.

2 Throughout this book the government majority is calculated as the number of seats held by the governing parties minus the number of seats held by all the other parties or independent Members. The Speaker is excluded when calculating the majority, but MPs who did not take their seats, for example Sinn Fein Members, are included (see Appendicies B and C).

3 Fortunately, this is a rich seam in Labour Party history, which includes, for instance, Kenneth O. Morgan's various biographies of figures such as Hardie, Michael Foot and Callaghan, David Marquand's work on Ramsay MacDonald, John Shepherd on George Lansbury, and John Bew on Attlee. K.O. Morgan, *Keir Hardie: Radical and Socialist*, Faber and Faber, 2011. K.O. Morgan, *Michael Foot: A Life*, HarperCollins, 2008. K.O. Morgan, *Callaghan: A Life*, Oxford University Press, 2007. D. Marquand, *Ramsay MacDonald: A Biography*, Jonathan Cape, 1977. J. Shepherd, *George Lansbury: At the Heart of Old Labour*, Oxford University Press, 2004. J. Bew, *Citizen Clem: A Biography of Attlee*, Riverrun, 2016.

4 For instance, the contributors in *Labour's First Century* evaluate Labour not against the standards of people who wanted it to be a revolutionary party, but 'against its own aims and values, and against what might reasonably have been achieved'. D. Tanner, P. Thane and N. Tiratsoo (eds) *Labour's First Century*, Cambridge University Press, 2000.

5 Brilliant examples are John Shepherd and Keith Laybourn's *Britain's First Labour Government* and *The Second Labour Government: A Reappraisal*, Palgrave Macmillan, 2011, edited by John Shepherd, Jonathan Davis and Chris Wrigley, and David Howell's *MacDonald's Party: Labour Identities and Crisis 1922–1931*, Manchester University Press, 2002.

6 On the origin and death question see Keith Laybourn, 'The History of the Labour Party', *History Today*, 66(1), January 2016.

7 R. McKibben, *The Evolution of the Labour Party 1910–1935*, Clarendon Press, 1983. K. Laybourn, 'The Rise of Labour and the Decline of Liberalism: The State of the Debate', *History*, 80, June 1995. P.F. Clarke, *Lancashire and the New Liberalism*, Cambridge University Press, 1971.

8 E. Hobsbawm, 'Forward March of Labour Halted?', Marx Memorial Lecture, 1978, reproduced in *Marxism Today*, September 1978.

9 It is a long-standing criticism of the Enlightenment that it overestimated our search for reason and progress in pursuit of an apparently linear history – the arc that bends in favour of progressive forces. For example, John Gray has suggested: 'The myth is that the progress achieved in science and technology can occur in ethics, politics or, more simply, civilisation. The myth is that the advances made in civilisation can be the basis for a continuing, cumulative improvement'. https://www.vice.com/en/article/qbwqem/john-gray-interview-atheism

10 Although we could go further back and suggest Labour has throughout its history been aware of its potential demise given the near-death experience of 1931.

11 R.H. Tawney, 'The Choice Before the Labour Party', in R.H. Tawney, *The Attack and Other Papers*, George Allen and Unwin, 1981, pp. 52–71.

12 Such as a strong Labour tradition concerned with gas and water municipal socialism within local government.

13 Sidney Webb, *Socialism: True and False*, Fabian Tract no. 51, 1894.

14 Although, as we shall see, only in the 1930s did Labour begin to formulate precise and workable nationalization policies through the work of a generation of young revisionists.

15 'TIGMOO' is a faintly tongue-in-cheek piece of jargon, used affectionately by those on the inside to describe the UK labour movement, standing for 'This Great Movement of Ours'.

16 E.P. Thompson, *The Making of the English Working Class*, Penguin Classics, 2013. E.P. Thompson, *William Morris, Romantic to Revolutionary*, Merlin, 2011. C.A.R. Crosland, *The Future of Socialism*, Vintage, 1956. P. Diamond, *New Labour's Old Roots: Revisionist Thinkers in Labour's History*, Imprint Academic, 2015. G. Foote, *The Labour Party's Political Thought: A History*, Croom Helm, 1985.

17 Henry Pelling was a quiet devotee of the ILP as well as a famous Labour Party and union historian.

18 D. Marquand, *The Progressive Dilemma*, Heinemann, 1991.

19 Rather than in individual countries such as Scotland and Wales.

20 Chesterton actually said – in *Orthodoxy*, Chapter Four 'The Ethics of Elfland' – 'Tradition means giving a vote to most obscure of all classes, our ancestors. It is the democracy of the dead'. G.K. Chesterton, *Orthodoxy*, Chump Change, 1908.

Chapter 2: Justice

1 Tanner et al. (eds) *Labour's First Century*, pp. 1–7.

2 M. Sandel, *Justice: What's the Right Thing to Do?*, Penguin, 2010.

3 J. Bentham, *An Introduction to the Principles of Morals and Legislation*, CreateSpace Independent Publishing, 2017. J.S. Mill, *Utilitarianism*, Oxford University Press, 1998. H. Sidgwick, *Methods of Ethics*, Hackett Publishing, 1981.

4 Francis Hutcheson, an Ulster Scot within the tradition of the Enlightenment, pre-figured attempts by Bentham to quantify the utility of any action and is generally credited with asserting that the benefits of any action should be calculated by how it maximizes the happiness of the maximum amount of people.

5 For obvious environmental reasons, they increasingly include intergenerational questions of future justice.

6 F. Klug, *A Magna Carta for All Humanity: Homing in on Human Rights*, Routledge, 2015, pp. 13–77.

7 Eleanor Roosevelt, Address to the United Nations General Assembly on the Adoption of the Universal Declaration of Human Rights, December 1948, published by the Department of State in *Human Rights and Genocide: Selected Statements; United Nations Resolution Declaration and Conventions*, 1949.

8 Neo-liberalism is best understood as a combination of the utility theory of neo-classical economics and philosophical concerns with liberty.

9 Leading some to question if it constitutes part of 'the left' at all. Marx, for example, mocked the 'so-called rights of man' and it is an approach widely abused by the reductive economistic left.

10 J. Rawls, *A Theory of Justice*, Harvard University Press, 1971.

11 M. Sandel, 'Populism, Trump and the Future of Democracy', *Open Democracy*, 9 May 2018, p. 5.

12 Cicero noted: 'virtue may be defined as a habit of mind in harmony with reason and the order of nature. It has four parts: wisdom, justice, courage, temperance'. M.T. Cicero, *De Inventrione*, Kessinger Publishing, 2004.

13 S. Yeo, 'A New Life: The Religion of Socialism in Britain, 1883–1896', *History Workshop Journal*, 4(1), 1977, 5–56.

14 Throughout, certain virtues and beliefs reappear, including the seven Christian virtues made up of the four *Cardinal Virtues* of prudence, justice, temperance and courage alongside the three *Theological Virtues* of faith, hope and charity.

A variation occurs within *Catholic Social Teaching* with an emphasis on social justice, questions of human dignity, especially regarding labour, a belief in solidarity for the common good, charity and subsidiarity, and preferential support for the poor. The key question remains, however, to quote MacIntyre: 'are there too many different and incompatible conceptions of virtue, for there to be any real unity to the concept or indeed to the history?'. A. MacIntyre, *After Virtue: A Study in Moral Theory*, University of Notre Dame Press, 1981, p. 169.

15 Although within early ethical socialist thinking there remained a tendency to insert a sense of divine certainty in the direction of social change in place of the economic certainties contained within other economistic traditions.

16 They can also be traced back to the enigmatic Thomas Carlyle – a major influence on Ruskin, Morris and Keir Hardie – with his conception of community consciousness, and the moral imperative to challenge the social order and a rejection of more restricted motivations of class.

17 In 1892, the *Labour Prophet* and the *Labour Hymm Book* both emerged out of the Labour Church, first founded in October 1891 by the Unitarian minister John Trevor.

18 P. Ackers and A.J. Reid, 'Other Worlds of Labour: Liberal-Pluralism in Twentieth-Century British Labour History', in P. Ackers and A.J. Reid (eds) *Alternatives to State-Socialism in Britain: Other Worlds of Labour in the Twentieth Century*, Palgrave Macmillan, 2016, p. 2.

19 More widely, the influence extended into groups such as the Garden City Movement, the work of libertarian left thinkers such as Colin Ward and into the arts, including the work of theatre director Joan Littlewood.

20 Sandel, *Justice: What's the Right Thing to Do?* A. Sen, 'Capability and Wellbeing', in M. Nussbaum and A. Sen (eds) *The Quality of Life*, Clarendon Press, 1993, pp. 30–53.

21 There are certain overlaps but also significant differences with the statist, collectivist and associational divisions within socialism identified by Stephen Yeo. See S. Yeo, *A Useable Past: A History of Association, Co-Operation and Un-Statist Socialism in 19th and Early 20th Century Britain. Volume 2: A New Life, the Religion of Socialism in Britain, 1883–1896: Alternatives to State Socialism*, Edward Everett Root, 2017.

22 K. Marx and F. Engels, 'Manifesto of the Communist Party', *Selected Works, Vol. 1*, Progress Publishers, 1969, pp. 98–137.

23 C.A.R. Crosland, *The Future of Socialism*, Jonathan Cape, 1956.

24 To recap, Crosland identified twelve socialist doctrines that existed before his own. Three cover the value theories of Mill, Ricardo and Marx as well as a Fabian tradition, a Soviet-inspired 'planning' framework and a 'welfarist' or 'paternalist' approach. He also highlighted an early nineteenth-century 'natural

law' doctrine of common land and a syndicalist or 'guild' tradition of industrial democracy. He added 'Owenism' – a utilitarian approach to economic cooperation – before concluding with an ethical Christian Socialist tradition, an ILP doctrine of fellowship and the separate one of William Morris. A rather cumbersome dozen socialisms to add to his own.

25 Assorted 'Marxisms' have been highly influential throughout Labour history including early organizational battles and factions shaping the creation of the party, the post-war influence of the New Left and present-day tensions and disagreements in and around 'Corbynism'.

26 E.P. Thompson, *William Morris: Romantic to Revolutionary*, Merlin Press, 1977.

27 R. Williams, *Culture and Society: 1780–1950*, Spokesman Books, 2013.

28 J. Ruskin, 'Lectures on Art. 1870', in E.T. Cook, and A. Wedderburn (eds) *The Works of John Ruskin, vol. 20*, George Allen, 1905, p. 39.

Chapter 3: Origins

1 It was Sidney Webb who, as Chairman of the party at the 1923 Conference, referred to the 'inevitable gradualness' of Labour's advance.

2 There was of course no payment of MPs at the time, obviously further discouraging working-class representation.

3 In 1898, West Ham Borough became the first ever Labour-controlled Council.

4 In 1892, Fred Jowett became the first socialist to be elected to Bradford City Council and, a few months later, founded a branch of the Independent Labour Party in the city.

5 In the first years of the twentieth century, Lansbury rediscovered his Christian faith and at the age of 45 re-joined the Anglican Church and left the SDF. For ten years he had been a leading figure in the party of the Marxist left and its salaried national organizer. In 1904, he joined the ILP, his 'natural home'. J. Shepherd, *George Lansbury: At the Heart of Old Labour*, Oxford University Press, 2002, p. 36.

6 K. Laybourn, *A Century of Labour: A History of the Labour Party, 1900–2000*, Sutton, 2000.

7 ILP, *Annual Conference Report*, 1898, p. 8.

8 Yeo, 'A New Life: The Religion of Socialism in Britain, 1883–1896', p. 17.

9 Ibid., p. 31.

10 Arthur Henderson was elected in 1903, MacDonald, J.R. Clynes, Snowden and Fred Jowett in 1906, J.T. Thomas, William Adamson and Lansbury in 1910.

11 This is a key point not just in the actual formation of Labour but throughout history – played out with *In Place of Strife*, the emergence of Thatcherism,

and the origins of New Labour. We will return to this, as it lies at the heart of Labour's purpose question – what is it there for? For many of the unions it has retained a deeply conservative purpose, a *collective laissez-faire*, to preserve the 1906 status quo and keep the law out of industrial relations.

12 The secret agreement was only revealed in the 1950s, with the availability of Gladstone's papers in the British Library.

13 This link between class reconciliation through growth and institutional maturity is a recurring theme throughout Labour history, including within the Fabian tradition, revisionism and Crosland and later the assumptions of New Labour.

14 Mark Garnett speaks to this 'double movement' in *The Snake That Swallowed Its Tail* when he identifies two rival modes of liberal thought; one he described as 'fleshed-out', the other 'hollowed-out': 'The former retains a close resemblance to the ideas of the great liberal thinkers, who were optimistic about human nature and envisaged a society made up of free, rational individuals, respecting themselves and others. The latter, by contrast, satisfies no more than the basic requirements of liberal thought. It reduces the concepts of reason and individual fulfilment to the lowest common denominator, identifying them with the pursuit of short-term material self-interest. For the hollowed-out liberal, other people are either means to an end, or obstacles which must be shunted aside. Instead of equality of respect, this is more like equality of contempt.' M. Garnett, *The Snake that Swallowed its Tail: Some Contradictions in Modern Liberalism*, Blackwell, 2004.

15 This is sometimes described as the Benthamite liberalism of 'enlightened self-interest', or the *laissez-faire* liberalism associated with the 'Manchester School'.

16 R.H. Tawney, *Equality*, George Allen and Unwin, 1931, p. 168.

17 T. Blair, *Let Us Face the Future – the 1945 Anniversary Lecture*, Fabian Pamphlet, 571, The Fabian Society, London, 1995.

18 Morgan, *Keir Hardie*, p. 9.

19 *Merthyr Pioneer*, 2 October 1915.

20 Morgan, *Keir Hardie*, p. 123.

21 Ibid., p. 170.

22 V. Bogdanor, *The Strange Survival of Liberal England: Politics and Power Before the First World War*, Biteback, 2022.

23 Tensions still existed, with the ILP remaining opposed to conscription, which Labour reluctantly accepted. Yet Labour could argue its wartime role helped working people by pushing for market regulation to fix wartime rents at pre-war levels, and 'fair share' price controls stabilizing the cost of food and outlawing profiteering and establishing the case for regulation of industry, as rail and coal were temporarily brought under state control.

24 A. Thorpe, *A History of the British Labour Party*, Macmillan International, 4th edn, 2015, p. 40.

25 The position of leader and chair of the PLP became the same after November 1922 when MacDonald beat Clynes to the position of party chairman by 61 votes to 56, an election that would define the next decade of Labour politics.

26 See Morgan, *Keir Hardie*, p. 266. Biblical references abound around Hardie. A Welsh supporter, Wil John Edwards, considered him a 'latter-day Jesus', whilst Ramsay MacDonald preferred a comparison with Moses navigating Labour towards a promised land.

27 At the 1918 Labour Party Conference, the Party adopted Clause IV into its constitution. Clause IV, then 3(d), stated: 'To secure for producers by hand or by brain the full fruits of their industry, and the most equitable distribution thereof that may be possible, upon the basis of the Common Ownership of the Means of Production and the best obtainable system of popular administration and control of each industry and service.'

28 Thorpe, p. 39.

29 Laybourne, p. 30.

Chapter 4: Minorities (1924–1931)

1 This figure includes three ILP MPs and three other unendorsed Labour MPs.

2 K.O. Morgan, *Labour People*, Oxford University Press, 1987, p. 11.

3 E.P. Thompson, 'Homage to Tom Maguire', in C. Winslow (ed.) '*E.P. Thompson and the Making of the New Left*', Monthly Review, 2014, pp. 263–90.

4 D. Howell, *British Workers and the Independent Labour Party, 1888–1906*, Manchester University Press, 1983.

5 Although the accuser Sidney Webb had himself backed the cuts to unemployment support in cabinet.

6 Since 1977, David Marquand and others have sought to establish a more balanced assessment of MacDonald and his immense contribution to party history.

7 Marquand, *Ramsay MacDonald: A Biography*, p. 795.

8 Ibid., p. 794.

9 Ibid.

10 D. Howell, *MacDonald's Party: Labour Identities and Crisis 1922–31*, Oxford University Press, 2002, p. 9.

11 In 1922, Lansbury had ensured that the *Herald* was handed over to the TUC and the party, after which it became the official publication of the TUC.

12 The 1922 election also saw the parliamentary arrival of Attlee and Sidney Webb, alongside four Co-operative Party MPs, anticipating the 1927 Cheltenham Agreement between the Labour and Co-operative Parties.

13 Quoted in Shepherd and Laybourn, pp. 31–2.
14 Marquand, *Ramsay MacDonald: A Biography*, p. 303.
15 Shepherd and Laybourn, p. 43.
16 Diary, 21 January 1924, quoted by Marquand.
17 The first Labour cabinet would have six ILP members – MacDonald, Snowden, Wheatley, Jowett, Trevelyan and Joshua Wedgewood – although only two, Wheatley and Jowett, could be described as left wing, and nine junior ministers. Many had opposed the war including Snowden and MacDonald. The latter had resigned as chair of the PLP even though the issue formally remained a matter of conscience. In reality, by the early 1920s, both had drifted away from the ILP and Labour's first government consisted mostly of moderates plus conservative and liberal lords. Principal Fabians in the cabinet were Webb and Oliver but a number had associations – Henderson, Noel-Buxton and Thomson. There were no women.
18 MacDonald became both Prime Minister and Foreign Secretary with Henderson as Home Secretary, Snowden Chancellor and Thomas Colonial Secretary. Clynes was appointed Lord Privy Seal, Sidney Webb President of the Board of Trade and Lord Olivier, Secretary of State for India. Willie Adamson became Scottish Secretary, Fred Jowett First Commissioner of Works and John Wheatley Minister of Health.
19 Documents released by the Public Records Office in 1998 finally revealed the letter to have been a forgery.
20 A union member was not able to contribute to the political fund unless they had actively given notice of their willingness to contribute to that fund (an 'opt-in' notice) rather than the previous system whereby union members had to actively contract out from paying into a political fund (an 'opt-out' notice). This administrative change had huge implications for Labour's finances.
21 Thorpe, p. 68.
22 Sidney Webb (Lord Passfield), 'What Happened in 1931: A Record', *Political Quarterly*, Jan–Mar 1932, 1.
23 Labour Party Conference Report, 1931, p. 201.
24 Howell, *MacDonald's Party*, p. 412.
25 Marquand, *Ramsay MacDonald: A Biography*, p. 610.
26 Ibid., p. 783.
27 Ibid., p. 785.
28 Yet MacDonald himself gave a Hampstead party that November – days before his death – where Walter Citrine in his diary noted how he failed to identify anyone associated with the Labour movement.
29 E. Shinwell, *Conflict Without Malice*, Odhams Press, 1955, p. 113.

30 R.H. Tawney, 'The Choice Before the Labour Party', in R.H. Tawney, *The Attack and Other Papers*, George Allen and Unwin, 1981, pp. 52–71.

31 R.H. Tawney, *Religion and the Rise of Capitalism*, Aaker Books, 2012, first published 1926.

32 R.H. Tawney, *The Acquisitive Society*, G. Bell and Sons, 1921. R.H. Tawney, *Equality*, George Allen and Unwin, 1931.

33 Tawney had joined the Fabians in 1906, the ILP in 1909 and Labour in 1918 after the introduction of individual membership.

34 R.H. Tawney, *R.H. Tawney's Commonplace Book*, Cambridge University Press, 1972, p. 52.

Chapter 5: Thirties (1931–1939)

1 W.H. Auden, 'September 1, 1939', *Another Time*, Random House, 1940.

2 M. Stears, *Out of the Ordinary: How Everyday Life Inspired a Nation and How It Can Again*, Belknap Press, 2021.

3 F. Field, *Attlee's Great Contemporaries: The Politics of Character*, Continuum, 2009, p. xxix.

4 Shepherd, pp. 2 and 362.

5 R. Holman, *Good Old George*, Lion Books, 1990. See also 'Socialism, which means love, cooperation and brotherhood in every department of human affairs, is the only outward expression of a Christian faith', G. Lansbury, *My England*, Selwyn and Blount, 1934, p. 37.

6 Shepherd, p. 286.

7 *Clarion*, 14 April 1934.

8 *Clarion*, 21 April 1934.

9 R. Postgate, *George Lansbury*, Longmans Green and Co., 1951.

10 C.R. Attlee, *As It Happened*, London, 1954, p.74.

11 F. Field, *Attlee's Great Contemporaries*, Continuum, 2009, p. xxix.

12 Ibid., p. xx.

13 Attlee, p. 21.

14 Ibid., p. 38.

15 Shepherd, p. 331.

16 M. Taylor, 'Patriotism, History and the Left in Twentieth Century Britain', *The Historical Journal*, 33(4), 1990, 971–87.

17 J.A. Hobson, *The Psychology of Jingoism*, G. Richards, 1901.

18 M. Stears, *Out of the Ordinary*.

19 P. Ward, *Red Flag and Union Jack: Englishness, Patriotism and the British Left 1881–1924*, Royal Historical Society/Boydell and Brewer, 1998. P. Ward, 'Preparing for the People's War: Labour and Patriotism in the 1930s', *Labour History Review*, 7(2), 2002.

20 We might also add to this figures such as Cecil Sharp and Vaughan Williams – socialists in search of authentic English musical traditions.

21 S. Brooke, *Labour's War: The Labour Party and the Second World War*, Clarendon Press, 1992. See also E. Durbin, *New Jerusalems: Labour Party and the Economics of Democratic Socialism*, Routledge & Kegan Paul, 1985.

22 Thorpe, p. 87.

23 Steel nationalization would remain contentious in the post-war Labour government. It was eventually secured despite opposition from Morrison and the steel union.

24 The ILP programme Living Wage policy sought to impose high minimum wages across all industries and nationalize all private enterprises which could not afford to pay them in order to resolve inter-war unemployment and poverty, which it held to be caused by underconsumption.

25 E.F.M. Durbin, *The Politics of Democratic Socialism: An Essay on Social Policy*, G. Routledge & Sons, 1940. See J. Bowlby, 'Psychology and Democracy', *Political Quarterly*, 17, 1946, 61–77. In 1939, Bowlby and Durbin published *Personal Aggressiveness and War*, Routledge and Kegan Paul.

26 J.M. Keynes, 'National Self-Sufficiency', *The Yale Review*, 22(4), 1933, 755–69.

Chapter 6: Jerusalem (1939–1951)

1 J. Harris, 'Labour's Political and Social Thought', in Tanner et al. (eds) *Labour's First Century*, p. 26.

2 William Beveridge, the economist and social reformer, in November 1942 published a report titled 'Social Insurance and Allied Services' that would provide the blueprint for social policy in post-war Britain. Beveridge had been drawn to the idea of remedying social inequality and the limits of philanthropy while working for the Toynbee Hall in East London. His vision was to battle against what he called the five giants: idleness, ignorance, disease, squalor and want. At the heart of Beveridge's plan was a comprehensive system of social insurance and welfare. Beveridge tasked the state with establishing a 'national minimum', a safety net below which no one could fall. Central to his plan was a contributory system which would entitle the population to maternity, child and unemployment benefits, state pensions and funeral allowances. Underpinning all of this would be a free at the point-of-use universal health care system regardless of personal circumstances.

3 R.H. Tawney, 'Social Democracy in Britain', in R. Hinden (ed.) *The Radical Tradition*, George Allen and Unwin, 1964.

4 D. Jay, *The Socialist Case*, 2nd edn, Faber and Faber, 1947, p. 258.

5 M. Bruce, *The Coming of the Welfare State*, 4th edn, Batsford, 1968.

6 Greenwood was both working class and an intellectual. Born in 1880 in

Leeds, largely self-taught, he became an economics lecturer. After a period as an Assistant Secretary at the Ministry of Reconstruction, in 1920 he became Secretary of the Joint TUC-Labour Party Research and Information Department. He entered Parliament in 1922, and in 1924 was given a junior post at the Ministry of Health. When the Labour Party set up its own Research Department in 1927, he became Head, and with only short breaks remained so until 1948. As Minister of Health in the second Labour government, he oversaw the 1930 Housing Act. Defeated in 1931, he re-entered parliament following a by-election in 1932. He aroused great affection across the party, 'although more of a back-room intellectual than a politician'. Elected as Deputy Leader in 1935, he stood in for Attlee in 1939 in opposing Chamberlain and, following his appointment to the War Cabinet in 1940, played a vital role in support of Churchill. See B. Pimlott, *Labour and the Left in the 1930s*, Cambridge University Press, 1977.

7 Bew, pp. 237–47.
8 From 1940 to 1942, Labour was the beneficiary of increased support in the polls. In 1942 Mass Observation estimated that 40 per cent of voters had changed their political opinion since the outbreak of war to the benefit of the party.
9 Brooke, pp. 55–103. 'MacDonaldism' was the charge used by Bevin against Lansbury in 1935 and would be used by Tribune against Gaitskell in the 1950s and regularly feature within Labour mythology.
10 A change that would bring with it a reorientation in economic policy. Dalton was a long-term advocate of active regional policy and economic intervention and remained critical of Keynesian macroeconomic policy, whereas Cripps was more willing to follow Keynes's lead.
11 Although the mutual arrangement proposed by Beveridge was not adopted. Here is how Frank Field characterized Beveridge's original ideas: 'Beveridge saw his welfare proposals as a means of moulding an active, independent citizenry that practised the virtues of hard work, honesty and prudence. His fundamental principle was that receipt of welfare was to be dependent on what a person had paid into the scheme.' Frank Field, 'Rebuilding Beveridge', *Prospect Magazine*, 19 September 2012, https://www.prospectmagazine.co.uk/magazine/rebuilding-beveridge-welfare-frank-field
12 As we shall see, this constitutional conservatism would only really be challenged decades later by the effects of nationalist movements and revisionist elements within both Labour's left and right wings as part of the wider movement for constitutional reform, including groups such as Charter 88 challenging Labour's traditional 'statism'.
13 Thorpe, pp. 124–7.

14 Ackers and Reid, p. 2.

15 C. Renwick, *Bread for All: The Origins of the Welfare State*, Penguin, 2018.

16 J. Gray, 'A Better Kind of Being', *New Statesman*, 11–17 February 2022.

17 Although anti-humanist thinking has made a comeback in modern debates on the left, regarding transhumanism see J. Cruddas, 'The Humanist Left Must Challenge the Rise of Cyborg Socialism', *New Statesman*, 23 April 2018.

18 Harris, *Attlee*, p. 172.

19 Bew, p. 401.

20 P. Hennessey, *Muddling Through*, Gollancz, 1996, p. 173; Field, p. xxvi; Bew, p. 403.

21 Bew, pp. 386–409.

22 Ibid., pp 382–3.

23 T.H. Marshall, *Citizenship and Social Class and Other Essays*, Cambridge University Press, 1950.

24 H.G. Wells, *The Rights of Man: Or, What Are We Fighting For?*, Penguin Special, 1940.

25 See Klug, pp. 18–28.

26 *International Covenant on Civil and Political Rights* and the *International Covenant on Economic, Social and Cultural Rights*, both adopted on 16 December 1966 and ratified ten years later.

27 R. Miliband, *Parliamentary Socialism: A Study in the Politics of Labour*, Merlin, 1973. C. Barnett, *The Collapse of British Power*, Sutton Publishing, 1984. K. Middlemas, *Power, Competition and the State, Volume 1: Britain in Search of Balance*, Palgrave Macmillan, 1986.

28 Stears, *Out of the Ordinary*.

Chapter 7: Waste (1951–1964)

1 Labour would be in power for only 11 of the next 46 years.

2 In the 1940s, Gaitskell was more of a technocrat than factional leader. From being Dalton's private secretary within the civil service in 1945, he would rise in a decade to the position of Labour leader.

3 The revisionists were not hostile to nationalization in principle, but rather argued it should be on a 'case by case' approach, although after the 1959 defeat this position did harden into pressing for the re-writing of Clause IV. See H.T.N. Gaitskell, *Socialism and Nationalisation*, Fabian Tract 100, Fabian Society, 1955. More generally, when compared to later revisionists or modernizers in the 1980s and 1990s, Gaitskell and Crosland had a much more positive view of the role of the state.

4 A. Bevan, *In Place of Fear*, William Heinemann, 1952. R.H.S. Crossman (ed.) *New Fabian Essays*, Turnstile Press, 1952.

5 Although it seems as much to do with hostility to Bevan as support for the Gaitskellites.

6 Despite these differences, Crosland tended to avoid factional arguments, preferring to remake the socialist case from first principles for the post-war era of affluence.

7 Presumably in a move that sought to attract the 'affluent' workers popular in post-war sociology, which many revisionists assumed helped account for Labour's unpopularity.

8 In the 1959 post-mortem, some revisionists such as Douglas Jay argued the name of the party should change as a dramatic symbol of Labour's renewal.

9 M. Adams and R. Rose, *Must Labour Lose?* Penguin, 1960, with commentary by Rita Hinden.

10 *Socialist Union* became the vehicle to uphold the ethical socialist tradition for the post-war era within revisionism with contributions from, amongst others, Michael Young, and Phyllis and Michael Wilmot.

11 A notable exception being John Kelly's biography. J. Kelly, *Ethical Socialism and the Trade Unions: Allan Flanders and British Industrial Relations Reform*, Routledge, 2011.

12 See the contributions in P. Ackers and A.J. Reid (eds) *Alternatives to State Socialism in Britain: Other Worlds of Labour in the Twentieth Century*, Palgrave Macmillan, 2016.

13 He also inspired numerous Labour politicians including Wilson, who in his memoirs said it was Cole who 'finally pointed me in the direction of the Labour Party'.

14 A case in point being that of the wartime social/political movement the libertarian socialist Common Wealth Party with its expressed belief in greater morality in politics, a rejection of Fabianism and an embrace of the guild tradition.

15 Ackers and Reid, p. 10.

16 A whole generation of revisionists had been attracted to Marxism including Denis Healey, Michael Young and Frank Horrabin. Crosland himself was strongly attracted to Marxism in the late 1930s. Clegg was formerly a member of the Communist Party and Flanders a former Trotskyite.

17 Especially in *Industrial Relations: What is Wrong with the System?* Faber, 1965; *Collective Bargaining: Selected Readings*, Penguin, 1969; and *Management and Unions: the Theory and Reform of Industrial Relations*, Faber, 1970.

18 Kelly, p. 94.

19 Lise Butler, *Michael Young, Social Science and The British Left, 1945–70*, Oxford University Press, 2020, p. 230.

20 Bowlby, 'Psychology and Democracy'; Bowlby and Durbin, *Personal Aggressiveness and War*.

21 M.D. Young, *Small Man, Big World*, Labour Publications Department, 1949.

22 See Butler, p. 79. In 1957, Young created the Consumer Advisory Service Which?, an idea which he had unsuccessfully suggested for inclusion in the 1950 manifesto.

23 M.D. Young and P. Willmott, *Family and Kinship in East London*, Penguin, 2007. R. Hoggart, *The Uses of Literacy: Aspects of Working-Class Life*, Penguin Modern Classics, 2009.

24 It was tacitly critical of core tenets of the post-war welfare state and legacy of the Attlee government by challenging the notion of a minimum level of subsistence/income to meet basic needs and overcome poverty. For these sociologists, it required a more nuanced approach to subsistence based on how people actually live.

25 Butler, p. 72.

26 E.P. Thompson's work *William Morris, Romantic to Revolutionary* was first published in 1955.

27 Thompson, *The Making of the English Working Class*, p. 7.

28 Although there remained fundamental disagreements. For instance, in a 1970 pamphlet entitled 'A Social Democratic Britain', Tony Crosland castigated the siren voices of the left who prioritize issues of 'alienation, communication, participation, automation, dehumanization, decentralization, the information network, student revolt, the generation gap or even Women's lib'. These are 'false trails' that focus attention away from the essentials of growth and distri- bution! C.A.R. Crosland, *A Social Democratic Britain*, Fabian Tract 404, Fabian Society, 1970.

29 B. Jackson, *Equality and the British Left*, Manchester University Press, 2007, pp. 185–7.

30 This argument can be overplayed, however, especially in regard to foreign policy. For instance, there remained fundamental disagreements over nuclear weapons. The New Left was involved in the creation of CND in 1958 alongside figures such as Michael Foot, resulting in revisionist dismay at the 1960 Conference support for unilateralism. In 1961, the New Left was active in the Committee of 100 and supportive of NATO withdrawal – strongly opposed by the party of Bevin and Attlee. However, these differences tended to fall away after the final Easter 1963 Aldermaston March as the left regrouped around Wilson in anticipation of the coming election.

Chapter 8: Strife (1964–1979)

1 The September 1965 National Plan aimed for a 25 per cent GDP uplift between 1964 and 1970, an average 3.8 per cent annual growth. The actual growth rate for the period averaged a more modest 2.2 per cent. Thorpe, p. 168.

2 The Sexual Offences Act was granted royal assent on 27 July 1967 yet only applied to England and Wales. Scotland, along with Northern Ireland, was excluded.

3 Tensions that would be repeated decades later in the ascent and disintegration of the left under Corbyn, a mixture of an older, often centralizing left and a younger movement attracted from a wider array of social movements – sometimes described as the 'new, new left' or 'post capitalist' left.

4 See, for example, K. Middlemas, *Politics in Industrial Society*, Andre Deutsch, 1979.

5 Corporatism in the sense of a collectivist political ideology which advocates the organization of society by corporate groups, labour, business or guild associations, on the basis of their common interests.

6 Pioneered in Allan Flanders's classic *The Fawley Productivity Agreements*, Faber and Faber, 1964.

7 Support greatly welcomed by Ted Heath, who needed their support given splits within his own ranks.

8 Jenkins was from the liberal revisionist traditions that emerged after the war, embracing human rights to remedy social and economic disadvantage. Crosland was from a more utilitarian, distributional, revisionist perspective, although both shared a focus on questions of personal freedom. Crosland sided with the Fabians rather than the old ILP ethical socialist traditions. He once wrote that the Webbs: 'were no doubt right to stress the solid virtues of hard work, self discipline, efficiency, research and abstinence: to sacrifice private pleasure to public duty, and expect that others should do the same: to put Blue Books before culture, and immunity from physical above all other virtues' because they are reacting against 'an unpractical, Utopian, sentimental, romantic, almost anarchist tradition on the left ... as stemming from William Morris'. *The Future of Socialism*, pp. 522–3.

Chapter 9: Wilderness (1979–1987)

1 https://www.cps.org.uk/research/stepping-stones/

2 Shadow Cabinet: Circulated Paper (Joseph, 'Notes towards the definition of policy'), 1975, Archive (Thatcher MSS), Declassified, House of Commons, MSS 2/6/1/156.

3 J. Cruddas and P. Nolan, *Labour and the Politics of Production: Reassessing Thatcher's Legacy*. Unpublished.

4 J. Cruddas, 'Labour Regulation and Productivity in the UK Since 1945: Debunking Myths about "Disease", "Miracles" and "Puzzles"', *National Institute Economic Review*, 262(1), 2022, 13–21.

5 E. Hobsbawm, 'Forward March of Labour Halted?, Marx Memorial Lecture, 1978', reproduced in *Marxism Today*, September 1978.

6 For instance, on policy the 1979 Conference voted both for unilateralist and multi-lateralist defence positions and against remaining in the European Community.

7 Morgan, *Michael Foot: A Life*, p. 407.

8 Ibid., pp. 400–10.

9 Although the Bennite left also embraced more orthodox distributional economics and the approach of Keynesian economists such as Wynne Godley and Francis Cripps.

10 See Foote, pp 308–36, on the hybrid quality of the Labour left in the 1980s and the influences on Benn.

11 Gathered largely at the instigation of Roy Grantham, general secretary of the clerical workers' union (APEX), the group included Bryan Stanley, general secretary of the postal engineers' union (POEU), and Frank Chapple, general secretary of the electricians' and plumbers' union (EETPU). Others among the seventeen who first met included Terry Duffy, president of the powerful engineering union (AEU); Sid Weighell, general secretary of the railwaymen's union (NUR); Tom Jackson, general secretary of the postal workers' union (UPW); Charlie Turnock, assistant general secretary of the NUR; Bill Sirs, general secretary of the steelworkers' union (ISTC); Bill Whatley, general secretary of the shop workers' union (USDAW); and Sandy Feather, also of the ISTC.

12 Rumours circulated about replacing Foot, especially after a disastrous by-election defeat in February 1983 in the safe seat of Bermondsey after an ugly homophobic campaign. A strong victory in another by-election, this time in Darlington in March, saw off the rumours, although Labour would go on to lose the seat at the general election.

13 This is a point also made by Colm Murphy in his reassessment of the 1983 manifesto, C. Murphy, 'What Did the 1983 Manifesto Ever Do For Us?', in N. Yeowell (ed.) *Rethinking Labour's Past*, I.B. Tauris, pp. 215–31.

14 'Neil Kinnock attacks Arthur Scargill for "suicidal vanity" over miners' strike', *The Guardian*, 12 March 2009.

15 Although in terms of general union modernization following the miners strike, it should be noted the task was aided by Norman Tebbit. Having legislated to force unions to ballot to retain their political funds, throughout 1985 and 1986 all 37 ballots successfully affirmed the funds, with 87 per cent of the 3.5 million votes cast in favour of retention.

Chapter 10: Revival (1987–1997)

1 More recently described as the 'Social Chapter', it was the name for the Protocol on Social Policy and the Agreement on Social Policy annexed to the Maastricht Treaty to extend qualified majority voting to aspects of social policy including employment protections.

2 For the purposes of full disclosure, I was the joint secretary of this review group.

3 P. Diamond, *The Crosland Legacy: The Future of British Social Democracy*, Policy Press, 2016.

4 R. Hattersley, *Choose Freedom: The Future of Democratic Socialism*, Penguin, 1987. On p. 214, Hattersley used Rawls's progressive social contract theory to make the case for supply-side socialism.

5 This is precisely the route chosen by Crosland himself to update *The Future of Socialism*. In *Socialism Now*, published in 1974, Crosland reinforced his concern for 'democratic equality' and 'distributive justice' but this time through a Rawlsian lens. A. Crosland, *Socialism Now*, Jonathan Cape, 1974, p. 1.

6 C. Hughes and P. Wintour, *Labour Rebuilt: The New Model Labour Party*, Fourth Estate, 1990, p. 74.

7 The commitment in the 1992 manifesto was for £3.40 an hour.

8 In parallel, 1989 also saw positive discrimination in Shadow Cabinet elections.

9 Charter 88, under the leadership of Lord Scarman and New Left activist Anthony Barnett, brought together under a single umbrella a wide range of innovative groups in support of a written constitution, including Liberty, the Labour Campaign for Electoral Reform, Campaign for Freedom of Information and many others.

10 As a demonstration of Kinnock's successful revisionism, Michael Young re-joined Labour in 1989.

11 The Campaign Group was not just a group of MPs but made up of key figures from across the left granted honorary membership, including MEP Les Huckfield, Vladimir Derer, secretary of CLPD, John McDonnell, Secretary of the Association of London Authorities, and Wendy Moore, the Secretary of the Women's Action Committee.

12 The LCC was intellectually aligned with Eurocommunist elements following splits within the Communist Party of Great Britain as well as parts of the New Left. In this period, it helped cultivate space in the party distinct from the orthodox utilitarian left and right factions. This coalescing of a soft or liberal 'left' with the revisionist 'right' in rejecting the orthodoxies of both the traditional factions reappears in the early New Labour period and for a time under both Miliband and Starmer.

13 Smith's Shadow Budget of 16 March 1992 sought to demonstrate that Labour could maintain budget discipline whilst making low- and middle-income families better off and investing in public services. No one earning under £22,000 a year would lose out. Yet the Conservatives sought to discredit the approach by claiming everyone would pay an extra £1,250 a year based on a widely exaggerated assessment of the £35 billion cost of Labour's total Policy Review, which formed the basis for their successful, yet dishonest, 'Tax Bombshell' campaign.

14 In September, Gould resigned from the Shadow Cabinet over Maastricht and in May 1994 stood down from his Dagenham seat. Gould was in many ways a leading revisionist, especially over issues of economic democracy, worker share ownership and industrial policy. In many respects he had more in common with 1950s revisionists than his contemporaries in the late 1980s and early 1990s in terms of economic intervention and an innate Euroscepticism. B. Gould, *A Future for Socialism*, Jonathan Cape, 1989.

15 In a Radio 4 *Sunday* programme while running for the leadership Smith said, 'I am an active and professing member of the Church of Scotland … It gives meaning to my political activities, because you have this sense of obligation to others'. In a Scotland on Sunday interview on 11 July 1992, he said, 'Just as the Christian stands by the fundamental tenets of Christianity, so the socialist should stand by the tenets of socialism. For me, socialism is largely Christian ethical values … Politics is a moral activity. Values should shine through at all times. You could either call it evangelism or salesmanship. I want the spirit of the evangel but the success of the good salesman.'

16 Giles Radice MP, in an influential '*Southern Discomfort*' pamphlet published by the Fabian Society in September 1992, examined attitudes towards the Labour Party in the south of England after the trauma of defeat, especially the concerns of voters in marginal constituencies regarding Labour's lack of economic credibility and fears of tax rises if the party came to power.

17 The Commission was effectively tasked with finding innovative social policy interventions to enhance equality beyond raising child benefit and state pensions. New Labour subsequently settled on the remedy of tax credits.

18 A. Barnett, 'John Smith and the Path Britain Did Not Take', *Open Democracy*, 12 May 2019.

19 For the purposes of full disclosure, I should note I was the secretary of this committee.

20 D. Ward, 'John Smith and the Mythology of "One More Heave"', Mile End Institute Lecture, 17 July 2022.

21 It should also be noted that Blair joined the Review Group to replace Gould in late 1992. In January 1993, in the only vote of the Review Group, Blair proposed the party programme be voted on by a national ballot of the membership and was heavily defeated – an issue he would return to in 1995 and 1996. See L. Minkin, *The Blair Supremacy: A Study in the Politics of Labour's Party Management*, Manchester University Press, 2014, pp. 106–7.

22 Although, of course, the reality was that despite individual delegate voting, union representatives still tended to vote in line with their agreed positions at the Party Conference rather than split their vote.

23 Smith had had a first heart attack two days after the 1988 Conference.

24 The wording of the amendment would eventually be placed on the membership card of every Labour member.

25 It might also have been an attempt to restate her socialist credentials years after the damage of *In Place of Strife*.

26 Lewis Minkin brilliantly describes how this occurred in *The Blair Supremacy*, pp. 191–7.

27 The *NEC at Work* group was convened by Maggie Jones of UNISON. *The Relationships in Power* by Mo Mowlem, *Strengthening Democracy* by Margaret Wall from the MSF and *Building a Healthy Party* by Diana Jeuda of USDAW. The academics Bob Fryer and Lewis Minkin acted as project facilitators, and Head of the General Secretary's Office Jon Cruddas acted as General Project Coordinator.

28 It led to the formation of the 'Grassroots Alliance' of CLPD and Labour Reform to challenge for seats in the CLP section

29 P. Mandelson and R. Liddle, *The Blair Revolution: Can New Labour Deliver?*, Faber and Faber, 1996.

30 The pledge card contained commitments to cut class sizes for infants, reduce waiting lists, ensure 250,000 young people found work, speed up the treatment of young offenders and maintain low inflation.

Chapter 11: Landslides (1997–2010)

1 M. Bevir, *New Labour: A Critique*, Routledge, 2005, p. 44.

2 This is especially the case with Philip Gould's New Labour 'bible', *The Unfinished Revolution*, Little, Brown, 1998.

3 S. Fielding, 'New Labour and the Past', in Tanner et al. (eds) *Labour's First Century*, pp. 367–92.

4 T. Blair, 'Why Modernisation Matters', *Renewal*, 1, 1993, 4–11.

5 It also has echoes of Harold Macmillan's use of the 'the middle way' in the 1930s and from the ILP James Maxton's call for a 'third alternative'. It was also a term used in the Prague Spring of 1968 to signal economic liberalization.

6 J. Kelly, *Ethical Socialism and the Trade Unions: Allan Flanders and British Industrial Relations Reform*, Routledge, 2011.

7 P. Diamond, 'The Road to 1997', Queen Mary Mile End Institute, 3 May 2022. https://www.qmul.ac.uk/mei/news-and-opinion/items/the-road-to-1997 .html

8 Yet even here it could be argued that he was reflecting the quieter ethical concerns of his predecessor John Smith.

9 MacIntyre, *After Virtue*. Sandel, *Justice: What's the Right Thing to Do?* C. Taylor, *Sources of the Self: The Making of the Modern Identity*, Harvard University Press, 1992. M. Waltzer, *On Toleration (Castle Lectures Series)*, Yale University Press,

1997. M. Waltzer, *Politics and Passion: Toward a More Egalitarian Liberalism*, Yale University Press, 2005.

10 See especially J. Macmurray, *Self as Agent*, Faber and Faber, 1957 and *Persons in Relation*, Faber and Faber, 1961.

11 Although many would argue that Blair's idea of the 'international community' was not so much a communitarian idea as a liberal construct to denote the values promoted by the US since Woodrow Wilson's fusion of idealism with nationalism. Blair's case for intervention was based on a liberal vision anchored in a Whig conception of history.

12 T. Blair, *Let Us Face the Future: The 1945 Anniversary Lecture*, Fabian Society, 1995.

13 Blair's analysis drew heavily on the work of David Marquand and was a compelling analysis, but its reading of history when implying it was Labour that was weakened by the split with liberalism is difficult to sustain.

14 P. Ashdown, *The Ashdown Diaries: Volume 1: 1988–1997*, Penguin, 2001, p. 429.

15 Although often poorly defined by politicians, the Third Way acquired a more specific meaning when defined by sociologist Anthony Giddens, who used it to describe an alternative to neo-liberalism and traditional social democracy in an era of globalization. For Giddens, it involved a commitment to the idea of a radical centre which could draw ideas from both left and right. The approach embraced a 'new mixed economy' along with public-private partnerships, private finance initiatives and consumer-friendly public service provision, and involved a commitment to build human capital to boost competitiveness. He emphasized a strengthened civil society and open participatory government that empowers the citizen, including a commitment to gender equality and 'equality of inclusion' rather than equality of outcome. The approach acknowledged that rights come with responsibilities. In terms of values, the Third Way celebrated cultural diversity and pluralism. It also involved a commitment to extending such cosmopolitan values into international arenas through a democratization of the institutions of global governance. See A. Giddens, *The Third Way: Renewal of Social Democracy*, Polity, 1998.

16 U. Beck, 'The Cosmopolitan Manifesto', *New Statesman*, 20, 1998, 38–50. See also the emphasis placed on personal identity as an organizing principle for the left by Tony Giddens in A. Giddens, *The Transformation of Intimacy: Love, Sexuality and Eroticism in Modern Societies*, Polity, 1993.

17 G. Brown, 'The Socialist Challenge', in G. Brown (ed.) *The Red Paper on Scotland*, EUSPB, 1975.

18 G. Brown, *Where There is Greed: Margaret Thatcher and the Betrayal of Britain*, Mainstream Publishing, 1989.

19 G. Brown and T. Wright, 'Introduction', in G. Brown and T. Wright (eds) *Values, Visions and Voices: An Anthology of Socialism*, Mainstream, 1995, p. 19.

20 See S. Lee, *Boom and Bust: The Politics and Legacy of Gordon Brown*, Oneworld, 2007.

21 The manifesto had stated this explicitly: 'We are a broad-based movement for progress and justice. New Labour is the political arm of none other than the British people as a whole. Our values are the same: the equal worth of all, with no one cast aside; fairness and justice within strong communities.'

22 Although there appeared little enthusiasm for regional devolution, which was eventually derailed following a heavy referendum defeat in the north-east in November 2004.

23 Although further reform proved elusive after a series of inconclusive votes on the subject in the House of Commons in 2003.

24 A 1997 White Paper had promised more robust legislation. Blair later described the Freedom of Information legislation as one of his 'biggest regrets', writing in his autobiography, 'I quake at the imbecility of it'. T. Blair, *A Journey*, Hutchinson, 2010, p. 909.

25 From the left a general criticism suggests New Labour simply built on a neo-liberal inheritance – by extending the market into public services, rejecting redistribution as an act of public policy, in deference to corporate power, with multiple privatizations and much more. Pushing on with Tory reforms exposed a liberal economic worldview. This line of attack is all a bit too easy. For instance, neo-liberal political economy asserts the state inhibits efficient market transactions whereas New Labour retained a benign belief in state intervention. Whilst the 'Third Way' sought to plunder ideas from both left and right, it is a bit simplistic to describe New Labour as simply neo-liberal.

26 In 2003, the Working Families Tax Credit was split into two benefits: a Working Tax Credit, which was payable to all those in work, and a Child Tax Credit, which was payable to all families with children, whether in work or not.

27 Although the then Archbishop of Canterbury Rowan Williams argued that the case for the invasion did not meet the ethical standards of Christian just war thinking. 'Attack on Iraq "cannot be defended as a just war"', *The Times*, 15 October 2003.

28 Between October 2002 and mid-2003, Blair's personal approval rating plummeted from 41 to 29 per cent. 'Labour's Lost Future: The Inside Story of a 20-Year Collapse', *New Statesman*, 2 September 2021.

29 Although given the decline in seat numbers in Scotland and boundary changes, these are notional figures.

30 By 2006, membership had collapsed to some 198,026, the lowest recorded since individual membership was first recorded in 1928.

31 G. Brown, speech to the Labour Party Special Conference, Manchester, 24 June 2007.

32 B. Hepple, 'The New Single Equality Act in Britain', *The Equal Rights Review*, 5, 2010, 11–24. See also G. Kirton and A.M. Greene, *The Dynamics of Managing Diversity and Inclusion: A Critical Approach*, Routledge, 2021.

33 Yet arguably it was an equalities agenda shorn of FDR's and Attlee's concerns of economic and social rights in their respective New Deals.

34 D. Miliband, 'Against the odds we can still win, on a platform of change', *The Guardian*, 30 July 2008.

35 G. Brown, Pre-Budget Report Statement, 25 November 2007.

36 G. Brown, Budget Statement, 21 March 2007.

37 For example, in his October 2006 Donald Dewar Memorial Lecture, his vision of politics appears to be one anchored within the Scottish Enlightenment and their embrace of the market; a positivist approach to human evolution through trade liberalization. His worldview appears increasingly reliant on liberal thinkers such as James Q. Wilson and Gertrude Himmelfarb.

Chapter 12: Isolation (2010–2024)

1 N. Lawson, *The View from No. 11: Memoirs of a Tory Radical*, Bantam Press, 1992, p. 64.

2 R. Leach, 'What is Thatcherism?', in M. Burch and M. Moran (eds) *British Politics: A Reader*, Manchester University Press, 1987, p. 157.

3 Despite at the height of the 1960s 'disease', average productivity growth at times approached 4 per cent.

4 Tony Blair, *A Journey*, Random House, 2010, p. 101.

5 See J. Muellbauer, 'The Assessment: Productivity and Competitiveness in British Manufacturing', *Oxford Review of Economic Policy*, 2(3), 1986, pp. i–xxv. D. Metcalf, 'Water Notes Dry Up', *British Journal of Industrial Relations*, 27(1), 1989, p. 27. See also G. Maynard, *The Economy Under Mrs Thatcher*, Basil Blackwell, 1988.

6 P. Nolan, 'The Productivity "Miracle"?' In F. Green (ed.) *The Restructuring of the UK Economy*, Wheatsheaf, 1989.

7 See https://www.telegraph.co.uk/news/politics/labour/8026708/Ed-Miliband-New -Labour-is-dead.html. The desire to move on – or at least suggest to the membership a desire to move – was shared by his brother David, who on announcing his own intention to run for the leadership also declared the New Labour era to be over. Blair himself later stated in a July 2011 speech that New Labour died when he left office and Brown assumed the leadership, claiming that from 2007 the party 'lost the driving rhythm'. https://www.theguardian.com/politics/2011/jul/08/tony-blair -new-labour-gordon-brown?CMP=share_btn_link

8 Both parents' families were Polish, although Ralph was born in Brussels.

9 Four years after David who was elected MP for South Shields in 2001.

10 M. Hasan and J. Macintyre, *Ed: The Milibands and the Making of a Labour Leader*, Biteback, 2012.

11 M. Glasman, J. Rutherford, M. Stears and S. White (eds) *The Labour Tradition and the Politics of Paradox*, Soundings, 2011.

12 The neologism 'omnishambles' dates back to a 2009 episode of the political satire *The Thick of It*. It was later used by Miliband at Prime Minister's Questions on 18 April 2012 to denote the total chaos triggered by the Budget.

13 The one notable exception to the safety-first strategy was in August 2013 with parliament recalled when Miliband stood firm against foreign intervention over Syria under pressure from Cameron and President Obama, helping defeat the government in the Commons vote on this issue. Although this was also more informed by the desire to preserve party unity and the difficulties the leader's office found in dealing with David Cameron than it was by political principle and exorcizing the legacy of Iraq.

14 At 2014 Conference, Miliband focused on the NHS, announcing Labour's proposal to fund more nurses, GPs, care workers and midwives, through a 'clampdown on tax avoiders and a new mansion tax'. T. Bale, *Five Year Mission: The Labour Party under Ed Miliband*, Oxford University Press, 2015, pp. 226–53.

15 T. Harris, *Ten Years in the Death of the Labour Party*, Biteback, 2018, pp. 103–18.

16 Including the author.

17 'Jeremy Corbyn's Votes Against Blair and Brown Showed His "Strength of Character" – Labour Chief Whip', *The Independent*, 17 October 2016.

18 P. Kellner, 'An Anatomy of Corbyn's Victory'. *YouGov*, 2015. Available at: https://yougov.co.uk/topics/politics/articles-reports/2015/09/15/anatomy-corbyns-victory

19 'Responses to an "Open Letter to the New New Left"', *The Nation*, 27 April 2020.

20 R.A. Ford, T. Bale, W. Jennings and P. Surridge, 'The Man Who Wasn't There: Labour Under Corbyn', in *The British General Election of 2019*, Palgrave Macmillan, 2021, pp. 107–57.

21 O. Eagleton, *The Starmer Project: A Journey to the Right*, Verso, 2022.

22 Not least because the NEC remained firmly under Corbyn's control. In 2018, all nine constituency members were elected from the pro-Corbyn slate.

23 S. Crossman, C. Emmerson and L. Kraftman, 'Labour's Nationalisation Policy', IFS Briefing Note BN271, 2019.

24 YouGov, 'How Britain Voted in the 2019 General Election, 17 December 2019. https://yougov.co.uk/topics/politics/articles-reports/2019/12/17/how-britain-voted-2019-general-election

25 The 2019 election result appeared to confirm a long-term decline in Labour's working-class base. Even in 1997, 58 per cent of working-class voters supported Labour, which was actually lower than the proportion in the 1940s and 1950s. This trend has continued since 1997. G. Evans and J. Tilley, *The New Politics of Class: The Political Exclusion of the British Working Class*, Oxford University Press, 2017.

26 T. Piketty, *Capital and Ideology*, Harvard University Press, 2020.

27 R. Ford and M. Goodwin, *Revolt on the Right: Explaining Support for the Radical Right in Britain*, Routledge, 2014.

28 Eagleton, p. 12.

29 K. Starmer, 'Labour can win again if it makes the moral case for socialism', *The Guardian*, 15 January 2020. https://www.theguardian.com/commentisfree/2020/jan/15/labour-socialism-values-election-economic-model?CMP=share_btn_link

30 https://keirstarmer.com/plans/10-pledges

31 P. Diamond, 'Is Keir Starmer Any Good? Don't Ask Londoners', Queen Mary University of London. Available at: https://www.qmul.ac.uk/media/news/2021/hss/is-keir-starmer-any-good-dont-ask-londoners.html

32 Ibid.

33 EHRC, *Investigation into Antisemitism in the Labour Party*. Equality and Human Rights Commission, 2020. Available at: https://www.equalityhumanrights.com/sites/default/files/investigation-into-antisemitism-in-the-labour-party.pdf

34 F. Hussain, and K. Pike, 'Public perceptions of Keir Starmer's performance suggest he has yet to produce a clear narrative of both the COVID-19 crisis and his leadership', British Politics and Policy at LSE. 2021. Available at: https://blogs.lse.ac.uk/politicsandpolicy/starmer-dilemma/

35 'The Guardian View on Sir Keir Starmer: Caught between scaring and inspiring voters | editorial', *The Guardian*, Guardian News and Media, 5 January 2023. Available at: https://www.theguardian.com/commentisfree/2023/jan/05/the-guardian-view-on-sir-keir-starmer-caught-between-scaring-and-inspiring-voters

36 J. Coman, 'British politics suddenly feels small – and the old order is "taking back control"', *The Guardian*, 6 December 2021.

37 J. Gray, 'David Cameron and the Great Sell-out', *The New Statesman*, 14 April 2021. Available at: https://www.newstatesman.com/politics/2021/04/david-cameron-and-great-sell-out

38 Although in August 2023 Labour diluted this 'single status' pledge to that of a consultation, one that would ensure a 'simpler framework' of employment protections that 'could properly capture the breadth of employment relationships in the UK'.

39 Eagleton, pp. 8–62.

40 P. English, 'Is the stereotypical image of "Red Wall" residents actually accurate?', *YouGov*, 17 May 2021.

41 https://www.electionpolling.co.uk/battleground/targets/labour

Chapter 13: Purpose

1 D. Cowling, *Can Labour Win the Next Election?*, 13 March 2023.

2 In 1929, Labour gained 136 seats but the percentage swing to it was much less because the 8.7 per cent swing from the Conservatives was split between Labour, with a 3.8 per cent increase in vote share, and the Liberals, with a 5.8 per cent increase in vote share.

3 'Yet recent events suggest the swing Labour requires to secure an outright majority could be much reduced due to three recent factors. First the rapid decline in support for Rishi Sunak. Second the decline in SNP support following the resignation of Nicola Sturgeon which was reflected in the scale of Labour's victory in the Rutherglen and Hamilton West byelection. The need for a 12 per cent swing was based on a straight Con-Lab swing across Britain. Assuming the SNP remained dominant north of the border, such a Britain-wide shift implied only limited Labour gains in Scotland. Things appear to have significantly altered north of the border which radically alters the challenge facing Labour outside Scotland. Third the increasing prominence of tactical voting revealed in recent byelections. Cumulatively these factors have led pollster Peter Kellner to suggest the target for an overall Labour majority has fallen to just a 5 per cent poll lead. https://www.prospectmagazine.co.uk/politics/63475/labour-keir-starmer-election-majority'.

4 Technically there was a third minority Labour government between February and October 1974, and following by-election defeats a fourth from 1977 to 1979.

5 Meaning the duration of time before being next elected, therefore excluding 1940–45 when part of the wartime coalition.

6 The figure of 23 includes acting leaders.

7 We can also include other significant figures who passed too soon. Cripps and Bevan both died at 62, Robin Cook was 59, Mo Mowlem 55 and Evan Durbin just 42.

Further Reading

There is, of course, a rich and fascinating literature on the Labour Party. For curious readers keen to follow up on some of the book's themes, I have put together the following guide to key works that have informed my own knowledge of Labour Party history and therefore the writing of this book.

In terms of the general history of the Labour Party: H. Pelling, *A Short History of the Labour Party*, 12th edn, Palgrave Macmillan, 2005. K.O. Morgan, *Labour People: Leaders and Lieutenants, Hardie to Kinnock*, Faber and Faber, 2011. J. Hinton, *Labour and Socialism: A History of the British Labour Movement, 1867–1974*, Wheatsheaf Books, 1983. M. Worley, *Labour Inside the Gate: A History of the British Labour Party between the Wars*, I.B. Tauris, 2005. E. Shaw, *The Labour Party since 1945*, John Wiley & Sons, 1996. G. Rosen, *Old Labour to New: The Dreams That Inspired, the Battles That Divided*, Politico's Publishing, 2005. J. Saville, *The Labour Movement in Britain*, Faber and Faber, 1988.

Books that cover Labour's pre-history include: H. Pelling, *The Origins of the Labour Party, 1880–1900*, 2nd edn, Oxford University Press, 1966. T. Paine, *The Rights of Man*, Hackett Publishing, 1992. R. Owen, *A New View of Society and Other Writings*, Penguin Classics, reprint edn, 1991. John Ruskin, *Unto this Last and Other Writings*, Penguin Classics, 1985. H.M. Hyndman, *England for All*, Wentworth Press, 2019. E. Carpenter, *The Selected Works of Edward Carpenter*, Lulu.com, 2021. W. Morris, *News from Nowhere and Other Writings*, Penguin Classics, 1993. J.B. Glasier and K. St. John Conway, *The Religion of Socialism*, Clarion Newspaper Co., 1890. R. Blatchford, *Merrie England*, Legare Street Press, 2022.

Labour's early years are considered in: E.F. Biagini and A.J. Reid (eds) *Currents of Radicalism: Popular Radicalism, Organised Labour and Party Politics in Britain, 1850–1914*, Cambridge University Press, 1991. F. Bealey and H. Pelling, *Labour and Politics: A History of the Labour Representation Committee*, rev. edn, Praeger, 1982. R.E. Dowse, *Left in the Centre: The Independent Labour Party, 1893–1940*, Northwestern University Press, 1966. P. Adelman, *The Rise of the Labour Party 1880–1945*, 3rd edn, Routledge, 1996. R. McKibbin, *Evolution of the Labour Party, 1910–1924*, Oxford University Press, 1974. D. Tanner, *Political Change and the Labour Party, 1900–1918*, Cambridge University Press, 1990.

Labour and socialist thought are covered in: H.M. Drucker, *Doctrine and Ethos in the Labour Party*, Routledge, 1979. J. Callaghan, *Socialism in Britain since 1884*, Wiley-Blackwell, 1990. R. Plant, M. Beech and K. Hickson (eds) *The Struggle for Labour's Soul: Understanding Labour's Political Thought since 1945*, Routledge, 2019. S. Fielding (ed.) *The Labour Party: 'Socialism' and Society since 1951*, Manchester University Press, 1997. M. Francis, *Ideas and Policies under Labour, 1945–51: Building a New Britain*, Manchester University Press, 1997. P. Diamond, *New Labour's Old Roots: Revisionist Thinkers in Labour's History 1930–1997*, Imprint Academic, 2004. D. Leonard, *Crosland and New Labour*, Palgrave Macmillan, 1998. J.K. Hardie, *From Serfdom to Socialism*, Franklin Classics, 2018. P. Snowden, *Labour and the New World Order*, Nabu Press, 2011. J.R. MacDonald, *Socialism: Critical and Constructive*, HardPress Publishing, 2019. J.R. MacDonald, *Socialism and Government*, Legare Street Press, 2022. G.D.H. Cole, *The World of Labour*, G. Bell, 1920. G.D.H. Cole, *Guild Socialism Restated*, Legare Street Press, 2022. H.J. Laski, *A Grammar of Politics*, Routledge, 2014. H.J. Laski, *Liberty in the Modern State*, Penguin, 1937. E.F.M. Durbin, *The Politics of Democratic Socialism*: *An Essay on Social Policy*, Routledge, 2020. H. Dalton, *Practical Socialism for Britain*, Routledge, 2022. J. Strachey, *Contemporary Capitalism*, Victor Gollancz, 1956.

Biography and autobiography: K. Laybourn, *Philip Snowden: A Biography*, Temple Smith, 1988. R. Skidelsky, *Oswald Mosley*, rev. edn, Papermac, 1990. B. Pimlott, *Hugh Dalton: A Life*, Jonathan Cape, 1985. K. Harris, *Attlee*, Weidenfeld and Nicolson, 1982. P.F. Clarke, *The Cripps Version: The Life of Sir Stafford Cripps*, Allen Lane, 2002. I. Kramnick and B. Sherman, *Harold Laski: A Life on the Left*, Allen Lane, 1993. A. Bullock, *Ernest Bevin, Foreign Secretary, 1945–51*, Oxford University Press, 1983. G. Radice, *Friends and Rivals: Crosland, Jenkins and Healey*, Little, Brown, 2002. G. Radice, *The Tortoise and* the Hares: Attlee, Bevin, Cripps, Dalton, Morrison, Politico's Publishing, 2008. J.M. Bellamy and J. Saville, Dictionary of Labour Biography, Palgrave, vols 1–10, 1972–2000. T. Judge, J.R. Clynes: A Political Life, CreateSpace Independent Publishing Platform, 2016. M. Jago, Clement Attlee: The Inevitable Prime Minister, Biteback, 2017. B. Donoughue and G.W. Jones, Herbert Morrison: Portrait of a Politician, Weidenfeld and Nicolson, 2001. M. Foot, Aneurin Bevan: A Biography, Faber and Faber, 2009. B. Brivati, Hugh Gaitskell: The First Moderniser, Metro Books, 2005. D. Healey, The Time of My Life, Methuen, 2015. A. Perkins, Red Queen: The Authorised Biography of Barbara Castle, Macmillan, 2003. R. Hattersley, Who Goes Home? Scenes from a Political Life, Time Warner Books UK, 2003. M. Westlake, Kinnock, Little, Brown, 2001. G. Drower, Kinnock: A Biography, Publishing Corporation, 1994. A. McSmith, John Smith: A Life, 1938–1994, Mandarin, 1994. A. Seldon, Blair, Simon & Schuster, 2005. G. Brown, My Life, Our Times, Bodley Head, 2017. J. Rentoul, Tony Blair, Little, Brown, 1995. A. Seldon and G. Lodge, Brown at 10, Biteback, 2011.

On Labour and the unions: L. Minkin, The Contentious Alliance: Trade Unions and the Labour Party, Edinburgh University Press, 1991. On the SDP: I. Crewe and A. King, SDP: The Birth, Life and Death of the Social Democratic Party, Oxford University Press, 1995. On Kinnock's modernization: R. Heffernan and M. Marqusee, Defeat from the Jaws of Victory: Inside Kinnock's Labour Party, Verso, 1992. On New Labour: P. Anderson and N. Mann, Safety First: The Making of New Labour, Granta Books, 1997. A. Rawnsley, Servants of the People: The Inside Story of New Labour, Penguin, 2001. A. Rawnsley, The End of the Party: The Rise and Fall of New Labour, Penguin, 2010.

From the Right: R. Jenkins, What Matters Now, HarperCollins, 1972. S. Williams, Politics is for People, Harvard University Press, 2014. D. Owen, Face the Future, Jonathan Cape, 1975. J. Golding, Hammer of the Left: The Battle for the Soul of the Labour Party, Biteback, 2016. D. Hayter, Fightback! Labour's Traditional Right in the 1970s and 1980s, Manchester University Press, 2005.

From the Left: R. Miliband, The State in Capitalist Society, Merlin, 2009. S. Holland, The Socialist Challenge, Quartet Books, 1975. T. Benn, Arguments for Socialism, Penguin, 1979. T. Benn, Parliament, People and Power: Agenda for a Free Society, Verso, 1982. H. Wainwright, Labour: A

Tale of Two Parties, The Hogarth Press, 1987. P. Seyd, *The Rise and Fall of the Labour Left*, Palgrave Macmillan, 1987. L. Panitch and C. Leys, *The End of Parliamentary Socialism: From New Left to New Labour*, Verso, 2001. R. Seymour, *Corbyn: The Strange Rebirth of Radical Politics*, Verso, 2017.

Index